THE COMPLETE IDIOT'S GUIDE® TO

Greens Cookbook

by Trish Sebben-Krupka

ALPHA

A member of Penguin Group (USA) Inc.

ALPHA BOOKS

Published by Penguin Group (USA) Inc.

Penguin Group (USA) Inc., 375 Hudson Street, New York, New York 10014, USA • Penguin Group (Canada), 90 Eglinton Avenue East, Suite 700, Toronto, Ontario M4P 2Y3, Canada (a division of Pearson Penguin Canada Inc.) • Penguin Books Ltd., 80 Strand, London WC2R 0RL, England • Penguin Ireland, 25 St. Stephen's Green, Dublin 2, Ireland (a division of Penguin Books Ltd.) • Penguin Group (Australia), 250 Camberwell Road, Camberwell, Victoria 3124, Australia (a division of Pearson Australia Group Pty. Ltd.) • Penguin Books India Pvt. Ltd., 11 Community Centre, Panchsheel Park, New Delhi—110 017, India • Penguin Group (NZ), 67 Apollo Drive, Rosedale, North Shore, Auckland 1311, New Zealand (a division of Pearson New Zealand Ltd.) • Penguin Books (South Africa) (Pty.) Ltd., 24 Sturdee Avenue, Rosebank, Johannesburg 2196, South Africa • Penguin Books Ltd., Registered Offices: 80 Strand, London WC2R 0RL, England

International Standard Book Number: 978-1-61564-315-8
Library of Congress Catalog Card Number: 2012953748

15 14 13   8 7 6 5 4 3 2 1

Interpretation of the printing code: The rightmost number of the first series of numbers is the year of the book's printing; the rightmost number of the second series of numbers is the number of the book's printing. For example, a printing code of 13-1 shows that the first printing occurred in 2013.

Printed in the United States of America

Note: This publication contains the opinions and ideas of its author. It is intended to provide helpful and informative material on the subject matter covered. It is sold with the understanding that the author and publisher are not engaged in rendering professional services in the book. If the reader requires personal assistance or advice, a competent professional should be consulted.

The author and publisher specifically disclaim any responsibility for any liability, loss, or risk, personal or otherwise, which is incurred as a consequence, directly or indirectly, of the use and application of any of the contents of this book.

Most Alpha books are available at special quantity discounts for bulk purchases for sales promotions, premiums, fund-raising, or educational use. Special books, or book excerpts, can also be created to fit specific needs. For details, write: Special Markets, Alpha Books, 375 Hudson Street, New York, NY 10014.

Publisher: *Mike Sanders*	**Cover Designer:** *Kurt Owens*
Executive Managing Editor: *Billy Fields*	**Book Designer:** *William Thomas, Rebecca Batchelor*
Senior Acquisitions Editor: *Tom Stevens*	**Indexer:** *Ginny Bess Monroe*
Development Editor: *Nancy Lewis*	**Layout:** *Ayanna Lacey*
Senior Production Editor: *Janette Lynn*	**Proofreader:** *Jan Zoya*
Copy Editor: *Amy Borrelli*	

Contents

viii   **The Complete Idiot's Guide Greens Cookbook**

Introduction

You've decided to include healthy, fresh greens in your diet. What a great choice! Get ready to enjoy improved digestion, lots of energy, radiant skin, healthy hair, a stronger immune system, and better overall health. Eating greens supports every system in your body, protecting your heart, brain, and eyesight, as well as purifying your blood and liver. Greens are rich in powerful antioxidants and phytochemicals, Omega-3 fatty acids, vitamins, and minerals.

Many of us are familiar with greens such as broccoli and spinach, but dig a little deeper and you'll find a whole universe of green goodness just waiting to be discovered.

So how do we include more fresh greens in our diet? The most obvious choice is to eat a salad, but a steady diet of raw greens will not nourish us completely, and may interfere with digestion. Summertime is the perfect season to enjoy fresh, raw dishes, but in the cooler months, warm, cooked food may be a better choice to nourish our bodies.

A great way to include more greens is by drinking fresh juice and smoothies. You'll find plenty of recipes and advice in this book for including green juice and smoothies in your daily routine.

How about snacks? A dehydrator allows you to create raw foods such as kale chips that can be eaten on the go. Raw food recipes can be found throughout this book. Look for the **R** symbol, which will let you know a recipe is raw.

All of the recipes that appear in this book are vegetarian. Many of them are vegan. While vegetarians avoid meat, and sometimes dairy and eggs, vegans do not consume any products that contain animal ingredients. Experiment with vegan recipes, where vegetables are the star ingredient. Vegan recipes can be identified by the **V** symbol.

Greens are enjoyed on every continent, in every cuisine. They are filling, highly nutritious, delicious, and, as we will learn, economical. They're also easy to grow yourself in a variety of climates and soil conditions.

This book will focus on greens in the North American diet, but our goal is to create global cuisine, influenced by dietary traditions from around the world.

We will enjoy soups and stews that have their roots in Mediterranean cuisine, such as Tuscan ribollita, Roman fava bean soup with puntarelle, and panzanella, the famous bread salad, which receives a nutritional upgrade through the addition of spinach. We'll also prepare a variety of pasta recipes.

African culture lends its spice to traditional American Southern cuisine. Cheesy grits with Southern greens, a collard and black-eyed pea soup based on Hoppin' John, and many recipes for stewed greens bring the South to your kitchen. The deliciously spiced Kenyan rice dish of pilau will receive a green makeover, too, bringing modern African influences into the mix.

Eastern Europe provides us with hearty, comforting flavors such as borscht, cabbage soups, stuffed cabbage, and, of course, sauerkraut. An old favorite gets a new twist in a deep-dish pierogi pie that must not be missed.

We'll travel extensively through Asia. India will offer inspiring curried dishes rich with flavor and anti-inflammatory spices, as well as Ayurveda's healing food, kitchari. Japanese, Chinese, and Thai cuisine will be represented amply with soups, dumplings, spring rolls, summer rolls, fresh salads, and stir-fries. We'll learn to make Korean kimchi, sauerkraut's spicy cousin.

Central and South American dishes, such as mole, fideos, and the traditional Lenten pie, pascualina, will mix with American-style Southwestern dishes such as tortilla lasagna.

American regional cuisine at its best is, of course, our primary focus. Our melting pot has brought us many traditions to make our own, and unlike our ancestors of all nations, we have access to fresh food thanks to our flourishing agricultural system. We will explore some current trends as well, including the raw food movement and farm-to-table issues. Our food choices affect the environment as well as the health of ourselves and our families, and ample advice for making the best choices will be provided throughout this book.

How This Book Is Organized

This book is organized into six parts. The first part focuses on providing you with the tools you need to get cooking, while parts 2 to 6 offer recipes for success. You'll learn over 200 ways to prepare greens. You'll never have to rely on boring steamed broccoli again!

Part 1, All About Greens, provides a detailed explanation of each green featured in this book. You'll learn everything you need to know about the culinary uses, history, and nutritional value of glorious greens. We will discuss the benefits of raw, vegan, and vegetarian diets, and review the economic values of a vegetarian diet that features greens as a staple food. You'll become more self-sufficient when you learn to stock your pantry, and grow your own garden regardless of where you live. We will also explore the benefits of freezing and dehydrating, and explore some basic recipes and techniques to get you on your way.

Part 2, Get Up and Go, offers fantastic breakfast and brunch recipes. We'll look at the benefits of adding fresh juice and green smoothies to your diet, and you'll find plenty of recipes and advice. Heartier fare is offered as well, including recipes for quiche, grits, home fries, omelets, and more.

Part 3, Super Salads and Starters, features recipes for both raw and cooked salads that can be enjoyed as appetizers, lunches, or main meals. You'll find party-pleasing dishes to share; protein-rich salads featuring lentils, eggs, or dairy; and a wide variety of techniques that you can mix and match to create your own salad style. Appetizers, snacks, and light fare will make it easy to pack a lunch or plan a party.

Part 4, Sensational Soups, offers plenty of recipes for my favorite thing to cook—soup! We'll enjoy raw, cooked, hot, and cold soups, from hearty peasant fare to a light bowl of miso broth with fresh veggies.

Part 5, The Main Event, will have you serving up incredible pasta, grain, and main-course dishes in no time at all. You'll travel the world with dishes from India, Asia, eastern Europe, Italy, Mexico, Kenya, and the Middle East, as well as classic American dishes that will warm your soul.

Part 6, Sides and Extras, helps you round out your meals with mouthwatering side dishes. I'll also give you a primer on pickling, which will add crunch and excitement to your meals. A chapter of extras such as pie pastry, pizza dough, and sauces and salad dressings will help you to make the recipes in this book in true homemade fashion. Finally, you'll find instructions for culinary techniques that are called for throughout the book.

Extras

In each chapter, you'll find helpful sidebars that provide facts, tips, and extra information:

HEADS UP!

Heads Up boxes bring potential problems and hot-button issues to your attention.

DEFINITIONS

Definition sidebars feature more information about terms you may not be familiar with.

THE LOWDOWN

These sidebars provide helpful information about all types of greens, as well as how to grow, shop, and eat close to home.

MAKE IT VEGAN

Make It Vegan sidebars appear in recipe chapters. Most recipes that contain eggs or dairy also include an option for "veganizing" the recipe.

Acknowledgments

Many people have helped to bring this book to you, and I owe a debt of gratitude to each of them. I offer my most sincere thanks to my agent, Marilyn Allen, of the Allen O'Shea Literary Agency; to senior acquisitions editor Tom Stevens, development editor Nancy Lewis, senior production editor Jan Lynn, and copy editor Amy Borrelli, for your thoughtful guidance and input throughout the creation of this book.

This book was reviewed by an expert for accuracy. My endless gratitude goes to Adriana Pecunia, who is a treasured friend, brilliant chef, and the technical reviewer for this work.

Thanks are also due to my husband, Jim, who washed many dishes, drank many smoothies, and endured too many takeout dinners while I was writing; Chelsea Bradley, for her valuable assistance with this project; my amazing family, for their love and support, and for eating everything—even the mistakes; my co-workers at the Viking Culinary Center and Carl Schaedel and Co. for being a wonderful sounding board for my ideas, and for doing without me so I could write this book; and Rebecca Doherty, my tiniest food critic, for eating green gazpacho and liking it.

This book is dedicated to the memory of Josephine Franceschini Sebben, my grandmother, friend, inspiration, and teacher. I love you always, Gram.

Special Thanks to the Technical Reviewer

The Complete Idiot's Guide to Greens Cookbook was reviewed by an expert who double-checked the accuracy of what you'll learn here, to help us ensure that this book gives you everything you need to know about cooking vegetarian and vegan dishes with greens. Special thanks are extended to Adriana Pecunia.

Adriana Pecunia is a graduate of The Culinary Institute of America. When she is not reading about food, she is probably out shopping for it or at work preparing something. In her free time she is home cooking for her husband, son, and dog. She wishes to thank Trish for letting her tag along on another of her adventures and says she's sorry for not helping with the dishes.

Trademarks

All terms mentioned in this book that are known to be or are suspected of being trademarks or service marks have been appropriately capitalized. Alpha Books and Penguin Group (USA) Inc. cannot attest to the accuracy of this information. Use of a term in this book should not be regarded as affecting the validity of any trademark or service mark.

All About Greens

Let's begin our journey into the wonderful world of greens! We'll start with an introduction to the vegetables featured in this book, including detailed nutrition information. Once you're familiar with the array of delicious, nourishing greens available and how they work to keep you healthy, read on to learn how to stock your kitchen, shop the farmers market, get the most from your grocery store, and even grow your own green garden.

Get ready to look and feel fantastic, maximize your food budget, and be kinder to animals and the planet. You'll find all the information you need right here.

The ABCs of Greens

In This Chapter

- Making healthy, economical choices
- Getting to know your greens
- Trying new greens

Throughout history, greens have offered an economical and easy way to feed our families and enjoy better health. We'll begin by reviewing the greens featured in this cookbook. Take some time to familiarize yourself with the history, practical applications, and substitutions for each green. We'll discuss ways to improve your diet, including choosing fresh, whole foods over processed junk food, and learn how budget-friendly greens can be.

Green Living

You've decided to include more healthy, fresh greens in your diet. What a great choice! Get ready to enjoy improved digestion, lots of energy, radiant skin, shiny hair, a stronger immune system, and better overall health. Eating greens supports every system in your body, protecting your heart, brain, and eyesight, and purifying your blood and liver. Greens are rich in powerful antioxidants and phytochemicals, omega-3 fatty acids, vitamins, and minerals.

Making greens an integral part of your diet plan is one of the best decisions you can make for your health. The USDA recommends five to nine servings of fresh vegetables and fruits every day, but remember that this is a minimum recommendation. Most health-care practitioners agree that you should include more. Getting your nutrients directly from *whole foods*, rather than manufactured supplements and processed goods with a list of ingredients as long as your arm, is the best way to fuel your body and protect your health.

DEFINITION

Whole foods are foods in their natural state—unprocessed, unrefined, and without additives. Some examples of whole foods are fresh fruits and vegetables, whole grains (such as brown rice, millet, buckwheat, barley, and oats), dried beans and legumes (such as lentils, kidney beans, mung beans, and chickpeas), nuts, and seeds.

It's no secret that a diet rich in whole foods is good for your health. Dr. Andrew Weil, Harvard-educated physician and integrative medicine specialist, includes plenty of dark, leafy, nutritious greens in his prescription for healthy living, the anti-inflammatory diet. Both Ayurveda and Chinese medicine, the world's oldest systems of natural medicine, tell us that a whole foods diet is paramount to maintaining good health. The vitamins in whole foods act much more effectively in your body than the synthetic vitamins present in manufactured supplements. By eating whole foods, one gains benefits beyond vitamins and minerals, which we will explore in Chapter 2.

THE LOWDOWN

Recent medical research confirms what natural health practitioners have known for years—chronic inflammation in the body is the root cause of many serious illnesses, including allergies, arthritis, gum disease, digestive ailments, and even some cancers. Inflammation is the body's natural response to injury and illness, but chronic inflammation is damaging to every cell in your body. Chronic inflammation is caused by stress, environmental toxins, a sedentary lifestyle, and, most importantly, poor dietary choices. Choosing to eat a diet primarily composed of unprocessed food is the best way to reduce inflammation in your body.

Less Expense Than You Think

Greens are an economical choice for the family cook on a budget. They deliver tremendous nutrition for little cost, and fill your belly with healthy fiber. Consider the cost of a fast-food meal: the average value meal is $4 to $7. Multiply this by a family of four, and you'll spend at least $22 to feed two adults and two kids. You'll also be getting something you didn't bargain for in the form of massive amounts of sodium, saturated fat, and processed ingredients.

In the amount of time it takes to drive to a fast-food restaurant, you can prepare a healthy, quick, and delicious meal for much less. Stir up a hearty, family-friendly chili featuring organic veggies such as kale, fire-roasted tomatoes, onions, and bell peppers, along with two cans of black beans. Served over brown rice with a spoonful of Greek yogurt, you'll pay about $8.50 (just over $2 per person), and you'll treat your family to a nourishing, kid-friendly feast that's on the table in a flash. If you're pressed for time, make use of a crock pot so dinner will be ready when you walk in the door after a busy day. Double the recipe and store some in the freezer so you can reap the benefits twice! We'll focus on freezing your own greens, as well as prepared recipes, in Chapter 5.

Chicory.

All About Greens

Let's begin by exploring the various greens that will be covered in this book. From amaranth to watercress, you'll find a rainbow of flavor, nutrition, and versatility.

Amaranth

Amaranth is a hardy annual plant grown throughout the world. It originated on the American content, and was once prized by the Aztecs, Incas, and Mayans as a staple food along with beans and maize. As amaranth was used not only as a staple food, but also as a component in religious ceremonies, the Conquistadors banned its cultivation, and it nearly disappeared. Luckily for us, its cultivation spread throughout the world during the seventeenth, eighteenth, and nineteenth centuries. Amaranth is valued in African, Caribbean, Asian, Indian, and Central and South American cuisine due to its high protein content and hardy nature.

Amaranth can be grown in nearly any climate, and is resistant to major diseases. It varies in color and size; green, pink, and purple leaves are all common, and plants can grow up to 10 feet. Leaves can be enjoyed in their young, tender form in salads and raw preparations. Large bunches of mature amaranth leaves may look tough, but their stems cook quickly to a tender consistency.

Amaranth.

Many natural-foods cooks are familiar with amaranth seeds, a gluten-free grain, but the leaves are enjoying renewed popularity. Look for them in Chinese, Mexican, and Caribbean markets, or easily grow your own. If amaranth is not readily available, spinach is an excellent substitute.

Arugula

Arugula, also known as rocket, is a peppery, assertively flavored green available in both cultivated and wild varieties. Its flavor is often described as mustardy. Available year-round, arugula leaves vary from tiny, mild-tasting greens that are excellent served raw, to large, fibrous, spicy greens that benefit from quick cooking.

Although arugula entered the American consciousness with a trendy splash in the 1990s, it has been planted in the United States since colonial times, and has been used for thousands of years in many cultures as both food and medicine. Arugula is particularly popular in Italian and Provençal cuisine.

Arugula varies throughout the seasons in size, tenderness, heat, and flavor. It is easy to grow, and highly perishable, so avoid waterlogged supermarket bunches in favor of home-grown or farm-fresh, recently harvested arugula. If arugula is unavailable, consider substituting escarole or dandelion greens.

Beet Greens

Beet greens are the leafy tops of beet root, a once-lowly root vegetable that has become the darling of the culinary world in recent years. Many people send their beet greens directly to the compost pile or trash can, but these delicious and nutritious greens should not be ignored.

Beets have been cultivated since the second millennium B.C.E., and were considered both a health food and an aphrodisiac in ancient Rome. Beets were once known primarily for providing hearty peasant fare in cold climates and lean times, served boiled, canned, in soups, or pickled. The trend toward farm-to-table culture and widespread cultivation of gorgeous varieties has brought new popularity to this earthy and healthful herbaceous biannual plant.

Beet greens can be young and tender, or large and somewhat tough. They are delicious steamed, sautéed, braised, or pickled. Add them to soups, pasta dishes, and fresh juices. Swiss chard is an excellent substitute for beet greens, as they are part of the same botanical family.

Belgian Endive

Belgian endive is not a true endive at all, but a leaf vegetable belonging to the *chicory* genus. Its pearly white, slightly bitter-tasting leaves are cultivated by forcing a second growth from cut chicory root, which was originally cultivated as a coffee substitute (it's still blended with coffee to create the signature New Orleans–style brew). It is excellent both in salads and cooked dishes.

Belgian endive is the fabled discovery of a farmer who realized that his chicory root stored in the cellar had sprouted unusual leaves. Its cultivation spread from Belgium to France in the mid-nineteenth century, and today, most Belgian endive is still imported from these countries.

Belgian endive is excellent when served raw, baked, or roasted, steamed, grilled, or braised. It is a sturdy green that is difficult to overcook. This succulent specimen can be prohibitively expensive for the cook on a budget. Viable substitutes include radicchio and the tender, inner leaves of escarole.

Bok Choy

Bok choy is a member of the genus *Brassica*. The term "bok choy" can be used for several stages of growth and different varieties of the same plant family. From tiny, tender seedlings found at the farmers market, to small varieties such as dwarf and Shanghai bok choy found in Asian markets and in upscale grocery stores (where it is often called baby bok choy), to the large, mature plants most frequently found in Western supermarkets, some form of bok choy is available throughout the year.

Bok choy was originally cultivated in China, but is now grown throughout North America as well. Its stems are crunchy and sweet, while its leaves have a somewhat more bitter quality. Some variety of bok choy should be easily available no matter your location or time of year, but if it's unavailable, Napa cabbage is a fine substitute.

Enjoy bok choy in salads or stir-fries, or use it in soups or spring roll fillings. Small, leafy seedlings can be cooked whole, while dwarf or baby varieties are nicest halved or quartered. Cut mature bok choy into equal-sized pieces for even cooking.

Broccoli

Broccoli is probably the most familiar *cruciferous vegetable*, one that is already in your repertoire, but its origins are unclear. While some linguists contend that the word "broccoli" is derived from an Italian word, *broccolo*, that means "a cabbage sprout," others cite the Dutch word *borecole*, which means "farmer's cabbage." To add to the confusion, a persistent legend (which is surely untrue) attributes the invention of broccoli to an eighteenth-century Italian family named Broccoli (of course). Whatever its provenance, broccoli in some form has been enjoyed in northern Europe for centuries, and has been grown in the United States since the 1920s.

While it is the flower portion (floret) of the vegetable that is most often eaten, broccoli stems are edible as well, although they often end up in the trash or compost pile. Don't waste them—peel them with a sharp vegetable peeler, and slice thinly. Many people find that the stems of broccoli are milder in flavor and more tender than the florets. If broccoli is unavailable, you may substitute cauliflower.

DEFINITION

Cruciferous vegetables are unique in the vegetable world, as they are a rich source of sulfur-containing compounds called glucosinolates, which are synthesized in the body to create powerful cancer-fighting substances. All members of the *Brassica* genus are cruciferous vegetables, but not all crucifers are *Brassica*. Arugula and watercress are also cruciferous vegetables.

Broccoli Rabe

Broccoli rabe, also known as rapini or broccoli di rapa, is a delicious cruciferous vegetable that stars in numerous Italian dishes. Despite its misleading name, it is more closely related to the turnip than to broccoli.

Italian immigrants in California began cultivating wild broccoli rabe in the 1930s, resulting in the small-leaved, juicy variety known in America today. This variety is different from its Italian counterpart, which is leafier and more bitter.

Broccoli rabe should always be cooked, as it is too strong-tasting and fibrous for raw preparations. Blanch, then sauté with garlic, hot pepper flakes and extra-virgin olive oil. It pairs well with strong flavors such as chile, garlic, and ginger, and also adds zip to pastas, potatoes, soups, and mild cheeses.

Distinct in flavor and readily available both at grocery stores and farmers markets, broccoli rabe knows no true substitute. If you can't find it, try turnip greens or mustard greens.

Broccoli rabe.

Brussels Sprouts

Brussels sprouts, another member of the *Brassica* family, are tiny, cabbagelike heads that grow on a large stalk. Over and undercooking has made them the scourge of children at dinner tables everywhere, so be sure to taste often, and don't wander away from the stove.

Until the early twentieth century, Brussels sprouts were grown in home gardens. Northern California growers began commercial cultivation to take advantage of the cool, misty climate, and today, this region produces 98 percent of the Brussels sprouts grown in the United States (the remaining 2 percent come from New York state).

Choose the tiniest, freshest specimens you can find. The very smallest are lovely steamed or boiled whole. Larger Brussels sprouts should be halved or quartered. If you separate each leaf (a time-consuming process), they can be sautéed very quickly. Also try Brussels sprouts roasted, stir-fried, or braised. Avoid serving them raw. If you can't find Brussels sprouts that suit your needs, consider cauliflower instead.

Cabbage

Cabbage, for the purpose of this book, refers to several varieties, including Napa, Savoy, red, and green. Each of these has its own characteristics and uses.

THE LOWDOWN

While cabbage is available year-round at your supermarket, its prime season is from November through April, when fresh, sweet, locally grown cabbages can be found at winter farmers markets everywhere. Cabbage is particularly well suited to root cellaring, making it the perfect winter staple for the locavore diet.

Napa cabbage is widely used in Asian cuisine, and is often called Chinese cabbage. These oblong, light-colored cabbages are excellent raw or cooked. Try Napa cabbage in stir-fries, soups, salads, dumpling and spring roll fillings, and kimchi. Bok choy is a good substitute for Napa cabbage.

Savoy cabbage is a lacy, wrinkled leaf cabbage that grows in compact, round heads. Enjoy it raw or cooked, in soups (especially minestrone), stews, casseroles, salads, and baked or stuffed preparations. Savoy cabbage is particularly tender and delicate when cooked.

Green cabbage is a smooth-leafed, firm *Brassica* that grows in heads ranging from 1 to 8 pounds. It is eaten throughout the world, and is perhaps best known in Western cuisine in its pickled, fermented form—sauerkraut—and its quintessential American raw preparation—coleslaw. In Britain, it pairs with salted beef to make "bubble and squeak," and it is used throughout eastern Europe as a dietary staple. Green cabbage can be enjoyed raw or cooked, in salads, soups, baked and stuffed variations, and, of course, pickled.

Red cabbage can be enjoyed raw or cooked, and is most often eaten in salads or coleslaw. When cooked, it will turn blue unless an acid such as vinegar is added to the preparation. Quickly sauté red cabbage with apples and onions, or braise with apple cider and vinegar for a hearty winter preparation.

Chicory

Chicory, also known as puntarelle, is similar to dandelion leaves in appearance and flavor. A traditional Roman preparation separates shoots and leaves, and soaks the shoots in cold water until they curl. Both leaves and shoots are then dressed with garlic, vinegar, olive oil, and anchovies. In the United States, this green is grown primarily in Italian American gardens. The name "chicory" is confusing, since it is also applied to curly endive, escarole, and chicory root (which is an entirely different plant—see the section "Belgian Endive," earlier in this chapter). Substitute dandelion greens when chicory is not available.

Collards

Collards are the quintessential American green, a staple in traditional Southern cuisine. These large, thick-leaved, sturdy vegetables are one of the earliest-known forms of cabbage.

Collards date back to prehistoric times, but were introduced in the Americas by African slaves brought to the colonies in the 1600s. Collard greens were also enjoyed in ancient times by the Greeks, Romans, and Celts, who brought them to Britain and France in the fourth century B.C.E.

THE LOWDOWN

Along with other greens such as mustard, turnip, and kale, collards continue to be a staple in Southern and African American cuisine. Several superstitions regarding collards are part of Southern folklore. Collards are eaten on New Year's Day with black-eyed peas for good luck and financial prosperity throughout the year. Hanging a collard leaf over your door is said to keep bad spirits away, and placing a collard leaf on your forehead is reputed to cure headaches.

Collards can be cooked low and slow until they are a soft mass of dark green pulp, braised in a flavorful liquid for a shorter period of time for a firmer texture, or thinly sliced and quickly sautéed with olive oil and garlic for a chewy, bright, fresh preparation.

Collards are available year-round, but this hardy, cool-weather vegetable is at its tender, flavorful best when the air is chilly. Vary your winter diet by substituting collards in recipes that call for cabbage leaves.

Curly Endive

Curly endive is also known as frisée or curly chicory, which helps to further confuse matters when it comes to greens referred to as chicory. Curly endive and escarole are both forms of *Chichorium endiva*, known as endive in the United States and Britain. Belgian endive is not an endive at all, but a misnamed chicory.

The term "frisée" commonly refers to the pale, tender, curly endive produced by *blanching*. Bittersweet and more delicate than its unblanched counterpart, curly endive, frisée is delicious when quickly tossed with a hot dressing. All varieties of curly endive also braise and sauté well, and are an excellent addition to vegetable soups.

DEFINITION

Blanching is a process commonly used by gardeners to cut the bitterness of both Belgian and curly endive. Cutting off light to the plant results in tender, mildly bittersweet leaves. Home gardeners can blanch plants simply by tying outer leaves up around inner leaves 1 week before harvest. The process of blanching that gardeners use should not be confused with the culinary term of the same name.

Most curly chicory sold in U.S. grocery stores comes from Italy or California. Look for damp, pale green leaves. It is normal to see some browning at the base, where it has been cut, but it should not be brown elsewhere. Escarole, since it is closely related, is an excellent substitute when curly chicory is not available.

Dandelion

Dandelion is available in both wild and cultivated forms. We will concern ourselves with wild dandelion, as many cultivated chicories are often referred to as "dandelion" (see the "Chicory" section for more about these varieties). True cultivated dandelion is grown in the spring, primarily in New Jersey. To enjoy the taste of wild dandelion greens, harvest them in early spring, before flowers are produced.

THE LOWDOWN

Many greens grow wild and can be foraged, but a little knowledge is necessary. Dandelion, chickweed, mallow, purslane, and over 70 additional varieties of wild green can be found growing in the United States. Use caution, however, as poisonous look-alikes abound. If you plan to forage, read a recently updated field guide, and do an internet search to find a foraging class or walking tour in your area. Dandelion greens are a great "starter" foraged food, since there are no poisonous look-alikes.

Dandelion greens can be assertively bitter. Add dandelion greens to your juice recipes. Drink straight in small quantities (incredibly healthy but not for the faint of heart), or mix with fruits and other greens to make the strong flavor more palatable. Tiny greens are excellent served raw, while larger leaves are best braised in a flavorful liquid until tender. Dandelion flowers are also edible, and were historically used to make dandelion wine. Choose an area free of pesticide contamination and animal waste if you plan to forage for wild dandelion. If dandelion greens are unavailable, try puntarelle or curly endive.

Escarole

Escarole is another member of the endive family, like its sibling, curly chicory (frisée). It is easily differentiated by its broad, firm leaves in a compact head. It is available year-round, but its flavor is at its best in autumn. Although it is native to Asia Minor, and has been cultivated in the West since the sixteenth century, it is perhaps best known for the role it plays in Italian cookery, particularly in bean soups and raw salads.

The center part of a head of escarole is white and tender, and can be served raw. Outer leaves are better cooked. Escarole lends itself particularly well to sautés, pastas, and soups. Substitute curly endive if escarole is not available.

Kale

Kale is the nutritional wonder of the *Brassica* family, and it has never been more popular. Kale is low in calories, high in fiber, and contains tremendous amounts of vitamins C, A, and K. It is also an excellent source of protein, calcium, magnesium, and minerals.

Kale has been cultivated for over 2,000 years. The most popular and readily available varieties are curly kale, which is frilly, dark green, and still too often used as an uneaten garnish, and Tuscan kale (lacinato, cavolo nero, or dinosaur are all common names), a dark, richly flavored kale that stews and sautés beautifully.

Both Tuscan and curly kale are excellent in soups, stews, sautés, and long-cooked preparations such as braises. Curly kale makes fantastic raw kale chips, as the frilly leaves catch all of the coating and make for a satisfying and flavorful snack. Kale is also particularly healthful when enjoyed raw, in juices, smoothies, and salads.

You may also find Russian red kale, or oak leaf kale, which is actually a member of a different species and has a very different flavor profile. Experiment with kale, and include a little in your diet every day for excellent health. If you don't have any kale on hand, Swiss chard is an excellent substitute.

Leaf Lettuce

Leaf lettuce is an annual plant that belongs to the same botanical family as sunflowers. It is easily cultivated in most climates in the spring and autumn, as the plants need cooler temperatures to prevent them from sprouting seeds and flowers, commonly known in gardening terminology as bolting.

Lettuces are excellent enjoyed raw, whether harvested when young and very tender, or allowed to grow to a full, mature head, but they are also well suited to cooking, and do particularly well in soups. If grown to maturity, leaf lettuces form heads of loosely bunched leaves. When picked very young, both red and green leaf lettuces join other baby greens to form the well-known and often imitated Provençal salad mix, mesclun.

Mizuna

Mizuna is a piquant, mildly peppery green that is commonly used in Asian cooking. It has been cultivated in Japan since ancient times, but may have originated in China.

Mizuna is an adaptable, attractive plant with dark green, serrated leaves and bright white stalks. It is difficult to find in supermarkets, but easy to grow yourself in a variety of climates.

Young mizuna leaves star in stir-fries and salads, while more mature leaves are a great substitute for Swiss chard or kale. No mizuna? No problem! Substitute arugula or tender, young mustard greens.

Mustard Greens

Mustard greens are strictly classified as a single species of plant, *Brassica juncea*, but many other varieties that vary in appearance, flavor, and heat are also classified as mustard greens. For our purposes, we will discuss Southern or American mustard, which is the most common type available in the United States.

Mustard greens are a traditional Southern green, often included with collards when stewing greens with "pot liquor" (the liquid they were cooked in). In their young, petite form, they are excellent served raw, while more mature varieties should be sautéed, stewed, braised, or steamed to tame their peppery assertiveness.

Mustard greens stand up to strong flavors, and work well in Chinese, Indian, and African dishes that feature plenty of spice. The leaves, flowers, seeds, and stems of this plant are all edible. Consider substituting mature arugula or mizuna for mustard greens.

Radicchio

Radicchio is a perennial leaf vegetable with white-veined, red leaves. It is commonly available in two varieties: chioggia, which has a compact, round head, and treviso, which has an elongated head that resembles Belgian endive, radicchio's closest relative.

Modern cultivation of radicchio began in northern Italy in the fifteenth century, but it wasn't until the nineteenth century that Belgian agronomist Francesco Van den Borre began blanching the leaves. The light deprivation of the blanching process deprives the plant of chlorophyll, which produces the familiar red and white color.

Radicchio can be served raw or cooked. It is particularly good when grilled over open coals, and can also be enjoyed in pasta dishes, risotto, and salads. Like Belgian endive, the root of the radicchio plant (chicory) can be used to flavor coffee. Belgian endive is an excellent substitute for radicchio.

Romaine Lettuce

Romaine lettuce, also known as cos lettuce, is ubiquitous for its use (and subsequent culinary abuse) in the classic Caesar salad. It grows in tall heads with a firm center stem, and is enjoyed throughout summer due to the heat-resistant nature of varieties such as *Jericho*.

Romaine lettuce is sturdy and firm, which makes it a good choice for heavy dressings, dips, and fillings. It also lends itself well to grilling. Be sure to try fattoush salad, a traditional Lebanese preparation that features romaine lettuce, fried pita, and tart, puckery sumac. Romaine is easy to find, but if you'd like to try something different, use butter lettuce.

Sorrel

Sorrel is a perennial herb that is cultivated for its leaves. It is remarkably easy to grow, and unchecked, will quickly establish its dominance over a corner of your garden.

Sorrel leaves have a lemony, tart flavor most commonly enjoyed in salads, soups, and sauces. Sorrel leaves are particularly high in oxalic acid, and can be toxic if consumed in very large quantities. If you're prone to kidney stones or arthritic conditions, you may wish to limit your intake of sorrel.

Many varieties of sorrel are considered weeds in the United States. Sorrel is best harvested in spring, as it can become increasingly bitter and unpalatable as heat changes its flavor. You can also sub arugula or spinach with a pinch of lemon zest.

Sorrel.

Spinach

Spinach is likely the best-known leafy green. Its small, tender leaves can be found in clamshell packages in every supermarket produce section, as well as bunches or bags of mature spinach leaves.

Spinach has a strong nutritional profile and is easily cultivated, widely available, and mild in flavor. It lends itself to a variety of dishes such as salads, soups, pasta dishes, risotto, stir-fries, fresh juices, and smoothies. It is enjoyed steamed, sautéed, boiled, wilted, and raw.

Spinach has been repeatedly cited by the Environmental Working Group as one of the dozen most heavily pesticide-contaminated foods. Look for organic spinach at your grocery store or farmers market, or grow your own during cooler weather. Spinach can even be cultivated throughout the winter in milder climates. If you'd like to vary your spinach recipes, substitute protein-rich amaranth, which is similar in flavor and texture.

THE LOWDOWN

Much has been made recently regarding oxalic acid, a naturally occurring compound found in plants and animals, including the human body. Greens that contain oxalic acid include amaranth, spinach, Swiss chard, beet greens, turnip greens, and sorrel. Oxalic acid exists in two forms—organic and inorganic. When consumed raw, oxalic acid remains organic and helps your body to assimilate calcium. When cooked, this compound becomes inorganic, and can cause issues for those with preexisting health conditions if consumed in large quantities. Studies show that calcium binds with oxalates to prevent absorption in your intestines. Consume adequate calcium, eat a variety of fresh whole foods in both raw and cooked form, and consult your health-care practitioner if you are concerned about oxalic acid in your diet.

Swiss Chard

Swiss chard, known also as silver beet, is closely related to the beet root. It is cultivated for its leaves, which are green, tender and nutritious. Chard stems are also edible, and vary in color from white or green to ruby and rainbow hues. Chard stems provide a good dose of iron, along with texture and beneficial fiber, and should not be wasted.

Chard can be picked when young or mature. It is easy to grow, and most plantings will provide three or more crops with continuous harvesting.

The first varieties of chard can be traced back to Sicily, and chard remains popular in Mediterranean cuisine. Young chard can be enjoyed raw, in salads, fresh juices, and smoothies. Very large, mature chard leaves will taste great when cooked, as they will develop a sweet, mild flavor comparable to spinach when braised or sautéed. Substitute spinach, kale, or beet greens in recipes that call for Swiss chard.

Tatsoi

Tatsoi, a dark, leafy Asian salad green known in many U.S. markets as spoon lettuce, is enjoyed throughout the world for its tender texture, and pleasantly mustardy, slightly sweet flavor. It is most commonly enjoyed in salads, but can also be sautéed, or added to soups and stir-fries toward the end of cooking.

Tatsoi grows in beautiful clusters of spoon-shaped leaves. It grows quickly from early spring through late fall. It is easy to find at farmers markets as well as Asian grocery stores. Although there is no substitute with the true flavor of tatsoi, spinach is an acceptable choice.

Turnip Greens

Turnip greens are the leafy tops of the turnip root. Like beet greens, they tend to receive short shrift in American kitchens, and are often disposed of uneaten.

This cruciferous vegetable is particularly high in calcium, as well as phytochemicals that work to prevent cancer and other chronic diseases. They often appear in Southern dishes, along with mustard greens and collards. Turnip greens are best when steamed until just tender, and then tossed in a flavorful dressing, or quickly sautéed.

If you've purchased turnip root with greens attached, remove them and store separately in the refrigerator. Mustard and beet greens both make perfect substitutes for turnip greens.

Watercress

Watercress is a semiaquatic perennial plant that is particularly well suited to hydroponic cultivation. This assertive leafy green grows both cultivated and wild, and in some parts of England and the American South was often the first fresh green vegetable eaten after months of wintered-over or root-cellared cabbages, or worse, deprivation, before modern food storage methods and widespread cultivation became the norm.

Many of us are familiar with watercress sandwiches, served at a traditional English afternoon tea, or perhaps watercress in a salad or as a garnish. But did you know that watercress has been used for its healing properties since ancient times? Today's food scientists value watercress for its anti-cancer and anti-inflammatory properties, as well as its ability to stimulate digestive processes. Enjoy watercress in salads, soups, and fresh juices. If watercress is unavailable, consider substituting young arugula leaves.

Take Care When Trying New Greens

While you should try to enjoy the full variety of greens available throughout the seasons, you may find that some of them simply don't agree with your system. Although some gas and intestinal discomfort are normal when shifting to a healthier diet that includes more greens, and thus more fiber, if a particular food bothers you consistently, listen to your body and skip it. When you're adding new foods to your diet, make changes gradually, and consider adding a probiotic supplement to avoid unpleasant digestive consequences.

The Least You Need to Know

- Including more greens in your diet is an easy way to improve your health.
- Greens are an economical choice for the cook on a budget, delivering maximum nutrition and filling, heart-healthy fiber for little cost.
- Choose minimally processed whole foods, such as fresh fruits, vegetables, whole grains, nuts, seeds, beans, and legumes.
- Greens are available around the world, in every climate and growing season. Familiarize yourself with each variety, and try to enjoy several servings per day.

Go Green for Your Health

In This Chapter

- Including greens in your diet
- Enjoying raw foods
- Discovering the truth about vegetarian nutrition

We all know that greens are good for us. Now, we'll take a closer look to see what nutrients each brings to the table. Greens have also been used as medicine throughout history, and we'll discover some of their healing properties.

Perhaps you've wondered about "eating raw." What's it all about? And is it for you? We'll explore the raw food movement, and discuss juicing, dehydrating, and incorporating raw foods into your daily routine.

Thinking about a vegetarian diet? You've probably wondered about protein, and whether you'll get enough. We'll learn about vegan, vegetarian, and transitional diets, and discuss the myths and facts surrounding nutrition and protein.

Vitamin Rich

Including fresh greens in your diet is one of the best things you can do for your health and well-being, and yet many of us simply don't do it. The USDA recommends eating just 3 cups of dark green vegetables per week, and shockingly, many Americans don't meet even this modest recommendation.

Recent research from the University of Leicester in the U.K. showed that by consuming a mere 1 ⅓ servings of leafy greens per day, study participants lowered their risk of type II diabetes by 14 percent. Imagine the health benefits of meeting your recommended daily allowance of five to nine servings of fruits and vegetables a day by including several servings of healthy, delicious greens. It's easy to do when you have the right information at your fingertips.

Leafy greens are a concentrated source of nutrition, including vitamins, minerals, and *phytonutrients*. Greens are low in calories and full of fiber, which helps to slow digestion and keep you feeling full longer, so they're the perfect food for weight reduction. Fiber also helps to regulate blood sugar levels. In addition, regularly including a variety of greens in your diet can help stave off other chronic illnesses such as arthritis, cancer, heart disease, artherosclerosis, high cholesterol, osteoporosis, and even depression. And, of course, greens are delicious, so why not enjoy them as often as possible?

> **DEFINITION**
>
> **Phytonutrients** are unique, protective compounds present in all plants. Phytonutrients act as antioxidants in your body, protecting cells against the effects of free radicals. Free radicals are damaging, disease-causing molecules produced by the body when digesting food, or when you are exposed to toxins such as pollution or radiation.

Break It Down

Greens are nature's health insurance, offering superior nutritional value. Eat (or drink) your greens, and you'll treat your body to rich stores of vitamins A, B, C, K, and E; plenty of iron, potassium, calcium, zinc, copper, and magnesium; plus disease-fighting antioxidants and phytochemicals.

Vitamin A

Vitamin A, also known as retinol, helps you maintain healthy vision, but that's only the beginning of the benefits you'll gain. It also stimulates white blood cell production for a strong immune system, and supports skeletal, reproductive, and respiratory functions. It is responsible for maintaining the health of your endothelial cells, which line the interior surfaces of your body, and is instrumental in preventing cancer by regulating cell division.

So why not just pop a multivitamin and forget about it? Preformed vitamin A has been linked to bone breakage, birth defects, and decreased absorption of vitamin D, as well as toxicity as high levels. By eating foods high in carotenoids, which your body converts to retinal, all of these problems are eliminated and your body has access to all of the benefits that vitamin A offers. If you do choose to add a multivitamin supplement to your diet, be sure that it contains beta-carotene, the carotenoid that is most efficiently made into retinal by your body.

We all associate carrots with high levels of beta carotene, but did you know that leafy greens are one of nature's best sources of this powerful antioxidant? Choose the brightest, most vividly colored greens for the highest content.

Spinach, broccoli, kale, endive, mustard greens, chicory, dandelion, escarole, watercress, turnip greens, and beet greens are all excellent sources of beta-carotene. Beta-carotene is fat soluble, so cooking it in a little oil will increase the nutrient's *bioavailability*.

DEFINITION

Bioavailability is the degree to with a nutrient becomes available to your body tissue after consumption. A fat-soluble vitamin is stored in your body's fat tissues, and will be better absorbed if ingested with a little oil. Water-soluble vitamins should be consumed every day, as they are dispersed in your body's fluids, and are not stored in quantity.

Beta-carotene is just one of several carotenoids—powerful antioxidant, cancer-fighting substances—found in dark leafy greens. Alpha-carotene, gamma-carotene, and beta-crypotxanthin all have vitamin A activity, allowing your body to convert them into retinal. Carotenoids are split into two classes: xanthophylis, which contain oxygen, and carotenes, which do not. A 1998 study in the *British Journal of Nutrition* showed that people with diets rich in carotenoids from fruits and vegetables were healthier, with lower incidences of cancer and mortality.

Spinach.

Vitamin B

Vitamin B is not just one compound, but a group of eight water-soluble substances that work together in your body to convert food into energy.

- Vitamin B_1 (thiamin) helps your body to turn carbohydrates into energy.

- Vitamin B_2 (riboflavin) helps the body to metabolize food into glucose, and provides antioxidant properties to combat disease.

- Vitamin B_3 (niacin) helps the body to produce energy, and is also essential for calcium absorption. Adequate niacin intake promotes healthy skin, nails, and hair.

- Vitamin B_5 (pantonthenic acid) turns food into energy, and builds the structures that carry oxygen through your body. The term "pantothenic" is derived from the Greek "pantos," meaning "everywhere," and as this suggests, this vitamin is available in a wide variety of foods, and deficiency is uncommon.

- Vitamin B_6 (pyridoxine) is essential for protein metabolism.

- Vitamin B_7 (biotin) helps your body to synthesize fats and metabolize protein.

- Vitamin B_9 (folic acid or folate) is a necessary nutrient that helps to produce and maintain new cells. It is particularly important in childhood, adolescence, and pregnancy. Adequate intake of folates has been shown to prevent birth defects, such as neural tube defects. It also helps to prevent cancer by preventing changes in your body's DNA, and helps with *homocysteine* metabolism.

- Vitamin B_{12} (cobalamin) is synthesized exclusively by bacteria and is necessary for the production of red blood cells, as well as growth and development in children. B_{12} is the only B vitamin that your body can store in the liver. Deficiency of B_{12} can cause pernicious anemia, a decrease in red blood cells caused by poor intestinal absorption, as well as permanent nerve damage. Since vitamin B_{12} is found primarily in meat, dairy, and egg products, those who follow a vegan diet should discuss B_{12} supplementation with their healthcare provider.

DEFINITION

Homocysteine is a toxic waste product produced in excess by our bodies when we are under stress. It damages blood vessels and contributes to high cholesterol and heart disease. Reducing homocysteine levels in the blood prevents blood clots and arterial plaque formation (artherosclerosis). It is a naturally occurring, sulfur-containing amino acid found in blood plasma. Its main purpose is in cellular metabolism and the manufacture of proteins.

Spinach, turnip greens, and bok choy are all excellent sources of B vitamins. To maintain maximum nutritional benefit, consider steaming your vegetables.

Vitamin C

Vitamin C (ascorbic acid) is a water-soluble vitamin that is needed for your body to grow and repair tissue. It also enhances iron absorption, and acts as an antioxidant to prevent free-radical damage and resulting disease.

This essential nutrient helps your body to make collagen, which is necessary for maintaining joint flexibility and preventing arthritis. Adequate collagen also keeps hair and skin looking healthy. Vitamin C may also prevent osteoporosis and reduce the risk of bone fractures.

We've all heard the advice to take vitamin C to prevent a cold. Recent research has shown that while increased vitamin C intake does not prevent colds, it may reduce their severity and duration.

If you're looking to increase your intake of vitamin C, you'll probably reach for a glass of orange juice. You might want to reach for iron-rich leafy greens instead, as consuming vitamin C and iron together enhances absorption. All fruits and vegetables include some quantity of vitamin C, so variety is the key to your healthy diet. Be sure to eat plenty of dark leafy greens, especially spinach, broccoli, green cabbage, turnip greens, and Brussels sprouts.

Vitamin K

Vitamin K (philoquinine) is derived nutritionally, and also made by the bacteria that live in our intestines. This fat-soluble vitamin is needed to help the blood to clot and prevent bleeding. Since vitamin K is stored in the liver, deficiencies are rare, but may be caused by chronic antibiotic use, Crohn's disease, celiac disease, gallbladder issues, and cystic fibrosis. Those who take blood thinners such as warfarin (Coumadin) must be especially careful to eat a variety of foods rich in vitamin K.

THE LOWDOWN

We know our bodies derive vitamin K from eating plants, but where do plants get their vitamin K? Chlorophyll is the substance that gives plants their green color, and provides them with vitamin K. Chlorophyll also strengthens the blood, detoxifies the body, fights infections, helps bad breath, and improves gastrointestinal function.

In addition to important blood-clotting activity, vitamin K has also been shown to strengthen bones. Studies published in the *American Journal of Clinical Nutrition* suggest that women who ate a minimum of 110 micrograms of vitamin K were 30 percent less likely to suffer a hip fracture than women who consumed less than this amount.

Data from the U.S. Department of Agriculture shows that one in four Americans does not get enough vitamin K from dietary sources. Vegetables rich in vitamin K include kale, broccoli, turnip greens, Swiss chard, mustard greens, romaine lettuce, spinach, cabbage, Brussels sprouts, and green leaf lettuce.

Vitamin E

Vitamin E actually consists of eight fat-soluble compounds called tocopherols. These compounds protect skin from ultraviolet rays, boost your metabolism, fight against cancer and free-radical damage, and provide anti-inflammatory benefits.

While vitamin E deficiency is rare, recent research suggests that a diet rich in these compounds may protect against Alzheimer's disease. A diet rich in vitamin E has also been recommended to reduce the risk of bladder cancer, which is the fourth-leading cause of cancer death among men.

Greens rich in vitamin E include spinach, dandelion, mustard greens, Swiss chard, watercress, and broccoli.

Iron

Iron is a mineral that is necessary for the production of hemoglobin in red blood cells, as well as myoglobin in muscles. Iron-deficiency anemia is common in young women and children. Common signs of anemia are exhaustion and shortness of breath.

Iron occurs in two forms—heme and nonheme. Heme iron is more easily absorbed in the body, and is found in eggs, meats, poultry, oysters, tuna, salmon, and dried fruits. Vegans and vegetarians get their iron from nonheme iron, which is found in fruits and vegetables. Nonheme iron is processed less efficiently by the body, so it is recommended that those who do not eat sources of heme iron increase their daily intake of iron-rich vegetables. Contrary to popular belief, studies show that vegetarians do not suffer from anemia any more frequently than the general population.

One easy way to increase iron in your diet is to cook food in a cast-iron frying pan. Greens rich in iron include spinach, kale, amaranth, Brussels sprouts, bok choy, and Swiss chard.

Potassium

Potassium is necessary to help your body balance water between cells and bodily fluids. It also builds proteins and muscle, and helps to control the electrical impulses of your heart.

Diets high in sodium and low in potassium have been shown to increase blood pressure levels. Increased potassium consumption decreases stroke risk, improves bone density, and helps your body to process calcium and avoid kidney stones.

HEADS UP!

Limiting sodium intake is a good call for your cardiovascular health, but you still need some sodium to support nerve and muscle function, and to work with potassium to regulate fluid in your body. The RDA (recommended daily allowance) of sodium for healthy adults is no more than 2,300 milligrams per day. Regularly exceeding this recommendation can lead to high blood pressure and other serious health problems.

People who should pay extra attention to potassium levels in their diet include cardiac patients who are on diuretics, athletes who regularly sweat profusely during workouts, and people with chronic kidney disease, especially those on renal dialysis.

Greens high in potassium include kale, collard, spinach, turnip greens, and mustard greens. Studies have shown that cooked greens offer superior bioavailable calcium content to their raw counterparts.

Calcium

Calcium, like potassium, is a mineral that acts as an *electrolyte* in your body. Calcium is necessary for developing and maintaining strong bones and teeth, and contributes to nerve and muscle function, cardiovascular health, and the balance of hormones and enzymes in your body.

DEFINITION

Electrolytes send impulses throughout your body, helping to regulate your heart and circulatory system, as well as your body's fluids and pH balance. Electrolytes are lost through dehydration, which first increases the balance of electrolytes in your system as water is lost, and then depletes them. Normal daily activity does not affect electrolyte balance, but those who regularly engage in vigorous athletic activity should pay attention.

Excessive sodium consumption and lactose intolerance can lead to calcium deficiency. In addition, your body needs vitamin D in order to absorb calcium. Vitamin D–fortified milk and nondairy milk substitutes (such as soy, rice, or hemp milk) are good choices to ensure adequate vitamin D consumption. Spending a few minutes in direct sunlight each day has also been shown to increase vitamin D levels. The elderly, in particular, benefit from increased vitamin D consumption, and simple blood tests can be performed to determine if supplementation is necessary.

Broccoli, collards, kale, mustard greens, Napa cabbage, and bok choy are all good sources of calcium.

Zinc

Zinc supports the immune system, brain function, and your body's reproductive ability. It also helps with wound healing, protects your eyesight, and maintains your ability to taste and smell. Some studies have shown that zinc can reduce the length and severity of the common cold, but evidence to the contrary exists as well.

Vegetarians and vegans must pay extra attention to their zinc intake, as compounds such as phytates, which are present in whole-grain breads, cereals, and legumes can decrease zinc absorption. Eating plenty of zinc-rich greens such as spinach, collards, broccoli, amaranth, and watercress, along with a varied and healthy diet, will help to prevent deficiency.

Copper

Copper is found primarily in the bloodstream, where it works with iron to form red blood cells. Copper is also essential to healthy nerve function, and formation of connective tissue and the skin pigment melanin.

Copper deficiency is rare, but high supplemental consumption of zinc or iron is often responsible. Anemia is a good indicator of the possibility of copper deficiency. Good sources of copper include amaranth, beet greens, turnip greens, and spinach.

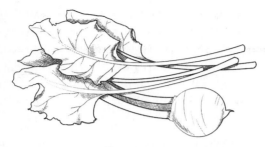

Beet greens.

Magnesium

Magnesium is necessary for more than 300 essential functions in your body. It strengthens your bones and immune system, assists with cardiac function, regulates blood sugar levels, and is necessary for nerve and muscle health.

Green, leafy vegetables are an excellent source of magnesium because they contain chlorophyll, as the center of the chlorophyll molecule contains magnesium. Greens with beneficial levels of magnesium include broccoli, spinach, cooked Swiss chard, kale, cooked bok choy, beet greens, and turnip greens.

The Raw Truth

Raw food aficionados believe that by keeping foods under 115°F, beneficial enzymes remain active. Enzymes are necessary for all of your bodily functions, particularly digestion. Raw foodists strive to consume a diet that consists of 75 to 100 percent uncooked, unprocessed foods, which help alkalize the body and remove acidic toxins.

Advocates of the alkaline diet, including raw foodists and natural health practitioners, maintain that as the natural state of the human body is somewhat alkaline, eating alkaline-producing foods, rather than acid-producing foods, will help you to maintain a state of optimal health, and fight cancer and other chronic diseases. While scientific evidence has not conclusively proved these claims, there is no disputing the fact that we can all benefit from a diet that features plenty of fresh vegetables, fruits, and unprocessed foods. Steer clear of diet plans that exclude many different foods, or prescribe fasts and nutritional supplements, and aim to enjoy a wide variety of fresh, unprocessed, whole foods.

You may not be ready for a completely raw lifestyle, but you can certainly benefit from including more raw foods in your diet. We've learned that some foods have more bioavailable vitamins and minerals when cooked, but many foods are better for you when eaten raw. Vitamin C and folates, as well as the cancer-fighting sulfur compounds in cruciferous vegetables, are all destroyed by heat. Enjoying plenty of fresh, raw recipes as part of a balanced diet will help you to maintain optimal health.

Eating a raw diet is not just about eating uncooked fruits and vegetables. Raw foodists enjoy a wide variety of sprouted grains, legumes, nuts, and seeds. Soaking or sprouting these foods releases nutrients, and sprouts are excellent for you due to their concentrated nutritional value. It's easy and economical to make your own sprouts at home—just start with organic foods, and soak in a clean glass jar, rinsing and draining several times. Germination times vary, so you might want to do some research. It's not necessary to purchase special equipment, but make sure you have a few simple items, such as cheesecloth and rubber bands, to make the process easier.

THE LOWDOWN

Sprouts are highly nutritious, easy to make, and economical. They are bursting with antioxidants, protein, chlorophyll, vitamins, minerals, and amino acids. Sprouts contain plenty of enzymes to keep your digestive system functioning optimally. They're fun to make, too, and kids will love doing a "science project" they can eat! If you'd like more information on making your own sprouts, visit a website such as www.sproutpeople.org, where you'll find extensive information on making your own delicious, nourishing sprouts.

Many raw food recipes call for blending or pulverizing food in a food processor or blender. This process will help you to make easily digested soups and sauces. Some blenders, such as Vitamix, even heat foods slightly, enhancing the flavor and appeal of some raw soups. Other raw recipes, such as gazpacho, are best enjoyed ice cold.

You'll find raw foods throughout this book, and not just the usual salads. Fresh juices, smoothies, raw snacks, entrées, soups, and desserts are all featured. Just look for the

ℝ symbol to find the right raw recipes for you.

The Veg Lifestyle

Vegetarians do not eat beef, pork, fish, shellfish, poultry, or animal flesh of any kind. Many people identify themselves as vegetarian, including *ovo-lacto vegetarians*, who consume milk and dairy products; *pescatarians*, who abstain from eating all animal flesh but fish; and *flexitarians*, who follow a primarily vegetarian diet, but occasionally eat meat, fish, or fowl.

THE LOWDOWN

Meatless Mondays, an initiative founded by former advertising executive Sid Lerner, aims to improve both public health and the environment by asking everyone to cut out meat consumption for one day a week. Lerner chose Mondays because of the day's association with a fresh start. Begin your own Meatless Monday tradition—have different family members cook dinner each week, or host a potluck for your friends—and join the revolution!

Vegans consume no animal products whatsoever, including the above, but also forgo honey, foods that have been processed with animal ingredients such as gelatin or wine, and foods that use animal products during production, like some refined sugars. The vegan lifestyle aims to do no harm to animals, the environment, and the people who produce food, so organic, sustainable practices are stressed. Most people who eat a vegan diet for ethical reasons also abstain from wearing leather and wool, or using cosmetics or household items that are tested on animals or contain animal products. If you're interested in learning more about the vegan way of life, see Appendix A, "Resources," in the back of this book for more information.

Vegan and vegetarian diets offer substantial variety, amazing flavors, and incredible health benefits. Choosing a plant-based diet can lower your cholesterol, prevent heart disease, and significantly reduce your risk for stroke, diabetes, and many cancers.

We can all benefit from the recipes and techniques that make vegetarian cuisine unique. If you haven't made the leap yet, try it a few days a week. Once you begin to enjoy better health, improved energy, and a revitalized appearance, you'll be hooked!

The Protein Myth

If you've ever shared your intention to go vegan or vegetarian, you've probably heard someone exclaim, *"But where will you get your protein?!"* You can feel free to assure them that most Americans consume far too much protein. Unless you are pregnant or engaging in extremely vigorous athletic activity for hours per day, you'll get enough protein without even trying.

In addition to greens such as broccoli, kale, spinach, amaranth, and beet greens, many vegetarian staple foods are excellent sources of protein. A diet rich in fresh vegetables, fruits, beans, legumes, whole grains, meat alternatives such as soy or tempeh, and low-fat dairy or dairy alternatives will provide more than adequate protein at any stage of life.

Much has been made throughout the years regarding protein combining. It was once believed that in order to replace the nine essential amino acids that form protein in your body, you had to consume foods such as beans, greens, and whole grains at the same meal. This is generally accepted as untrue, although some people still practice these combinations because particular foods actually combine well to make a satisfying meal.

Think of your diet in terms of a day, or even several days, and keep track of your nutrition. If you find that you are particularly deficient in any particular nutrient, consider making dietary changes based upon the information provided in this book, or add fortified foods or supplements to your diet. If you have concerns, or are pregnant, talk to your health-care provider about your dietary choices.

The Least You Need to Know

- Eating more greens improves immunity, eyesight, and cardiovascular health, strengthens muscles and bones, balances hormones and enzymes, and protects your cells against certain cancers.
- Greens are low in calories and high in fiber, making them great for digestion and weight loss.
- Incorporate more raw foods into your diet as part of a healthy lifestyle.
- Consider a vegan or vegetarian diet for optimal health.
- All of the protein you need can be found in plant foods. Make sure to eat a wide variety.

Stocking Your Green Kitchen

In This Chapter

- Buying the freshest, most nutritious greens
- Choosing locally grown, organic foods
- Stocking your pantry with ingredients for fast, fresh meals
- Storing foods properly for nutrition, economy, and freshness
- Planning meals to save time and money

Before you jump into healthy, fresh cooking with greens, you'll need to learn a few basics, such as how to select and store the freshest produce. Every great meal starts at the market, so tips for shopping in season will help you tune in to nature every time you enter the kitchen.

You may ask which is better—eating organic, or eating locally? We'll explore both options, and discuss strategies for eating the cleanest meals possible without busting your food budget!

Shopping is an art and a science. Once you've learned to choose your produce wisely, you'll need some basic items that will allow you to prepare great food on a moment's notice. Stock your pantry with staples such as pasta, grains, and legumes, and you're on your way to fast, healthy, delicious meals!

At the Market

When shopping for greens, you'll want to make sure you get the freshest, most tender produce available. Check the stems; they should be fresh and pliable, not woody and dried out. Give the leaves a shake—do they seem resilient, or floppy and wilted?

Colors should be bright and vibrant, not yellowed or brown. Take a good sniff, too, and ensure that your greens smell fresh and bright. Never purchase musty-smelling or slimy greens.

HEADS UP!

Many supermarkets will mist your greens with water throughout the day. While this keeps them fresh and appetizing-looking to shoppers, it also accelerates spoilage and can leave you with a wet mess in your grocery cart. Give your greens a good shake at the market before you put them in a bag, and watch out for showers when you're reaching into the bins to search for the freshest produce!

When selecting your greens, consider their intended use. Packaged greens of all kinds are available in your supermarket, offering convenience to the cook on the run. They may not be the best choice, however, if you intend to enjoy your greens in a raw preparation such as a salad or smoothie. Packaged greens have been known to harbor food-borne contaminants such as E. coli. Contamination can occur during harvesting, processing, and packaging, and the chances of contamination increase the longer the product sits in your fridge. Whatever your choice, be sure to wash all produce well, even if it says "prewashed" on the package.

Tune In to Nature

Eating food that is grown locally and sustainably is one of the best things you can do for your health, and greens are one of the few fresh foods that are always in season. Choosing vegetables and fruits that are in season locally can save money and help the environment, too. Reducing the distance food has to travel to get to your plate saves energy, and buying directly from farmers in your area benefits your community. For the least environmental impact, choose foods that are organically or transitionally grown whenever possible.

According to the USDA, organically grown produce must be grown without synthetic fertilizers or pesticides. Organic produce must also be free of GMOs (genetically modified ingredients) and sewage sludge, and cannot be irradiated. Transitional produce has been grown to organic standards, although the farm may not yet have met the 36-month pesticide-free criteria or completed the licensing process. While organic foods are not always more nutritious than conventionally grown produce, organic is the best choice for most people. Chemical pesticides, fungicides, and fertilizers have been linked to cancer and other diseases, and the long-term effects of GMOs are unknown.

THE LOWDOWN

Organic food is better for your health, as well as our planet. Buy organic whenever possible. If you need to stretch your budget, check out "The Dirty Dozen" and "The Clean 15" at www.ewg.org/foodnews. These annual lists, compiled by the Environmental Working Group, will help you to decide which organic foods are must-haves, and which conventionally grown fruits and veggies are safer to buy.

In the spring, enjoy tender young spinach, amaranth, and arugula, as well as baby lettuces of all kinds. Summer brings a bounty of delicious greens, such as bok choy, mizuna, mustard, beet, and turnip greens. In autumn and winter, hardy greens such as kale, cabbage, and escarole carry us through the chilly months with their vibrant flavors and excellent nutrition profile.

Not everyone is lucky enough to have a farm nearby, but nearly every city features a farmers market that offers fresh, local produce in season. The USDA offers a searchable database of farmers markets throughout the United States at http://search.ams.usda.gov/farmersmarkets/, or you can check your local newspaper's events section. When shopping the farmers market, be sure to talk to the farmers. Ask questions, and know where your food is coming from. The folks at the farm stand can also be a great source of recipe ideas. If they're growing it, you can bet they're eating it, too!

La Vida Locavore

If you're a locavore, your goal is to only eat seasonal foods grown within 100 miles of home, avoiding anything flown from far away, grown out of season, processed, or packaged. Although the locavore lifestyle can present some challenges, especially in the winter months, locavorism is a worthy goal. Eating locally produced food supports your local economy; protects family farms; encourages a healthy, seasonal diet; and helps the environment, too.

Green cabbage.

Savoy cabbage.

The following table can help you eat like a locavore by giving you a better idea of when different greens are in season and how long you can keep them in storage. Peak season indicates when each green is at its best throughout most of the United States. Some hardy greens, such as cabbage, are excellent almost year-round. If you're lucky enough to live in a temperate climate, you will find that the majority of these greens may be available to you throughout the year:

Vegetable	Peak Season	Storage
Amaranth	Spring–Autumn	Use immediately
Arugula	Spring, Autumn	Bunches: 3 days; Packaged: follow expiration date
Beet Greens	Summer–Winter	Use immediately
Bok Choy	Year-round	5–7 days
Broccoli	Spring–Fall	3 days
Broccoli Rabe	Spring–Fall	3 days
Brussels Sprouts	Fall–Winter	2 days
Cabbage	Summer–Winter	Heads: 1–2 weeks; Sliced: 5–6 days
Chicory (Puntarelle)	Fall–Winter	3 days
Curly Endive (Frisee)	Spring, Fall	3–4 days
Collard	Summer–Winter	5–7 days
Dandelion	Spring	2 days
Endive (Belgian)	Year-round	1–2 weeks
Escarole	Fall–Spring	3–4 days
Kale	Fall–Spring	4 days
Leaf Lettuce	Spring, Fall	3–4 days
Mizuna	Year-round	3 days
Mustard	Year-round	3 days
Radicchio	Fall–Spring	7 days
Romaine	Spring, Fall	7 days
Sorrel	Spring–Fall	7 days
Spinach	Spring–Fall	Bunches: 3 days; Packaged: follow expiration date
Swiss Chard	Summer–Fall	3–5 days
Tatsoi	Year-round	3 days
Turnip	Summer–Winter	Use immediately
Watercress	Year-round	Use immediately

Clean Your Greens

Greens are often grown in sandy soil, and their many layers of leaves provide hiding places for grit, so you'll need to wash them well. As soon as you get home, remove them from the bag and submerge them in several changes of cold water, either in a large bowl or a well-cleaned and sanitized sink. Lift the greens out of the water, and you'll see plenty of grit left behind. Repeat the process until no grit or dirt is left behind.

Dry the greens in your salad spinner, wrap them in a paper towel to absorb excess moisture, and store in your vegetable crisper in a resealable plastic bag. Most greens that have been washed and stored properly will keep in the crisper for several days.

The Well-Stocked Pantry

A well-stocked pantry allows you to create fast, nourishing meals featuring nutritious, versatile greens any day of the week. Start with basic staples such as rice, dried and canned beans and legumes, pasta, canned tomatoes, oils, vinegars, and commonly used herbs and spices.

As you become more comfortable, expand your repertoire with more exotic ingredients such as curry powder, canned chipotle chiles, Moroccan harissa paste, flavored vinegars, and luxury items such as truffle salt.

Start building your pantry with these ingredients:

> Oils: olive, grapeseed, sunflower, coconut
>
> Vinegars: apple cider, red wine, sherry, champagne, balsamic
>
> Flours: all-purpose, whole-wheat pastry, gluten-free blend
>
> Pastas: whole wheat, semolina, gluten-free varieties
>
> Rices: brown basmati, arborio
>
> Grains: quinoa, millet, farro, bulgur wheat, barley
>
> Condiments: vegetarian Worcestershire, mustard, raw honey or agave nectar, hot pepper sauce
>
> Herbs, Spices, and Extracts: vanilla extract, oregano, thyme, bay leaves, crushed red pepper, smoked and sweet paprika, curry powder, ginger, cinnamon, cumin, black peppercorns
>
> Beans and legumes: dried lentils, dried and canned white beans, black beans, and chick peas

Pantry-stable vegetables: onions, garlic, potatoes

Miscellaneous: dried chiles, dried mushrooms, canned tomatoes, jarred olives

Store your pantry items carefully. Airtight containers, such as glass jars, ensure a long shelf life. Don't buy in large quantities unless you know you'll use the ingredient frequently. Take advantage of bulk bins at your local market. These allow you to only buy as much as you will need, and you won't waste time and money throwing away unused pantry items that have been on the shelf forever.

The fats in oil, flour, rice, nuts, and seeds can turn rancid quickly. Store oils such as canola, grapeseed, sunflower, and coconut in the refrigerator for maximum freshness. Rice that is used regularly does fine in an airtight container in the pantry, but if you buy specialty rice, such as sushi rice, that you'll use once in awhile, the fridge is a great place to keep it fresh. Infrequently used flours, nuts, and seeds keep best in an airtight container in the freezer.

Pantry-stable vegetables such as potatoes, onions, and garlic will keep for a long time when stored in a dark, well-ventilated, cool place. Don't store them together, though, as the gases in potatoes and onions work to turn one another mushy.

Dried herbs, spices, and extracts should be stored away from light and heat, in airtight containers. That cabinet over the stove seems like a convenient place to store those spices, but they'll last longer and retain maximum flavor if you choose a cooler spot.

With a well-stocked pantry and a little knowledge at your local market, you'll soon be preparing fresh, healthy dinners that are on the table in a snap.

Fill Your Fridge

Now that you've learned the best way to purchase and store fresh greens, and you've stocked your pantry with staple ingredients, you'll need to fill your refrigerator so that you're always ready to make a fresh, healthy meal starring delicious and nutritious greens.

Pay close attention to expiration dates, and ensure freshness by using a strict policy of "first in/first out" when using items from your refrigerator. You might find that keeping a list of ingredients in your refrigerator and freezer helps you to use all items before they expire. Plan meals based not only on what is fresh at the market, but what you already have on hand.

A properly stocked refrigerator includes dairy or dairy substitutes, fruits, vegetables, and perishable ingredients. You'll be ready to cook a variety of dishes when you choose from this list of common refrigerated foods:

> Dairy and Dairy Substitutes: milk (cow's milk or nondairy beverages such as rice, soy, coconut, or hemp milk), butter (cow's milk or vegan butter substitute), cheese (cheddar, Monterey jack, Parmesan, vegan cheese substitutes such as Daiya), half and half or soy creamer, plain yogurt (cow or goat's milk, soy, or coconut milk). If you choose to eat eggs, aim for local, pasture-raised eggs whenever possible.

> Fruits and Vegetables: Apples, berries, cucumbers, peppers, tomatoes, parsley, scallions, lemons, and limes.

> Miscellaneous: tofu, mayonnaise (traditional or vegan), ketchup, Worcestershire sauce, hot sauce (such as Tabasco), Dijon mustard, whole-grain mustard, soy sauce or tamari, sesame oil.

Convenience from the Freezer

Convenience items abound at your local supermarket. It's now easy to find organic fruits and vegetables in the freezer aisle, along with veggie burgers, shelled edamame, pizza dough, bagels, and pita bread. Fill your freezer with foods you know your family will consume within 3 months. Many commonly used ingredients, such as milk, butter, cheese, shortening, nuts, flours, and chocolate can be frozen to extend shelf life and take advantage of sale prices.

How you stock your freezer will depend on how much you value cost savings over convenience, and whether locally grown produce is available for you to freeze yourself. Doubling the recipe when making soups, sauces, and casseroles is a great way to fill your freezer with nutritious foods that will save you on busy days when takeout seems the only option. In Chapter 5, we'll discuss how freezing your own ingredients and prepared dishes can help to save you money and time, and recipes throughout this book will provide suggestions for making ahead and freezing.

To ensure that healthy, nutritious greens are always a part of your diet, keep a selection of frozen vegetables such as spinach, cauliflower, broccoli, and collard greens. Unless you are growing your own veggies or shopping at your local farmers market, buying frozen vegetables can be a smart choice. While produce in your supermarket is picked days or even weeks before it hits the shelves, frozen foods are picked and processed at peak ripeness to ensure product quality, resulting in excellent flavor and nutritional value, especially during winter months.

Your freezer will run most efficiently when it is full. To maintain the quality of the food in your freezer, and save on energy costs, place plastic jugs filled ¾ of the way with water in your freezer to fill empty spaces.

THE LOWDOWN

Having a well-organized meal plan and grocery list makes a trip to the store or market a snap! From a simple notebook on the kitchen counter to online meal planning and grocery list tools, the possibilities are limitless. Organize your list by category, and consider your supermarket's layout—produce, dairy, bread, and frozen items are usually at the perimeter of the store, with staple items and pre-pared foods in the middle. If you're headed to the farmers market, know what's in season and keep an open mind about trying new items. Sticking to the list keeps your budget in check, but having a little flexibility allows you to take advantage of a great bargain or produce of excellent quality when you see it.

The Least You Need to Know

- Choose the freshest greens available. Sniff, poke, and shake your greens to ensure that they are bright, vital, and moist, with pliable stems.
- Wash greens in several changes of cold water, wrap loosely in paper towels, and store in plastic bags in the vegetable crisper as soon as you get home from the market.
- Stock your pantry with staple ingredients, buy in-season produce, and plan your meals in advance to save time and money.
- Take advantage of frozen fruits and vegetables during winter months, and keep a few home-cooked meals stored in the freezer for days when you don't have time to cook from scratch.
- Make a meal plan and grocery list, and stick to it.

Grow Your Own

In This Chapter

- Gardening ideas for every home
- Planting tips
- Creating compost and fertilizers
- Employing natural pest control

There are many reasons to start growing your own greens. Perhaps you're interested in sustainability, self-sufficiency, or a fun project to get your kids interested in eating their veggies. Whether you live in a city apartment, a suburban neighborhood, or out in the country, this chapter will show you it's simple to grow fresh greens for your family with a little know-how.

It Starts with a Seed

Seeds are available everywhere—at garden centers, your local farm, in catalogs, and even your local grocery store. Try to find organic or heirloom seeds. Heirloom seeds are created from open pollination, not in a lab. Seeds labeled heirloom, organic, or heritage are free of genetically modified ingredients (GMOs).

You can also save seeds from previous organic crops to plant during the next growing season. My grandparents were always certain to save the seeds from a select few tomatoes deemed the "cream of the crop" each season, in order to select traits that they enjoyed. The seeds from particularly delicious specimens would be carefully dried, then put away in an airtight container. In the spring, they would plant these seeds, and the strongest seedlings would be placed in the garden to repeat the cycle.

Organizations such as Seed Savers Exchange are dedicated to the preservation of heirloom (also known as heritage) seeds. They operate one of North America's largest seed banks, offering a huge variety of non-GMO, organic heirloom seeds. Members are offered education, and encouraged to save and exchange heirloom seeds to be enjoyed for generations to come.

The Plot Thickens

Now that you know where to find great seeds, you'll need to decide where to plant your garden. Window boxes, raised beds, garden plots—even an old whiskey barrel can be the site of your green garden.

Container Gardening

Container gardening is a great choice if you live in an apartment, have very little usable garden space, or have poor soil conditions. Containers can vary from window boxes, a few pots on your fire escape, or a collection of repurposed vessels on your patio or front lawn. Be creative!

When planting your miniature garden, be sure to purchase organic soil made especially for containers. You'll want to be sure your container has good drainage as well, so that water does not accumulate in the bottom. Some might advise you to place rocks or broken shells in the bottom of your container, but this can actually create the conditions you are trying to avoid—heavy, sludgy soil blocking drainage at the bottom of the pot.

The best soil choice for container gardening is an organic potting mix with peat moss, which will ensure drainage. Unlike nonorganic soils, organic potting mix can be reused because it contains living organisms that nourish the soil.

Hydroponic Gardens

No room for a window box? If you have a little counter space to spare, consider an indoor hydroponic garden. Purchase one ready to use out of the box, or make your own using old clamshell salad containers, a shelf, and a few grow lights. Put several inches of soil-free potting mix in the bottom of each container, and then add seeds and water. Leave them covered for a few days, then poke holes in the bottom of the clamshell containers, remove the lids and place them underneath as watering trays. Fill the lower trays with an inch of water. You'll be able to grow baby greens of all kinds, in all weather, and in every home using this method.

Raised Beds

Raised beds are perfect if you have a little extra space outside, as you'll be able to grow a variety of crops in close quarters. Build your own raised beds, or find them ready to assemble in most gardening catalogs.

Raised beds are just that—raised above the soil. If your soil is poor, or you are unable to dig a permanent garden bed, raised beds are the way to go. They're also easier for many people to manage, and can be built at heights that are accessible for the elderly, small children, or those with disabilities.

Raised beds are also more pest resistant than in-ground beds, as bunnies and gophers can't tunnel underneath to snack on your produce. It's more difficult for weeds to invade your raised beds as well, so you'll probably only need to weed once or twice each season (after your plants have sprouted and grown a few inches, since you don't want to accidentally weed your crop!).

THE LOWDOWN

It's important to consider depth when choosing or building containers and raised beds. Herbs, microgreens, and baby salad greens can be planted in shallower containers, but to accommodate the root system of most vegetable plants, you'll need about 10 to 12 inches of depth.

In-Ground Beds

In-ground beds are the perfect inexpensive option, but you will need plenty of room and good-quality soil. To prepare an in-ground bed, use a tiller to turn over and aerate the soil. You can purchase a small tiller for a reasonable price, or use a hoe and pitchfork if you are ready for a serious workout, but many people choose to visit their local hardware or farm supply store to rent a larger, mechanized tiller if preparing beds of substantial size.

In-ground beds will need to be weeded more often, but you'll have plenty of room to plant a variety of crops, from perennials such as sorrel that return each year, to row after row of cabbage, broccoli, Swiss chard, and as many lettuces as your heart desires.

If you live in an area with lots of deer and bunnies, you may need to surround your in-ground beds with wire fencing to protect your crop. If bunnies are your bane, sink fencing at least 4 inches deep in soil to keep them from tunneling right under. Are deer driving you to distraction? You'll need a 4-foot-high fence to discourage them. Try planting a patch of delicious greens far from the fenced area to share with your animal friends and keep them away from your garden. If you'd rather surround your garden with nature, plant coarse, prickly specimens such as daisies, aster, or echinacea around your garden's perimeter for a beautiful alternative to fencing. Deer will avoid plants with strong odors or irritating textures. A few unpleasant nibbles from your border plants is usually all it takes for them to move on to more tender foliage.

Ready, Set, Grow!

Growing greens is easy. You can germinate your seeds first by placing them in a warm spot between layers of damp paper toweling for a day or two before planting, or sow them directly in your chosen container or garden plot. Moistening them first will speed the germination process, but directly sown seeds will germinate just as well in a slightly longer period of time. Your seed packet will probably tell you to plant in rows with a specified distance between each seed, but the easy way to plant greens is to scatter the seeds randomly in your plot or container, then cover with an inch or two of soil.

When shoots emerge, thin the plants until they are 1 inch apart. Thin plants by cutting them at the soil line with a sharp scissor. These first tender sprouts are highly nutritious and delicious, so enjoy them immediately in a salad. As your plants grow larger, thin them again when they are the size of baby lettuce greens.

HEADS UP!

While this simple method works for most leafy greens, others require particular attention. Larger plants such as broccoli and cabbage, as well as root vegetables such as turnips and beets, will require more room, and are sometimes easier to grow if planted from seedlings, healthy plants that have begun to grow and are ready to transplant into the soil, rather than from seed. Amaranth, in particular, can grow in bushes up to 5 feet, and must be sown according to instructions on the seed packet for the variety you are planting.

Broccoli.

When you thin plants for the second time, give the remaining ones appropriate growing space to grow to maturity. (Refer to the following chart, or check your seed packet for recommended growing space.)

Many leafy greens that grow in loose heads, such as leaf lettuce or Swiss chard, can be harvested several times by cutting the outer leaves, leaving the inner leaves intact.

The inner leaves will continue to produce new growth. In this manner, you will provide yourself with quite a few meals from one small packet of seeds.

You'll know your leafy greens have stopped producing when they form a flower stalk. This is called bolting; it happens at the end of the growing season, or when the weather has become too hot. Your greens will taste bitter and unpleasant after bolting, and will stop producing new growth, so pull them up, and put them in your composter. If your crop of greens was planted in the spring, replace them with warm-weather plants such as tomato or cucumber seedlings. In the autumn, cover the bed or container with a fresh layer of compost or mulch to nourish and protect the soil during the winter months. When springtime returns, work in a fresh layer of compost, and your soil is renewed and ready to begin the cycle again.

This handy chart will provide the basics. If you're serious about helping your garden grow, check some books about gardening out from your local library, or contact your state's cooperative extension for more information on the best growing practices in your region.

When reading the chart below, you may wish to have a farmers almanac handy. It will give you valuable information, such as frost dates for your area. For instance, in my part of New Jersey, the first fall frost occurs around November 7, so I'll want to get hardy fall plantings such as broccoli into the ground during the first week of October. The last spring frost is projected for April 13, so I'll be able to begin sowing lettuce directly into the ground sometime around March 30.

These are general guidelines, and weather patterns can vary. Use the chart, but use some common sense, too. If March 30 arrives with a blizzard, I'll probably wait a few weeks before I put my lettuce in the ground.

Vegetable	Germination	Begin Harvest	Container	Planting Notes
Amaranth	1–7 days	4–6 weeks	No	Plant when soil reaches 65°F in well-fed soil. Fertilize often.
Arugula	4–8 days	3–4 weeks	Yes	Plant as soon as soil is warm enough to dig. Sow additional seeds throughout the season for a continuous crop.
Beet Greens/ Turnip Greens	1 day	3 weeks	Yes	Plant as soon as soil is warm enough to dig. Begin to harvest greens as soon as they reach 2 inches. Harvest roots after 8 weeks.

Vegetable	Germination	Begin Harvest	Container	Planting Notes
Bok Choy	7–10 days	6–7 weeks	Yes	Plant as soon as soil is warm enough to dig. Plants will survive a frost. Start second crop in late summer.
Broccoli	1–7 days	8–9 weeks	Yes	Sow seeds directly in ground 8 weeks before first frost in well-fed soil. Fertilize often.
Broccoli Rabe	*See* Broccoli.			
Brussels Sprouts	1–7 days	12 weeks	No	Plant seedlings that have been started indoors 90 days before first frost. Keep soil moist and well fertilized. Remove leaves at bottom of plant as sprouts develop, and be vigilant for worms and aphids.
Cabbage (Green/Red)	1–7 days	12–14 weeks	No	Begin seeding in late spring, and continue planting seeds through mid-June for continuous harvest. Fertilize often, and cover in early growth stages to discourage pests.
Chicory	1–7 days	6 weeks	Yes	Sow seeds in early spring. If you wish to blanch your chicory for tender, white hearts, transfer to pots when the plants reach 6 inches, cover with another pot, and continue to grow for another 3–5 weeks.
Curly Endive	1–7 days	6 weeks	Yes	Sow seeds in early spring. If you wish to blanch leaves, as for frisée, tie up outer leaves at 5 weeks using twine, and leave in ground for 5–7 more days.

continues

continued

Vegetable	Germination	Begin Harvest	Container	Planting Notes
Collard	1–7 days	12 weeks	Yes	Plant hardened-off seedlings in well-fertilized soil 3–4 weeks before last frost. Water regularly, and mulch base of plants to keep leaves clean and soil cool. Plant 8 weeks before first frost for autumn harvest.
Dandelion	N/A	N/A	N/A	Dandelion is a wild edible. Harvest in early spring, from areas free from animal waste and pesticide use. Pick leaves before flowers form for best flavor.
Endive (Belgian)	1–7 days	*See* planting notes.	Yes	Belgian endive must be planted twice—once outdoors for the root, then indoors for the tender, white leaves. Plant in early spring, in rich soil, with 6 inches between each seed. After 12 weeks, gently unearth roots. Cut leaves off 2 inches above roots, and feed leaves to your compost. Pack roots upright in a bucket, cover to keep light out, and place in a very cool spot, such as your unheated garage or shed. Three weeks before you want your first harvest, move to a warmer spot, about 60°F (such as your basement). After 3 weeks, endive should be ready for harvest.

Vegetable	Germination	Begin Harvest	Container	Planting Notes
Kale	1–7 days	8 weeks	Yes	Plant as soon as soil is warm enough to dig. Can be grown throughout winter months for spring harvest if covered with straw. Does not grow well in warm weather.
Leaf Lettuce	1–7 days	6 weeks	Yes	For spring plantings, plant seeds in cold frames 8 weeks before last frost, or sow directly in ground 2 weeks before last frost. Plant autumn crop as soon as temperatures average 75°F or lower. Seeds can be saved for the next season— harvest seed heads, dry and sift to separate seeds from chaff.
Mizuna	1–7 days	4–6 weeks	Yes	Tolerates frost and heat. Plant in early spring, and sow seeds every few weeks for continuous harvest.
Mustard	1–7 days	4–6 weeks	Yes	Sow seeds continuously from early spring to late summer. If plants bolt due to excessive heat, harvest flowers for salads, and dry some to save seeds.
Napa Cabbage	1–7 days	7–10 weeks	No	*See* planting notes for Cabbage.

continues

continued

Vegetable	Germination	Begin Harvest	Container	Planting Notes
Radicchio	3–10 days	Varies	Yes	Sow seeds 4–6 weeks before last frost. Older varieties should be planted in early spring, and then forced in late summer by cutting back leaves. Harvest 6 weeks later. Newer varieties do not need to be forced. Consult your seed packet. After autumn harvest, cover with mulch. If conditions are mild, you may get another growth.
Romaine	*See* Leaf Lettuce			Many romaine varieties are heat tolerant, and may be planted for summer harvest.
Savoy Cabbage	*See* Cabbage			
Sorrel	1–7 days	8 weeks	Yes	Sow sorrel 3 weeks before first frost. In milder climates, sorrel will return as a perennial. Divide plants in spring every 3–4 years, to renew growth. Remove flowers to continue harvest through autumn.
Spinach	1–7 days	6 weeks	Yes	Plant as soon as soil is warm enough to dig. Plants will survive a frost. Sow successively until first frost. Choose bolt-resistant varieties for summer planting. If planted in a cold frame, can be grown throughout winter in milder climates. Plant in-ground in late autumn and mulch heavily for early spring harvest.

Vegetable	Germination	Begin Harvest	Container	Planting Notes
Swiss Chard	1–7 days	7–8 weeks	Yes	Plant 2–3 weeks before last frost. Continue to sow successively for continuous harvest. Plants will not bolt in hot weather. Harvest by cutting outer leaves. When leaves become tough, cut entire plant back to 2 inches to force another growth.
Tatsoi	*See* Mizuna.			
Turnip Greens	*See* Beet Greens/ Turnip Greens.			
Watercress	8–12 days	8 weeks	Yes	Watercress can be planted in natural water, such as a stream, but grows easily in pots. Place rocks in bottom of pots to prevent soil loss, then fill with soil. Sow seeds, and place pots in a large tub with several inches of water. Do not let plants dry out. Watercress can be grown any time the temperature is above freezing.

DEFINITION

To *harden off* seedlings that have been started indoors, bring them outside for a few hours during the warmest part of the day, then bring them back indoors as the temperature begins to drop. Leave them outside for longer periods of time over a 7-10 day period, and water less frequently. This will give them time to become accustomed to strong sunlight and varying temperatures, and will raise the survival rate for your transplants.

Curly endive.

Dig That Compost!

Composting is a method of breaking down food scraps, grass clippings, dead plants, and leaves. This practice doesn't just feed your plants—it's also great for the environment. A large percentage of greenhouse gases in landfills are produced by food waste, which could have been used to nourish your soil instead. Anyone can compost their food scraps, regardless of space. Both indoor and outdoor systems are available.

The health of your soil determines the nutritional value of the food that you grow, so composting is also an investment in the health of your crops. It can be used as mulch, or to feed your garden and lawn soil. You can also stir some finished compost into your houseplants.

The cheapest and easiest method of composting is the good old compost trench. Choose this option if you have a fair amount of property, and can keep the pile a distance from your house. Waste is buried in a trench, and then covered with soil. Turn your compost pile whenever you add to it, and soon, you'll have a batch of rich material ready for use.

Bins, tumblers, and wire basket systems all make composting easier on smaller properties. Bins and tumblers keep compost out of sight (and smell) range, and are available in sizes to suit every household.

If you live in an apartment, consider a bokashi composting unit, which allows you to compost indoors by fermenting food scraps. Some detractors of bokashi composting complain about the smell, which is said to be picklelike. You will also need to sprinkle the fermentation bacteria every time you add food to the composter, so costs may add up. If your food smells rotten, your container is not properly sealed. An airtight container will prevent lingering unpleasant odors and ensure that fermentation is occurring.

> **HEADS UP!**
>
> Compost your fruits, vegetables, leftovers, yard waste, egg shells, and coffee and tea grounds. You should never compost cat and dog waste, kitty litter (even if it's biodegradable!), meat, or animal bones.

Wormeries are a fun and fascinating compost option. Children love composting with worms! Worm composting, or vermiculture, can be done indoors or outdoors, making it a fantastic choice if you live in an apartment or want to compost year round. Keep your wormery between 40°F and 80°F. In extreme weather, keep it indoors, or well insulated in a shed or garage.

> **THE LOWDOWN**
>
> Make a funky, economical home for your worms by recycling an old dresser or trunk. Drill holes in the bottom to ensure adequate drainage (make sure you have a container beneath to catch the compost tea, a nutrient-rich liquid that you can use to water plants) and line the drawers with biodegradable bedding such as shredded newspaper, cardboard, or dried leaves. Be sure to moisten bedding before adding worms.

You'll need about 2 pounds of worms for every pound of food waste you produce per day. Red wriggler worms are the best choice for populating your wormery, which should be made of wood if possible. Don't use the big earthworms found in your garden soil, as they won't survive. You can find red wrigglers in manure or existing compost piles, or they can be purchased by the pound at garden centers or bait shops.

It's All In the Timing

If you're growing your plants indoors, you can enjoy fresh greens year-round. Keep your plants warm. As long as temperatures are above freezing, cool weather crops such as spinach and lettuce will do well. The perfect temperature for indoor growing is from 65°F to 70°F. Your plants will need 6 to 8 hours of sunlight per day. South-facing windows are the best choice, or you can augment with a grow light.

If you're sowing seeds outside, wait until the soil has warmed enough to dig before planting most greens. Many seeds can be started indoors, and then transplanted to the garden. Some crops, such as spinach and arugula, do not transplant well and are best sown directly into the ground.

If you'd like to extend your outdoor growing season, consider building a cold frame, a small structure with a transparent roof used to protect plants from cold temperatures. Both greens and root vegetables grow brilliantly in cold frames, and in many climates, this option will allow you to produce food nearly year-round.

To build a simple cold frame, create a box, then top it with a repurposed window attached to hinges to facilitate access to the interior. A simple box is fine, but if you have a little carpentry know-how, you might wish to angle the top of the box so it can be placed to capture maximum sunlight. You can even purchase an in-ground electrical cable to add heat to the soil.

Cold frames are portable, and can be used for both in-ground and raised beds. If you don't relish the thought of a do-it-yourself project, ready-made cold-frame kits can be purchased from garden centers or online catalogs.

Feed Me!

If you want to feed yourself, you'll need to feed your plants first. They will thank you for keeping their soil nourished by providing you with a bountiful crop. Fertilizers range from the homemade, such as compost, to store-bought mixes and ready-to-use soil.

Beware of chemical fertilizers! Synthetic fertilizers may be cheaper in the short term, as they contain a more concentrated mix of nutrients, but the chemical residue left behind is damaging to the health of your soil, and future crops will be affected.

The best fertilizer you can use is compost, which is practically free and made from waste you have created. If your soil is lacking in particular nutrients, you can enrich it with organic fertilizers available at your garden center. Many garden centers will test your soil and provide advice for building your soil using organic methods. You can also use simple tricks. For instance, pepper plants love extra sulfur in the soil. Planting a single match 1 inch below each pepper seedling will bring a bountiful pepper harvest later in the season.

Coffee grounds and crushed eggshells can be worked directly into the soil. If you aren't a big coffee drinker, check with your local coffee shop. Most will be happy to supply you with a big bag of grounds to take home.

Pest-Free, Naturally

Once your garden is growing, you'll need to prevent pest infestation. Critters such as aphids, loopers, cutworms, cabbage worms, and spotted cucumber beetles are waiting in the wings to munch on your tasty greens, so be on the lookout. You'll want to avoid commercial pesticides, of course, so what should you do?

The first line of defense is a good offense. Encourage beneficial insects and plants to live in your garden. Plant a praying mantis or two, and release ladybugs into the area. You should be able to get both at your garden center. Crops planted in the summer and autumn are most susceptible to insect predators, so be sure to add more ladybugs later in the season.

Inspect your plants regularly. If you see worms or other insects clinging to your plants, pick them off and water well. Cutworms can be thwarted by creating a collar at the base of the plant while it is still a seedling. To create an easy cutworm collar, cut a vertical line up the side of a paper cup, starting from the bottom, and stopping 2 inches from the top. Cut around the cup. You should be left with a 2 inch tall ring. Place one collar around each seedling to keep cutworms at bay.

If an infestation spins out of control and you must use pesticide, be sure it's organic. Neem oil, as well as soap-based products, are best for your plants, the environment, and your health. Bacterial pesticides are also available. Misting plants with cayenne pepper water will discourage some critters. Whatever method you choose, be sure to wash your crop well before you sit down to eat.

Fungus and mold can also affect your greens. Ask about diseases common to your geographic area at your garden center, particularly if you live in an area with heavy rain. Be vigilant about fungal diseases, as many can live in the soil for years, destroying crop after crop. Water plants in the morning, and if you must use a fungicide, be sure it is an organic product.

The Least You Need to Know

- Choose organic (heirloom or heritage) seeds over genetically modified varieties.
- Avoid commercial fertilizers and potting mixes. Choose organic soil.
- Plant in containers, raised beds, or in-ground beds outdoors; use hydroponic gardens, containers, or window boxes for indoor gardening.
- Compost your food scraps, lawn trimmings, and leaves.
- Employ natural methods of pest control, such as removal by hand, beneficial insects and bacteria, or natural pesticides.

Cooking and Preserving

In This Chapter

- Following some basic recipes
- Freezing for nutrition and economy
- Dehydrating 101

You have your greens, and you're ready to cook! Start by familiarizing yourself with some basic cooking techniques, and learn to freeze and dehydrate so you can enjoy your greens year round.

Simple Techniques

Greens can be boiled, blanched, steamed, sautéed, braised, or roasted. But what do these terms mean? Let's explore each cooking method, and learn how to use each to bring out the best in your greens.

Boiled Greens

Boiling your greens will yield a soft, tender mass of goodness, but some greens are too delicate for this process. You may also find that your greens lose flavor when cooked in this manner. Collards, mustard greens, kale, mature beet greens, cabbage, and turnip greens are good candidates for boiling. Boiled greens can be drained and dressed with olive oil or butter, or served in the liquid they were cooked in, known as "pot liquor" in Southern cuisine. While boiling your greens may cause the loss of more fragile, water-soluble vitamins, they still offer protein, fiber, and minerals, and can be an easily digestible choice for older folks or those who just don't like the texture of crisp-tender veggies.

Blanched greens are boiled greens that are removed from the cooking water and immediately plunged into a bowl of ice and water (ice bath) to stop the cooking process. You'll blanch greens when using them later on in a recipe. The ice bath sets the bright green color of your greens, and stops the enzymatic processes that occur during cooking. Blanching is also the preferred method for preparing food for storage in the freezer.

Southern-Style Boiled Greens with Pot Liquor

Collards and mustard greens offer a slightly bitter savory flavor in this traditional Southern delight. Serve with a pan of cornbread for a down-home supper.

Yield:	Serving size:	Cook time:	Prep time:
8 cups	2 cups	10 minutes	20–60 minutes

1 qt. water

2 bunches collards, tough stems removed, cut in small pieces

1 bunch mustard greens, tough stems removed, cut in small pieces

1/2 tsp. crushed red pepper flakes

1 tsp. sugar

1 tsp. kosher salt, or to taste

2 garlic cloves, crushed

½ tsp. smoked paprika

1 tsp. fresh lemon juice

1. Bring water to a boil in a large stockpot over high heat.

2. Add collards, mustard greens, crushed red pepper flakes, sugar, kosher salt, garlic, and smoked paprika. Return to a boil, then reduce heat to medium low.

3. Cook, stirring occasionally, until greens are as tender as you like, anywhere from 20 minutes to 1 hour. Stir occasionally.

4. Remove from heat, and stir in lemon juice. Taste greens for seasoning, and add additional kosher salt if desired. Ladle greens and cooking liquid into bowls, and serve immediately.

THE LOWDOWN

The American Southern tradition of serving slowly stewed greens with a cup of "pot liquor" (also spelled "pot likker") that is drunk separately has its roots in African tradition. The slave trade brought approximately half a million Africans to the New World, and their culinary tradition of including plenty of fresh greens in the diet are credited with saving their "masters" from malnutrition and often starvation in the years during and after the Civil War.

Steamed Greens

All of the greens in this book can be steamed. Steaming is a gentle method of cooking, and delicate flavors remain intact. Food that has been steamed retains more nutrients than food has been boiled. Many recipes call for steaming greens before another cooking method, such as sautéing, is employed. To make weekday meals a snap, consider steaming a few different greens, chilling them in ice water, draining, and storing in the refrigerator. They'll be ready when you are!

Steamed greens can be served simply, dressed with butter, olive oil, or a bit of lemon juice. Offer steamed spinach or kale as a side dish, or lightly steam bok choy before adding to stir-fries to make it more digestible.

Steamed Broccoli with Butter and Lemon

The flavor of buttery, lemony broccoli shines through in this simple preparation.

Yield:	Serving size:	Cook time:	Prep time:
4 cups	1 cup	6 minutes	5 minutes

1 large bunch broccoli	1 TB. lemon juice
1 TB. butter, softened	¼ tsp. kosher salt
1 tsp. lemon zest	¼ tsp. freshly ground black pepper

1. Separate crowns of broccoli into small florets. Trim tough bottom end of stem. Peel remaining stem with a sharp vegetable peeler, and cut into ½-inch slices.

2. Fit a steamer basket into a medium sauce pan with a tight-fitting lid. Add 2 inches of water, then add broccoli florets and stems.

3. Bring water to a boil over high heat, cover, and reduce heat to medium. Steam broccoli until tender, about 6 minutes.

4. Meanwhile, stir together softened butter, lemon zest, and lemon juice in a medium serving bowl. Drain broccoli thoroughly, and add to butter mixture. Season with salt and pepper, and serve immediately.

> **DEFINITION**
>
> **Lemon zest** is simply the outer, yellow part of a lemon peel, which contains oils that provide an intense citrus flavor (the inner, white part of the peel is called the pith, and is very bitter). A microplane grater makes zesting a lemon easy. This relatively inexpensive kitchen tool grates the zest, leaving the pith behind. You can find an even less expensive substitute at the hardware store, by purchasing a small wood rasp.

Sautéed Greens

Sauté is a French word meaning "jump in the pan." To sauté, one cooks food in a hot pan with a little bit of fat and optional flavorings such as garlic, shallots, onions, or herbs.

Sautéing greens will result in plenty of flavor, but stay close to the stove, because you'll need to mind your greens and stir them often so they don't burn.

Brazilian-Style Sautéed Collard Greens

Fresh, slightly chewy collard greens are highlighted by plenty of garlic in this quick and easy sauté.

Yield:	Serving size:	Cook time:	Prep time:
6 cups	1 cup	10 minutes	5 minutes

2–3 bunches collards (about 3 lbs.), tough stems removed

2 TB. extra-virgin olive oil

3 cloves garlic, peeled and thinly sliced

1 tsp. red-wine vinegar

1 tsp. kosher salt

½ tsp. freshly ground black pepper, or to taste

1. Slice or tear collards into bite-size pieces.

2. Heat olive oil in a wide sauté pan over medium-high heat. Add garlic slices and cook, stirring constantly, until garlic just begins to color. Add half of collards, and cook, stirring frequently, for 2 minutes.

3. Add remaining half of collards, and continue to cook, stirring often, for 5 minutes. Remove from heat, season with vinegar, salt, and pepper. Serve immediately.

> **HEADS UP!**
>
> If you haven't cooked greens before, you're probably thinking that the measurements in these recipes have to be wrong. Leafy greens cook down significantly, so starting a recipe with 18 cups of greens will yield only 6 cups at the end of the cooking time. Don't be skimpy—greens are good for you!

Braised Greens

When food is braised, it is cooked, covered, in a small amount of flavorful liquid such as vegetable stock. Additions such as butter, olive oil, salt, and sugar enhance the flavor of braised foods.

Braised Kale with Olives and Tomatoes

Kale, garlic, tomato, and salty olives combine in this delicious side dish. You probably won't need to add extra salt, as the olives will season both the kale and the braising liquid with plenty of briny flavor.

Yield:	Serving size:	Cook time:	Prep time:
4 cups	1 cup	10 minutes	15 minutes

2 bunches curly kale, tough stems removed (about 12 cups)

2 TB. extra-virgin olive oil

2 cloves garlic, minced

1 cup diced ripe tomato (about 1 medium)

¼ cup pitted kalamata olives

1 cup vegetable stock (See Chapter 16 for recipe)

½ tsp. freshly ground black pepper, or to taste

1 tsp. fresh lemon juice

1. Slice or tear kale into bite-size pieces.

2. Heat olive oil in a medium stock pot over medium-high heat. Add garlic and cook, stirring constantly, until garlic just begins to color. Add half of kale, and cook, stirring frequently, for 2 minutes.

3. Add remaining half of kale, tomato, and olives. Cook, stirring often, for 2 minutes. Add vegetable stock. Cover and cook until tender, about 10 minutes more.

4. Remove from heat, season with black pepper and lemon juice, and serve immediately.

Roasted Greens

Roasting brings out the earthy flavors of sturdy greens such as Belgian endive, Brussels sprouts, radicchio, and even romaine lettuce. To roast greens, toss with olive oil, salt, and pepper, and roast in a hot oven until tender.

Roasted Brussels Sprouts

When Brussels sprouts are roasted, their flavor is slightly sweet and nutty. Try this dish if you're reluctant to add Brussels sprouts to your repertoire—it will make a believer out of you.

Yield:	Serving size:	Cook time:	Prep time:
4 cups	1 cup	10 minutes	15 minutes

4 cups Brussels sprouts (about 1 lb.)

2 TB. extra-virgin olive oil

½ tsp. kosher salt

¼ tsp. freshly ground black pepper

1. Preheat oven to 400°F. Trim stem end of Brussels sprouts, and carefully cut into quarters.

2. Toss Brussels sprouts in a large bowl with olive oil, salt, and pepper. Transfer to a parchment-lined baking sheet and roast, stirring occasionally, for 10 to 15 minutes, until just tender and beginning to brown. Pierce sprouts with a fork after 10 minutes. You'll know they're done when the fork meets little resistance, but the sprouts still retain a firm texture.

3. Serve immediately.

HEADS UP!

It's often a great idea to rely on frozen veggies in a pinch, but Brussels sprouts from the freezer section tend to be mushy and unpleasant tasting. Take the extra few minutes to wash and trim fresh sprouts. You'll be glad you did.

Freeze Now, Enjoy Later

Freezing is an easy and economical way to enjoy seasonal foods throughout the year, take advantage of the low prices of in-season vegetables, and have a selection of convenient, ready-to-heat meals available for busy days.

It's important to remember that freezing does not improve the quality of food. When freezing vegetables, select the freshest, best-quality specimens. All plants contain enzymes, proteins that facilitate ripening and maturation. Enzymes continue their job even after harvesting, and freezing does not stop enzymatic activity. To halt this process, food must be cooked.

Freezing also results in some nutrient loss. Ten to twenty percent of water-soluble vitamins are lost during the freezing process. This pales in comparison, however, to the nutrient loss that occurs when vegetables are shipped long distances to sit on your grocer's shelf. A recent study by the Institute of Food Research showed that vegetables lose as much as 45 percent of their nutritional value by the time they hit your supermarket's produce department!

Preparing greens for the freezer is simple. Select the best-quality, freshly picked produce you can find. Wash well, and discard any under- or overripe specimens. Wash your containers as well.

Suitable containers for freezing include rigid plastic containers, glass jars with wide mouths and straight sides, and plastic bags and wraps that are specifically labeled for freezer use. Plastic wraps and bags not specified for freezer use are not moisture and vapor resistant, so using them will result in *freezer burn*.

DEFINITION

Freezer burn is spoilage caused by exposure to air. Food dries out and becomes odd smelling and inedible. Freezer burn is caused by improper wrapping, or puncturing of wrapping material. Be sure to use freezer-safe wraps, bags, and containers to avoid freezer burn.

Vegetables must be blanched before freezing in order to halt all enzymatic activity. Vegetables that are not blanched will continue to spoil even after freezing. Prepare a boiling water bath using 1 gallon of water. Add a teaspoon of kosher salt if desired. Blanch greens for 1-2 minutes, then immediately transfer to a large bowl of ice water to cool. Place cooled greens in a colander to drain, and repeat the process until all greens are blanched. To freeze 7 quarts of leafy greens, you'll need to start with about 14 pounds of raw produce, so plan to spend some time in the kitchen.

Once vegetables have been blanched, transfer to freezer-safe containers, label, and chill in refrigerator. Foods should be packed with a 2-inch headspace to allow for expansion in the freezer. Cover with a small piece of parchment or plastic wrap before affixing the lid or sealing the bag. If using plastic freezer bags, insert a straw and suck out the air before sealing completely to prevent freezer burn.

Transfer to the freezer when cold. This will prevent large crystals from forming during the freezing process, which can cause leakage, nutritional loss, and uneven texture. Quick freezing results in small crystal formation, ensuring better quality.

Prepared foods such as soups and casseroles can be frozen as well. Plan to use prepared foods within 3 months. Pack in freezer-safe containers. Foods that will be baked, such as lasagna, can be frozen directly in freezer-safe baking dishes (such as Pyrex).

Spices in prepared foods can change in flavor over time. Avoid freezing heavily spiced foods, and consider adding spices after defrosting to soups and stews. Just add a label to the package indicating the spices you need to add when heating.

Prepared foods should always be defrosted in the refrigerator before cooking. Defrosting foods on the kitchen counter seems like a quick and easy alternative, but keeping food between 40 and 140°F encourages bacteria and other spoilers to flourish, exposing you to the risk of food-borne illness. Always heat frozen foods thoroughly before eating.

Drying Foods

Dehydrating, or drying, is the oldest method of food preservation. Drying foods removes moisture, which halts spoilage and slows down enzyme activity. As when freezing, vegetables should be blanched or pretreated with an acid such as lemon juice before drying.

If you're dedicated to the raw lifestyle, you may wish to purchase a dehydrator and begin drying foods. Making smoothie powder out of fresh, local greens is a great starter project.

Green Smoothie Powder

Out of fresh greens? Add a few tablespoons of dried greens to your smoothie with this convenient powder.

Yield:	Serving size:	Cook time:	Prep time:
1 1/2 cups	2 TB.	10 hours	15 minutes

1 qt. cold water

2 TB. lemon juice, bottled

1 bunch curly kale, washed, tough stems removed

1 bunch Tuscan kale, washed, tough stems removed

2 bunches spinach, washed, tough stems removed

1. Prepare a citrus bath with water and lemon juice. Cut greens into evenly sized pieces. Dip greens in citrus bath, and drain in a colander.

2. Place greens in a single layer on trays in your dehydrator. If you don't have a dehydrator, set your oven to the lowest setting, preferably below 150°F.

3. Dry greens, checking occasionally, until they are brittle.

4. Condition greens to be sure they are completely dry. Place in tightly sealed plastic container overnight. If any moisture appears, your greens are not thoroughly dried and you will need to return them to the dehydrator or oven.

5. Place dried greens in bowl of food processor, and pulse until reduced to a fine powder. Store your Green Smoothie Powder in a sealed glass jar in your pantry. Use within 1 year.

THE LOWDOWN

Kale chips are another great use for your dehydrator. You'll find recipes for Raw Cheezy Kale Chips and Oven-Baked Kale Chips in Chapter 9.

The Least You Need to Know

- Cooking methods for greens include boiling, blanching, steaming, sautéing, braising, and roasting.
- Freezing foods supports your locavore lifestyle, helps control your food budget, and keeps a variety of foods available for your convenience.
- Freeze foods in appropriate containers, removing as much air as possible to prevent freezer burn.
- Dry foods to support a raw lifestyle, and make your own smoothie powder to enjoy the power of fresh greens regardless of seasonal availability.

Get Up and Go!

Experts agree that a healthy breakfast is the building block of good health. In Part 2, you'll learn to start your day right with fresh smoothies, nourishing juices, and delicious breakfast and brunch dishes to share with family and friends.

Whether you're on the go on a busy weekday, curling up in your pajamas for a lazy Saturday breakfast, or inviting friends for an impressive Sunday brunch, these chapters will provide everything you need for the most important meal of the day.

Drink Your Greens!

In This Chapter

- Knowing when and why to choose smoothies or juice
- Making fast and filling smoothies
- Preparing fresh, nutritious juices

Smoothies and juice provide an easy way to pack more nutritious greens, fruits, and veggies into your diet. Quick to prepare and easy on your digestion, both smoothies and fresh juices provide a concentrated source of vitamins, minerals, digestive enzymes, phytochemicals, and antioxidants from raw fruits and vegetables. While expert opinions abound touting the superiority of juices and smoothies, it's worthwhile to include both in your diet. This chapter provides you with numerous recipes for juices and smoothies—we'll let you determine your favorites.

Which Do I Choose?

Smoothies and juices both offer tremendous health benefits. Liquid foods are more easily assimilated than solid foods, and consuming your produce raw is the best way to get maximum nutritional "bang for your buck."

Smoothies are whole fruits and vegetables blended with liquids such as coconut milk, hemp, or soy milk or yogurt to form a thick, satisfying beverage. Since they retain all of the fiber of the foods that go into them, smoothies are filling enough to make a meal or hearty snack. Fiber also promotes regularity and regulates blood sugar.

Juice is extracted from fruits and vegetables, separating the cellular walls from the content within, making juice a highly concentrated and quickly digested source of powerful nutrients. Since the insoluble fiber is removed when juicing, it's easy to consume large quantities. It's much easier to drink a pound of spinach than to eat it!

Whether you're making a smoothie or juice, it's best to drink it right away. Blending or juicing your fruits and vegetables exposes the cellular matter to oxygen, which immediately begins to break down the nutrients you've released. Luckily, smoothies and juices take just minutes to make, and they're portable, too, making them the perfect breakfast or snack on the go. If you can't consume your juice or smoothie immediately, freezing is the best bet.

The Right Stuff

While smoothies are made in a blender, an appliance that appears on nearly every kitchen countertop, juicing requires special equipment. A great blender can last for many years, with a relatively modest investment. Juicers, on the other hand, range in price from under $100 for a basic centrifugal juicer to thousands for a heavy-duty masticating or hydraulic press juicer. Consider your budget, as well as the nutritional benefits, when choosing these products.

When using a centrifugal juicer, you'll notice an inch or two of foam at the top of your juice. This is caused by oxidation, and although harmless to drink, does indicate that nutrition is lost when using a centrifugal juicer. Don't let it be your only deciding factor when investing in a juicer, though, as your juice is still very good for you. You can drink the foam, or use a straw if the taste or texture is off-putting.

Once your equipment is in place, you're ready to drink your way to better health. Begin with the recipes in this chapter, then move on and create your own juice and smoothie masterpieces!

Ⓥ Green Banana Date Smoothie

Banana, dates, and spinach combine with hemp milk and vanilla yogurt to form a mildly sweet and filling smoothie that will keep you going until lunch.

Yield:	Serving size:	Prep time:
2 cups	1 cups	5 minutes plus soaking time for dates

4 pitted dates

½ cup almost boiling water

1 medium banana, frozen if desired

½ cup hemp milk

¼ cup vanilla-flavored nondairy yogurt (such as coconut milk)

2 TB. flax meal

1½ cups baby spinach

6 ice cubes (optional)

1. Place dates in a small bowl, and cover with water. Soak for at least 20 minutes (or overnight).

2. Combine dates, soaking water, banana, hemp milk, yogurt, flax meal, baby spinach, and ice cubes in a blender. Blend on medium setting for 1 minute, then blend on highest speed until smooth. Divide smoothie between two glasses. Serve immediately.

THE LOWDOWN

Dates are one of nature's perfect foods. Since they contain both natural sugars and high fiber, they sweeten and provide energy while maintaining steady blood sugar levels and keeping "sugar crashes" at bay. Dates are extraordinarily rich in potassium, B vitamins, and polyphenols, which neutralize free radicals to protect cells from cardiovascular disease, cancer, Alzheimer's disease, and other life-threatening illnesses.

Ⓥ Great Pumpkin Smoothie

Pumpkin and cinnamon evoke the sweet flavors of autumn, making this smoothie a wonderful fall breakfast or afternoon snack.

Yield:	Serving size:	Prep time:
2½ cups	1¼ cups	5 minutes

¼ cup plus 2 TB. organic canned pumpkin (not pie filling)

¼ cup vanilla-flavored nondairy yogurt (such as coconut milk)

2 TB. pumpkin seeds

1 cup spinach leaves, lightly packed

½ medium banana, frozen if desired

½ tsp. ground cinnamon

¼ tsp. freshly ground nutmeg

½ cup hemp milk

7 ice cubes (optional)

1. Combine canned pumpkin, yogurt, pumpkin seeds, spinach leaves, banana, cinnamon, nutmeg, hemp milk, and ice cubes (if using) in blender.

2. Blend on medium setting for 1 minute, then blend on highest speed until smooth.

3. Divide smoothie between two glasses. Serve immediately.

THE LOWDOWN

Carotenoids from spinach, pumpkin, and pumpkin seeds join forces with cinnamon to reduce inflammation, while magnesium and calcium keep bones healthy and strong.

Ⓥ Ⓡ Gorgeous Glow Green Smoothie

Enjoy this lightly sweet, creamy, and pineapple-licious smoothie. Your skin will glow from within thanks to pineapple enzymes, beneficial fats from avocado and flax, and the intense hydration provided by coconut water.

Yield:	Serving size:	Prep time:
3 cups	1½ cups	5 minutes

1 cup pineapple, frozen

1 avocado, peeled and diced

3 kale leaves, stems removed, torn into 1-inch pieces (or 2 TB. kale powder)

2 TB. *flax meal*

12 oz. chilled coconut water

1 TB. raw agave nectar

1. Combine pineapple, avocado, kale leaves, flax meal, coconut water, and agave nectar in blender.

2. Blend on medium speed for 2 minutes, then blend on highest setting until smooth.

3. Divide smoothie between two glasses. Serve immediately.

Variation: For a frozen treat, add 2 additional tablespoons each of flax meal, vanilla-flavored nondairy yogurt (such as coconut), and raw agave nectar to the ingredients. Blend as directed. Pour into a freezer-safe container. Freeze for 1½ to 2 hours, stirring occasionally with a fork. Stir vigorously at end of freezing time. Serve immediately. Makes six ½-cup servings.

DEFINITION

Flax meal, or simply ground flax seeds, are rich in fiber, omega-3 fatty acids, and phytochemicals called *lignans*. In their whole form, flax seeds pass through the digestive system intact. In order to enjoy their myriad benefits, buy organic flax meal or grind flax seeds. Refrigerate flax meal or whole seeds to keep them fresh and nutritious.

Lignans are antioxidant phytoestrogens found in many plants, such as flax, pumpkin seeds, and whole grains. Studies have indicated that lignans fight cancer, lower blood pressure, and treat artherosclerosis. Those at high risk for developing hormone-dependent cancers should consult their doctor regarding lignan consumption.

ⓋMatcha Super Green Smoothie

Matcha is ground whole green tea leaves, and its flavor comes to the forefront in this very "green-tasting" smoothie that offers an early-morning boost of energy and antioxidants.

Yield:	Serving size:	Prep time:
2 cups	1 cup	5 minutes

1 tsp. matcha powder

1 TB. kale powder (see Chapter 5 for recipe)

1 ripe banana, frozen

1 cup lightly packed spinach leaves, tough stems removed

¼ cup vanilla-flavored nondairy yogurt (such as coconut milk)

½ cup coconut water

1 TB. raw agave nectar

4–6 ice cubes

1. Combine matcha powder, kale powder, banana, spinach, yogurt, coconut water, agave nectar, and ice cubes in blender.

2. Blend on medium speed for 1 minute, then blend on highest setting until smooth.

3. Divide smoothie between two glasses. Serve immediately.

HEADS UP!

The taste of matcha can be intense if you're not familiar with it, so feel free to use only ½ teaspoon or add a bit more agave if you don't love the green tea flavor.

ⓋCacao-Coconut Green Smoothie

Who doesn't love chocolate, cinnamon, and coconut? This satisfying, antioxidant-packed smoothie is great for breakfast or an afternoon snack.

Yield:	Serving size:	Prep time:
2 cups	1 cup	5 minutes plus soaking time for dates

4 pitted dates

2 TB. unsweetened dried coconut

½ cup coconut water

2 TB. raw organic cacao nibs or powder

½ tsp. ground cinnamon

1 cup lightly packed baby spinach leaves

½ frozen banana

½ cup hemp milk

1. Place dates and coconut in a small bowl. Cover with coconut water. Soak for 2 hours or overnight.

2. Place soaked dates and coconut in blender with their soaking water. Add cacao nibs, cinnamon, spinach leaves, banana, and hemp milk.

3. Blend on medium speed for 2 minutes, then blend on highest setting until smooth.

4. Divide smoothie between two glasses. Serve immediately.

THE LOWDOWN

Since you are soaking your dates and coconut in room-temperature coconut water, choose the longest soaking time possible, preferably overnight. Soaking will ensure that the dates blend smoothly, instead of making a sticky mess in your blender. Dried coconut benefits from longer soaking times, especially if you don't like texture in your smoothie. If you don't mind having to chew your smoothie a little, a shorter soaking time may be acceptable to you. If you're particularly averse to texture in your smoothie, use cacao powder rather than nibs, and omit the coconut.

Ⓥ Coffee Cacao Jumpstart Smoothie

If you can't live without your morning cup of joe, this is the smoothie for you! You get a thick, creamy, and satisfying breakfast shake with the delightful flavors of coffee and chocolate.

Yield:	Serving size:	Prep time:
2 cups	1 cup	5 minutes

½ cup chilled brewed coffee
½ cup hemp milk
1 frozen banana
2 TB. raw organic cacao nibs

1 TB. chia seeds
1 TB. raw agave nectar
3 leaves kale, ribs removed, torn into 1-inch pieces

1. Combine coffee, hemp milk, banana, cacao nibs, chia seeds, agave nectar, and kale in blender.

2. Blend on medium speed for 2 minutes, then blend on highest setting until smooth.

3. Divide smoothie between two glasses. Serve immediately.

THE LOWDOWN

Hemp milk is an extremely nutritious dairy substitute that offers rich stores of Omega 3 and Omega 6 fatty acids, as well plenty of other vitamins and minerals. Cup for cup, it's the healthiest milk substitute. Don't worry that it will make you silly—hemp seeds do not contain THC, the psychoactive substance found in marijuana.

ⓥ Digestive Detox Green Smoothie

If you've overindulged in unhealthy foods or beverages (we all do once in awhile!), get your system back on track with this sweet, soothing tropical smoothie packed with the unique flavor and cleansing properties of papaya.

Yield:	Serving size:	Prep time:
2 cups	1 cup	5 minutes

1½ cups ripe papaya, cut into chunks, partially frozen

½ cup coconut water

½ cup vanilla-flavored nondairy yogurt, such as coconut milk

1 cup spinach leaves, loosely packed

2 TB. flax meal

1 TB. fresh lime juice (about 1 small lime)

1. Combine papaya, coconut water, yogurt, spinach, flax meal, and lime juice in blender.

2. Blend on medium speed for 2 minutes, then blend on highest setting until smooth. This smoothie is particularly thick and creamy, so you may need to stop the blender and stir a few times to fully combine ingredients.

3. Divide smoothie between two glasses. Serve immediately.

THE LOWDOWN

Nondairy yogurt provides active cultures to replenish your body's natural flora, while spinach detoxifies your liver with chlorophyll without overwhelming your taste buds. Coconut water and lime juice cleanse and hydrate. Finally, the omega-3 oils in flax meal will prevent your body from absorbing any toxins you've ingested. That large cheese pizza and pint of ice cream will soon be a distant memory!

Ⓥ Ⓡ 60/40 Juice

This tart, fresh, lemony juice fits the bill perfectly with the flavors of celery, cucumber, chard, parsley, and kale backed up by a touch of sweet mango. A perfectly balanced green juice should contain about 60 percent greens and veggies to 40 percent fruits.

Yield:	Serving size:	Prep time:
10 oz.	10 oz.	5 minutes

2 ribs celery	1 ripe mango, peeled and seeded
½ large cucumber, seeds removed	½ lemon, peel removed
3 kale leaves	1 cup fresh flat-leaf parsley leaves
3 Swiss chard leaves	

1. Chop celery, cucumber, kale, chard leaves, mango, lemon, and parsley into large pieces that will easily fit in the chute of your juicer.

2. Turn juicer on. Push all ingredients through juicer.

3. Pour juice into a large glass. Stir; serve immediately.

Swiss chard.

THE LOWDOWN

Vary the greens in your juices and smoothies based on what is fresh and in season. In the spring and summer, try spinach, watercress, and the many varieties of lettuce available from your garden or local farmers market. In autumn and winter, enjoy hardier varieties such as kale, collards, and Swiss chard.

ⓥ ⓡ Peachy Green Juice

Sweet peaches meet spicy ginger and watercress in this zingy refresher. If you can't take the heat, replace the watercress with additional spinach.

Yield:	Serving size:	Prep time:
10 oz.	10 oz.	5 minutes

2 ripe peaches, pitted and sliced

1-inch piece fresh ginger, peeled

1 cup spinach leaves

½ cup watercress

1. Turn juicer on. Push peaches, ginger, spinach, and watercress through juicer.

2. Pour juice into a large glass. Stir; serve immediately.

ⓥ ⓡ Sweet Beet Juice

The sweetness of beets and carrots mingles deliciously with the fresh flavors of beet greens and cucumber in this juice.

Yield:	Serving size:	Prep time:
10 oz.	10 oz.	5 minutes

1 cup beetroot (1 large or 2 small)

½ cup carrot (1 small)

3 cups beet greens, roughly

chopped (about ½ bunch)

¾ cup seeded cucumber (about ½ medium)

1. Turn juicer on. Push beetroot, carrot, beet greens, and cucumber through juicer.

2. Pour juice into a large glass. Stir; serve immediately.

THE LOWDOWN

Eat your beets! Beet root is a rich source of glycine betaine, a phytochemical that compound that lowers homocysteine levels in your blood, protecting your cardiovascular system. Both the root and greens of the plant are an excellent source of folate when consumed in their raw form, so juicing is the perfect way to reap the benefits of beets.

Ⓥ Ⓡ Ginger Kale Juice

The sweet, perfectly spicy flavor of this *ginger*, apple, and kale juice is the perfect way to start your day.

Yield:	Serving size:	Prep time:
10 oz.	10 oz.	5 minutes

2 medium Honeycrisp apples, cut into chunks

1½ cups kale or kale stems, chopped
1-inch piece fresh ginger

1. Turn juicer on. Push apples, kale, and ginger through juicer.
2. Pour juice into a large glass. Stir; serve immediately.

Variation: Add ½ cup sparkling water or seltzer for a **Fizzy Ginger Kale Soda.** Serve over ice, and garnish with fresh mint.

> **DEFINITION**
>
> **Ginger** or **ginger root** is the rhizome (stem formed underground) of the plant *Zingiber officinale*. Long used as a folk remedy for nausea and indigestion, recent studies have also showed that ginger may also reduce muscle pain after exercise, protect the body from free radicals, reduce inflammation related to arthritis, and reduce the risk of colon cancer. Unless very young and tender, ginger root tends to be fibrous and very strong in spicy flavor.

Ⓥ Ⓡ Iron-Boost Power Juice

If you're feeling tired and run down, consider this tart, iron-and-protein-rich juice to give you a boost of energy. It's bright and tangy, with the flavor of lemon and cherries.

Yield:	Serving size:	Prep time:
8 oz.	8 oz.	5 minutes

¾ cup pitted sweet cherries (about 12)
½ cup watermelon chunks
½ lemon, peel removed

1 cup amaranth leaves (or spinach)
1 cup kale leaves or stems, chopped

1. Turn juicer on. Push cherries, watermelon, lemon, amaranth, and kale through juicer.

2. Pour juice into a large glass. Stir; serve immediately.

Ⓥ Ⓡ Post-Workout Refresher

Replenish your strength and oxygenate tired muscles with a delicious glass of this sweet papaya pleaser. Amaranth's powerful punch of protein makes this juice a real "body builder."

Yield:	Serving size:	Prep time:
12 oz.	12 oz.	5 minutes

1 cup papaya chunks

1½ cups amaranth leaves (or kale)

1½ cups Swiss chard leaves and
    stems, chopped

½ cup watermelon chunks

½ lemon, peel removed

1-inch piece ginger

1. Turn juicer on. Push papaya, amaranth, chard, watermelon, lemon, and ginger through juicer.

2. Pour juice into a large glass. Stir; serve immediately.

HEADS UP!

When making fresh juice, wash all produce well, and make only as much juice as your will be able to consume immediately. This not only ensures maximum nutritional content, but also protects you against harmful bacteria that can quickly grow in unpasteurized fresh juice. If you can't drink all of your juice as soon as you make it, freeze it immediately to maximize vitamin retention and food safety.

Ⓥ Ⓡ Spicy Green Lemonade

Rehydrate while enjoying this spicy, slightly sweet, lemony refresher. Cayenne pepper and ginger add zip, and work with lemons and kale to reduce inflammation in your body.

Yield:	Serving size:	Prep time:
16 oz.	16 oz.	5 minutes

1 cup kale leaves and stems	¼ tsp. cayenne pepper, or to taste
1 lemon, peeled and cut in half	8 oz. cold, filtered water
1-inch piece of ginger	Sprig of fresh mint (for optional garnish)
1 tsp. agave nectar, or to taste	

1. Turn juicer on. Push kale, lemon, and ginger through juicer.

2. Pour juice into a large glass. Add agave nectar, cayenne, and water. Stir; garnish with fresh mint if desired. Serve immediately.

THE LOWDOWN

In Ayurvedic medicine, ginger and lemon are both recommended for increasing your body's digestive power. Ayurveda is a popular form of alternative medicine that has been practiced in India for thousands of years. Ayurvedic principles also suggest drinking beverages at room temperature, as ice cold or very hot beverages are believed to interfere with digestive processes.

Breakfast and Brunch

In This Chapter

- Making quick, easy breakfast recipes
- Preparing hearty dishes for weekend breakfasts and brunch

It's often said that breakfast is the most important meal of the day, but why? Studies show that people who eat breakfast perform better on cognitive tests, have more energy, and are better nourished than those who skip this meal. Eating breakfast also helps you to maintain a healthy weight. Your body needs fuel to function properly, and the time between dinner and breakfast is your longest fast of the day.

A quick breakfast of fruits and veggies, or perhaps an omelet, is a great weekday option. On the weekend, or when you have more time, make the first meal of the day an occasion with quiche, home fries, and other specialty items. Invite your friends and make it a party.

If you're particularly time-crunched in the morning, you might want to prep your breakfast ingredients the night before, or even prepare your meal in advance. Eat breakfast every day. You'll be glad you did!

Cheesy Grits with Beet Greens and Pan-Roasted Corn

Sunday mornings are special when you stir up a pot of creamy, cheesy corn grits studded with garlicky, tender beet greens and smoky pan-roasted corn.

Yield:	Serving size:	Prep time:	Cook time:
8 cups	2 cups	10 minutes	50 minutes

2 TB. plus 1 tsp. unsalted butter

¾ cup yellow onion, diced (about 1 medium onion)

¼ tsp. plus ½ tsp. plus ½ tsp. kosher salt, or to taste

5 cups room-temperature water

1 cup stone-ground corn grits (not quick cooking)

1½ cups fresh corn kernels (from about 2 cobs), or frozen corn

¼ tsp. sweet paprika

¼ tsp. smoked paprika

½ tsp. freshly ground black pepper, or to taste

1 TB. extra-virgin olive oil

2 cloves garlic, finely chopped

5–6 cups of beet greens, including stems, chopped into 1-inch pieces (about 2 small bunches)

1 TB. apple cider vinegar

½ cup Parmesan cheese, grated

½ cup sharp cheddar cheese, grated

1 tsp. Asian-style hot sauce, such as Sriracha (optional)

1. Heat 2 tablespoons butter in a large sauce pan over medium-high heat. When butter is sizzling, add onion, ¼ teaspoon kosher salt, and pepper. Cook, stirring occasionally, for 10 minutes, or until onions are begin to soften and color.

2. Add water, turn heat to high, and immediately whisk in corn grits and ½ teaspoon kosher salt.

3. Bring to a boil, then reduce heat to low. Simmer for 35 minutes, whisking frequently, until most of the liquid is absorbed and grits are tender.

4. Meanwhile, heat a medium sauté pan (preferably cast iron) over medium-high heat. Add 1 teaspoon butter, corn, sweet paprika, smoked paprika, and ¼ tsp. black pepper. Cook for 5 minutes, stirring occasionally. Set corn aside in small bowl.

5. In same cast-iron pan, heat olive oil over medium-high heat. Add garlic. Stir constantly for 1 minute. Add beet greens, ¼ teaspoon kosher salt, and ¼ tsp. black pepper. Reduce heat to medium and cook, stirring occasionally, for 10 minutes, or until beet greens are tender.

6. Season beet greens with apple cider vinegar. Remove from heat and set aside.

7. When grits are tender and water is nearly absorbed, add corn and beet greens to grits mixture. Cook, stirring frequently, for another 5 minutes.

8. Remove grits from heat. Stir in Parmesan and cheddar cheeses. Add hot sauce if using.

9. Ladle grits into bowls. Serve immediately.

MAKE IT VEGAN

It's incredibly easy to "veganize" this recipe. Just substitute vegan margarine or more extra-virgin olive oil for the butter, and use a meltable vegan cheese alternative, such as Daiya, in place of Parmesan and cheddar cheeses. For a huge flavor boost, whisk in 1 teaspoon nutritional yeast.

Ⓥ Ⓡ Tropical Chia Pudding

Chia pudding is a fantastic weekday breakfast, since you can mix it up the night before and then enjoy in the morning. The sweetness of banana and agave blend with the tropical flavors of coconut, lime, and mango, while chia seeds provide a tapioca-like texture. Try it for dessert, too!

Yield:	Serving size:	Prep time:
4 cups	1 cup	10 minutes, plus 1 hour soaking time for cashews and 4 hours to overnight for pudding in refrigerator

1 small ripe banana (about ¾ cup)	3 TB. raw agave nectar or honey
1 cup spinach leaves, tough ribs removed	½ tsp. grated lime zest
½ cup raw cashews, soaked for 1 hour	½ cup chia seeds
	2 TB. unsweetened dried coconut
2 cups filtered water	1 ripe mango, peeled and cut into ½-inch cubes

1. Place banana, spinach leaves, cashews, water, agave nectar, and lime zest in blender. Blend on high speed until smooth, about 5 minutes.

2. In a quart-sized Mason jar (or plastic container), combine chia seeds and coconut. Shake well.

3. Pour banana-lime mixture over chia seeds, and shake well to combine.

4. Refrigerate for at least 4 hours, or overnight, shaking jar occasionally during the first hour.

5. When ready to serve, shake jar one last time. Serve in small bowls topped with mango.

DEFINITION

Chia seeds are rich in protein, dietary fiber, omega-3 fatty acids, and several essential minerals. You may be familiar with chia seeds from the commercials that popularized them as "pets," with nutritious (and uneaten) chia sprouting from clay animals in windowsills everywhere. Chia has been used as a food since ancient times, and was used by the Aztecs as an athletic endurance food due to its ability to absorb water and balance electrolytes in your system. Try chia pudding as an easily digested breakfast or dessert, or add some seeds to your smoothies for a nutritional boost. Chia seeds can also be sprouted or added to baked goods as you would use flax seeds.

Spinach Omelet

Fluffy eggs and spinach star in this easy and delicious breakfast. Add your choice of cheese if you like.

Yield:	Serving size:	Prep time:	Cook time:
1 6-inch omelet	1 omelet	5 minutes	5 minutes

1 tsp. unsalted butter

2 eggs, beaten with a fork until well combined

1 cup steamed baby spinach leaves, cooled and squeezed dry

1 pinch kosher salt, or to taste

1 pinch black pepper, or to taste

1. Place butter in a 6-inch nonstick sauté pan. Heat over medium-high heat until butter is sizzling.

2. Pour eggs into pan, and shake to evenly distribute.

3. Season spinach with salt and pepper.

4. Using a rubber spatula, lift edges of egg mixture while tilting pan, to allow uncooked egg to run underneath.

5. When omelet has nearly set, add spinach to center third of omelet. Use spatula to quickly fold outer edges over center, folding the omelet in thirds.

6. Turn onto a plate and serve immediately.

Variation: Add your choice of cheese, such as cheddar, feta, or Swiss, when spinach is added.

Ⓥ Sweet Potato and Kale Home Fries

Serve up a down-home nutritional powerhouse with this filling skillet of home fries brimming with sweet potato, kale, and onions.

Yield:	Serving size:	Prep time:	Cook time:
6 cups	1½ cups	10 minutes	25 minutes

2 TB. sunflower oil

1 large sweet potato, unpeeled, diced into ½-inch pieces (about 2 cups)

1 large yellow onion, diced

1 medium red bell pepper, diced

1 poblano chile, diced

2 cloves garlic, minced

1 bunch curly kale, tough ribs removed, torn into 1-inch pieces

½ tsp. kosher salt

¼ tsp. freshly ground black pepper

¼ tsp. smoked paprika

1. Heat sunflower oil in a large sauté pan over medium-high heat. Add sweet potato, onion, bell pepper, and poblano chile. Cook, stirring occasionally, for 15 minutes.

2. Add garlic, kale, salt, pepper, and smoked paprika to pan. Continue cooking, stirring frequently, for an additional 10 minutes. Serve immediately.

Ⓥ Ⓡ Fruity Spinach Salad

Salad for breakfast? Absolutely, if it's this fruity concoction of healthy raw spinach sweetened with ripe fruit and the crunch of almonds. A tangy dressing with the fresh zip of lime will wake up your palate!

Yield:	Serving size:	Prep time:
4 cups	2 cups	5 minutes

2 cups baby spinach

1 small ripe banana, sliced

1 kiwi, peeled and sliced

1 medium apple, such as Honeycrisp, sliced

2 TB. fresh lime juice (about 2 small limes)

1 TB. flax oil

1 tsp. raw agave nectar or honey

¼ cup raw almonds, roughly chopped

1. Divide baby spinach, banana, kiwi, and apple between two bowls.

2. Combine lime juice, flax oil, and agave nectar in a small jar. Shake well.

3. Pour dressing over spinach mixture, and top each serving with half the almonds. Serve immediately.

THE LOWDOWN

Make this salad into a healthy, packable lunch. Just place dressing in the bottom of a container with a lid. Add fruit next, then spinach, and top with almonds. When you're ready for lunch, just shake and enjoy!

Ⓥ Tofu Quiche with Swiss Chard and Tomatoes

Tofu replaces eggs in this healthy quiche featuring the savory flavors of Swiss chard, onion, and tomato.

Yield:	Serving size:	Prep time:	Cook time:
1 quiche	$\frac{1}{8}$ of quiche	30 minutes	45 minutes

½ recipe pie pastry (see Chapter 16)

1 TB. extra-virgin olive oil

1 bunch Swiss chard, tough ends of stems removed, cut or torn into 2-inch pieces

1 cup grape tomatoes, halved

1 small yellow onion, halved and thinly sliced

1 clove garlic, minced

¼ tsp. plus ¼ tsp. kosher salt

1 pound firm organic silken tofu

½ cup organic soy milk

½ tsp. Dijon mustard

2 TB. nutritional yeast

½ tsp. freshly ground black pepper

1. Preheat oven to 350°F. Roll pie pastry to fit a 9-inch pie pan. Carefully transfer to pie pan, and trim crust so that there is a ½-inch overhang. Fold crust inward to create an edge, and crimp to seal with fingers or a fork. (Alternately, use a frozen premade vegan pie crust.) Chill in freezer for 15 minutes.

2. Use a fork to prick bottom of pastry all over. Line with parchment paper or aluminum foil. Fill with dried beans or pie weights; bake for 10 minutes. Remove from oven and set aside.

3. In a medium sauté pan, heat olive oil over medium-high heat. Add Swiss chard, grape tomatoes, onion, garlic, and ¼ teaspoon kosher salt. Cook, stirring often, until mixture has reduced and chard is tender, about 10 minutes. Set aside.

4. Place tofu, soy milk, Dijon mustard, ¼ teaspoon kosher salt, nutritional yeast, and black pepper in blender or food processor. Process on high speed for 5 minutes, or until smooth.

5. Combine Swiss chard mixture with tofu mixture. Pour into prepared crust, and bake for 45 minutes. Serve hot or cold.

HEADS UP!

Approximately 90 percent of soy grown in the United States is from genetically modified seed. Since GMO soy has been linked to many health issues, purchasing organic soy and soy products is a wise choice. Avoid processed food whenever possible, as soy is a hidden ingredient in most convenience foods.

Quiche Lorraine

A classic receives a vegetarian twist with smoky onions and mushrooms standing in for bacon in this creamy, cheesy quiche with plenty of fresh spinach flavor.

Yield:	Serving size:	Prep time:	Cook time:
1 quiche	⅛ of quiche	30 minutes	50–55 minutes

½ recipe pie pastry (see Chapter 16)

2 TB. unsalted butter

1 yellow onion, halved and thinly sliced

1 10-oz. package baby bella mushrooms, thinly sliced

¼ tsp. smoked paprika

¼ tsp. plus ¼ tsp. kosher salt

6 cups spinach leaves, tough stems removed, steamed and squeezed dry

8 large eggs

¼ cup heavy cream

½ cup shredded Gruyere cheese

½ tsp. freshly grated nutmeg

½ tsp. freshly ground black pepper

1. Preheat oven to 350°F. Roll pie pastry to fit a 9-inch pie pan. Carefully transfer to pie pan, and trim crust so that there is a ½-inch overhang. Fold crust inward to create an edge, and crimp to seal with fingers or a fork. (Alternately, use a frozen premade vegan pie crust.) Chill in freezer for 15 minutes.

2. Use a fork to prick bottom of pastry all over. Line with parchment paper or aluminum foil. Fill with dried beans or pie weights; bake for 10 minutes. Remove from oven and set aside.

3. In a medium sauté pan, heat butter over medium-high heat. Add onions, mushrooms, smoked paprika, and ¼ teaspoon kosher salt. Cook, stirring often, until mushrooms and onions are golden brown. Stir in spinach. Set aside.

4. Using a wire whisk, beat eggs, heavy cream, Gruyere, nutmeg, ¼ teaspoon kosher salt, and black pepper until well combined and creamy, about 5 minutes.

5. Gently combine mushroom-spinach mixture with eggs. Pour into prepared crust, and bake for 50 to 55 minutes. Serve hot or cold.

Frittata with Escarole, Potato, and Onion

This classic Italian omelet makes a satisfying brunch, but the hearty flavors of escarole and potato make it a lovely light supper as well.

Yield:	Serving size:	Prep time:	Cook time:
1 frittata	$\frac{1}{8}$ of frittata	20 minutes	15 minutes

1 medium russet potato

1 TB. plus 1 tsp. extra-virgin olive oil

1 medium yellow onion, halved and thinly sliced

1 head escarole, tough outer leaves trimmed, cut into 1-inch ribbons

2 cloves garlic, minced

$\frac{1}{4}$ tsp. plus $\frac{1}{4}$ tsp. kosher salt

$\frac{1}{4}$ tsp. crushed red pepper flakes

$\frac{1}{2}$ tsp. freshly ground black pepper

8 large eggs

$\frac{1}{4}$ cup tomato sauce (see recipe in Chapter 16)

2 TB. fresh Italian parsley, chopped, or 1 tsp. dried parsley

$\frac{1}{2}$ cup shredded mozzarella cheese

1. Place potato, unpeeled, in small saucepan. Cover with water, and bring to a boil over high heat. Cook, about 10 minutes, until potato is tender. Set aside to cool slightly.

2. Meanwhile, heat 1 tablespoon olive oil in an oven-safe 10-inch nonstick sauté pan over medium-high heat. Add onion and cook, stirring occasionally, until tender and translucent, about 5 minutes. Add escarole, garlic, $\frac{1}{4}$ teaspoon kosher salt, red pepper flakes, and pepper, and reduce heat to medium. Continue to cook for another 10 minutes, or until all liquid has evaporated and escarole is tender. Stir occasionally.

3. Peel potato, and cut into 1-inch chunks. Add to escarole mixture in sauté pan, stir well, and remove from heat.

4. Using a wire whisk, beat eggs, tomato sauce, $\frac{1}{4}$ teaspoon salt, and parsley until well combined, about 2 minutes. Add mozzarella and escarole mixture to eggs, and stir well.

5. Heat broiler. Wipe nonstick sauté pan clean with a paper towel. Heat 1 teaspoon olive oil over medium-high heat, add egg mixture, and reduce heat to medium low. Cover and cook until eggs are nearly set.

6. Place frittata in oven 8 to 10 inches away from broiler. Cook, checking often, until frittata has puffed and eggs are set. The top of your frittata should be a light golden color.

7. Remove from oven carefully using an oven mitt or potholder. Set on a hot pad to cool slightly.

8. Carefully slide frittata onto a serving plate, cut into wedges, and serve hot or cold.

Escarole.

MAKE IT VEGAN

For a vegan frittata, replace the eight eggs with 1 pound firm silken tofu. Purée tofu in food processor or blender with tomato sauce and parsley. Omit mozzarella, and stir in ½ cup vegan mozzarella shreds (such as Daiya) when adding vegetables. Omit stovetop cooking. Bake frittata at 350°F for 40 minutes, or until set. Serve hot or cold.

HEADS UP!

Mind the handle on your frittata pan as it cools on the counter—it's blazing hot! Help remember to keep hands off by draping a folded kitchen towel over the handle to remind you (and unsuspecting family members) that the pan is hot. Keep safety in mind whenever you're working in the kitchen, and you'll avoid unpleasant accidental burns.

Broccoli-Cheddar Crustless Quiche

The popular flavor combination of broccoli and cheese with a touch of zing from mustard and cayenne pepper makes this dish a breakfast or brunch sensation.

Yield:	Serving size:	Prep time:	Cook time:
1 9-inch quiche	⅛ of quiche	20 minutes	15 minutes

1 head broccoli

1 TB. unsalted butter, melted

½ cup fresh whole-wheat bread crumbs, from about 1 slice bread

8 large eggs

¼ cup half-and-half

½ tsp. dry mustard powder

Pinch cayenne pepper

½ tsp. kosher salt

¼ tsp. freshly ground black pepper

1 cup coarsely grated sharp cheddar cheese

1. Trim tough ends from broccoli. Peel remaining stem. Separate broccoli crown into 1-inch florets, then slice peeled stem into ½-inch pieces.

2. Preheat oven to 350°F. Grease a 9-inch pie pan with cooking spray. Pour butter over bread crumbs and mix well. Sprinkle bread crumbs over bottom and sides of pie pan, and set aside.

3. Pour 2 inches of water into a medium sauce pan with a tight-fitting lid. Fit a collapsible steamer insert into pot. Bring to a boil over high heat, then add broccoli and cover. Steam for 5 minutes, or until broccoli is bright green and just tender. Remove broccoli and cool in an ice bath, then drain and set aside.

4. Whisk eggs, half-and-half, mustard, cayenne, salt, and pepper in a large bowl until foamy and well combined, about 3 minutes. Gently stir in broccoli and cheddar cheese. Pour into pie pan, and bake for 45 minutes, or until quiche has set and center no longer jiggles when gently shaken.

5. Remove from oven, cool slightly, and cut into wedges. Serve hot, room temperature or cold.

THE LOWDOWN

You can purchase a steamer basket, which looks like a large, collapsible sink strainer, in the kitchen department of nearly any grocery, big box, or dollar store. Choose one made of stainless steel—they're inexpensive, are dishwasher safe, and will last a very long time.

ⓥ Swiss Chard-Filled Potato Galette

Filled with Swiss chard and onions, this crispy potato galette is fragrant and crispy, with a touch of rosemary. Top with Greek yogurt and fresh chives or scallions for a satisfying main dish.

Yield:	Serving size:	Prep time:	Cook time:
1 9-inch galette	⅛ of galette	15 minutes	20 minutes

1 bunch Swiss chard (about 10 oz.)

1 large russet potato, unpeeled

1 TB. plus 1 tsp. plus 1 tsp. extra-virgin olive oil

½ medium yellow onion, thinly sliced

1 clove garlic, minced

¼ tsp. plus ¾ tsp. kosher salt

½ tsp. freshly ground black pepper

½ tsp. finely chopped fresh rosemary, or ¼ tsp. dried

1. Trim tough stems from Swiss chard. Slice leaves into 1-inch ribbons, or *chiffonade*, and thinly slice tender stems.

2. Shred potato using the large holes on a box grater. Place in a bowl with cold water to cover, and set aside.

3. Heat 1 tablespoon olive oil in a 9-inch nonstick skillet over medium-high heat. Add onion and cook, stirring occasionally, until onions are tender and translucent, about 5 minutes. Add garlic, and cook for 1 minute more. Add Swiss chard, ¼ teaspoon kosher salt, and pepper and cook, stirring frequently, for 10 minutes. Remove chard mixture to a small bowl and wipe pan clean.

4. Drain shredded potato in a fine mesh colander, and use several layers of paper toweling to press all liquid out of potato. Stir rosemary and ¾ teaspoon kosher salt into potato.

5. Heat 1 teaspoon olive oil over medium-high heat. Add half of potato mixture, pressing evenly with a spatula to evenly cover the bottom of the pan. Distribute Swiss chard mixture evenly over potato, leaving a ½-inch border. Add remaining potato to pan, and press evenly to cover Swiss chard mixture and seal edges.

6. Reduce heat to medium. Cook, gently pressing galette with spatula every few minutes, for 10 minutes. Lift edge carefully to ensure that galette is golden brown. If it is not, increase heat to medium high and cook several minutes more, checking frequently.

7. Carefully slide galette out of pan onto a flat plate or inverted baking sheet. Return pan to stovetop, and heat 1 teaspoon oil over medium-high heat. Flip galette back into pan, uncooked side down, reduce heat to medium and cook for 10 more minutes.

8. Slide galette carefully onto serving plate, cut into wedges, and serve immediately.

> **DEFINITION**
>
> To make a **chiffonade** cut, stack leaves, then roll into a tight cylinder like a cigar. Slice cylinder with a sharp knife, then unroll for ribbons of greens.

Ⓥ Spinach and Scallion Scones

These scones highlight the savory flavors of spinach and scallions with just a bit of heat from pepperjack-style vegan cheese shreds.

Yield:	Serving size:	Prep time:	Cook time:
8 scones	1 scone	10 minutes	15 minutes

1 TB. apple cider vinegar (or lemon juice)

1 cup plus 4 TB. organic soy milk

3 cups all-purpose flour

2 TB. vegan sugar

1 tsp. baking soda

1 tsp. kosher salt

4 TB. vegan butter substitute, well chilled and cut into small pieces

¼ cup shredded vegan pepperjack cheese

¼ cup sliced scallions, green parts only

1 cup blanched spinach, cooled, squeezed dry and chopped (see Chapter 5)

1. Preheat oven to 400°F. Grease a 9-inch cake pan with cooking spray.

2. Mix vinegar or lemon juice with 1 cup plus 3 tablespoons soy milk. Allow to stand.

3. Combine flour, sugar, baking soda, and kosher salt in a medium bowl. Rub butter substitute into the flour mixture by hand, until it resembles coarse crumbs. Stir in vegan pepperjack and scallions.

4. Stir spinach into soured soy milk. Make a well in the center of the flour mixture, and add the soy milk mixture all at once. Using a rubber spatula, mix, turning the batter until the flour is just incorporated. Do not overmix!

5. Divide dough into eight even balls. Place balls in cake pan, spaced evenly apart, then pat them until they are just touching. Brush scones with 1 tablespoon soy milk.

6. Bake for 15 minutes, until scones are light golden brown.

HEADS UP!

If you're following a vegan diet, you'll want to use sugar that is specifically labeled "vegan." Sugar, and other processed sugars, are often refined with bone char, so those avoiding animal products in their diet will want to keep a sharp eye when choosing ingredients.

ⓥ Cheesy Twice-Baked Sweet Potatoes with Amaranth

Tender young amaranth leaves and sweet potato combine with luscious vegan cream cheese, onion, and nutmeg for a satisfying, protein-rich breakfast dish.

Yield:	Serving size:	Prep time:	Cook time:
8 potato halves	½ potato	15 minutes	1 hour, 10 minutes

4 medium sweet potatoes, well scrubbed

1 TB. extra-virgin olive oil

1 small yellow onion, diced (about ½ cup)

½ tsp. kosher salt

¼ tsp. freshly ground black pepper

6 cups young amaranth leaves

1 tsp. fresh lemon juice

½ cup vegan cream cheese

½ tsp. freshly grated nutmeg

¼ tsp. cayenne pepper, or to taste

1. Preheat oven to 375°F. Place sweet potatoes on a parchment-lined baking sheet and bake for 40 minutes, or until easily pierced with a fork. Remove from oven to cool slightly.

2. While potatoes are baking, heat olive oil over medium heat in a large sauté pan. Add onion, salt, and pepper. Cook, stirring frequently, until onions are golden and soft. Add spinach to pan. Cook, stirring frequently, until amaranth is soft and liquid has evaporated from pan. Remove from heat, stir in lemon juice, and cool slightly.

3. In a medium mixing bowl, stir vegan cream cheese, nutmeg, and cayenne pepper until well combined. Cut sweet potatoes in half lengthwise, and carefully scoop out flesh with a soup spoon, leaving about ¼ inch of flesh inside potato skins to hold them together. Place potato skins back on baking sheet.

4. Stir sweet potato flesh and spinach mixture into cream cheese. Spoon mixture back into potato skins, dividing evenly, and bake, uncovered, for 30 minutes. Serve immediately.

Variation: To make **Cheesy Twice-Baked Sweet Potatoes with Spinach,** use spinach in place of amaranth.

> **HEADS UP!**
>
> Microwaving a sweet potato will result in stringy, watery flesh. If possible, bake your sweet potato in the oven for superior flavor and texture.

Torta Pascualina

Pascualina is traditionally served in Uruguay and Argentina during Lent, but you'll want to enjoy this delicious dish much more frequently!

Yield:	Serving size:	Prep time:	Cook time:
1 10-inch pie	⅙ of pie	20 minutes	45–50 minutes

2 TB. extra-virgin olive oil	3 large bunches Swiss chard, tough stem ends removed, sliced
1 medium yellow onion, finely diced	1 package puff pastry (2 sheets), thawed
1 medium yellow bell pepper, finely diced	6 large eggs
3 cloves garlic	1 TB. milk
½ tsp. kosher salt	
¼ tsp. freshly ground black pepper	

1. Preheat oven to 400°F. Heat olive oil in a large sauté pan over medium-high heat. Add onion, bell pepper, garlic, salt, and pepper. Cook, stirring frequently, until onions and peppers have softened, about 5 to 7 minutes. Add Swiss chard and continue to cook, stirring often, until chard has softened and is tender to the bite, about 8 to 10 minutes. Remove from heat and cool slightly. Place greens in a fine mesh sieve, and press to remove excess liquid.

2. Butter a 10-inch deep-dish pie pan. Roll and trim one sheet puff pastry into a 14-inch circle. Transfer to pie pan. Prick pastry all over with a fork. Fill with Swiss chard mixture. Make six equal-size wells in filling, then carefully crack an egg into each well, leaving yolk unbroken. Roll and trim second sheet of puff pastry into a 10-inch circle, and gently cover pie. Fold overhang of bottom crust up, and crimp to seal. Brush top and edges of pie with milk.

3. Bake pie for 45 to 50 minutes, until golden brown all over. Cool slightly, then slice and serve. May be enjoyed hot, warm, or cold.

MAKE IT VEGAN

Most commercial puff pastry is vegan—just read the label to be sure. Replace butter with vegan margarine, and omit eggs.

Super Salads and Starters

A great meal deserves a great beginning. In Part 3, you'll find recipes for salads, appetizers, and amazing party foods. Enjoy a light lunch, or impress your guests with a dazzling array of starters that will tickle their taste buds while packing a nutritional wallop.

Recipe and tips abound to take your salads from the same old lettuce and tomato to an unbelievable array of flavor and texture: raw "uncooking," warm dressings, cooked salads, and crunchy palate pleasers.

Rev up your appetite with incredible appetizers, chips, dips, little bites, and snacks. Whether lunchtime or cocktail hour, you'll find that perfect something for every occasion.

Sensational Salads

In This Chapter

- Preparing seasonal raw salad recipes
- Making hearty, warm, cooked salads
- Putting together potlucks and party pleasers

When most people think of salad, what comes to mind? Probably a boring bowl of iceberg lettuce, topped with a sad slice of cucumber or tomato. Spoon on a blob of unhealthy dressing from the refrigerator, and you've seen it all, right? Wrong!

Get ready to explore the wonderful delights that salad has to offer: cooked or wilted greens with warm dressings, a Caesar salad for every mood and diet, and hearty salads such as panzanella that make a great main course or party dish.

Get Ready

Take a few minutes to prep your greens. This can be done an hour before serving, or even a day in advance. Wash your greens well in several changes of cold water, then spin them dry in a salad spinner. Cover, and place in the fridge until you're ready to use. This will ensure that your greens are crisp, cold, and clean when it's time to serve them.

Some of the recipes that follow are quite simple, and some feature a few more steps. Always be sure to read your recipe through and assemble all ingredients and equipment before you begin food preparation. Chefs call this *mise en place*, and if you do it, you'll find that you're producing better food in less time.

Ⓥ Frisée and Dandelion Salad with Warm Shallot Dressing

The pleasant bitterness of frisée and dandelion is tempered with a savory, slightly sweet shallot vinaigrette.

Yield:	Serving size:	Prep time:	Cook time:
10 cups	2 cups	10 minutes	5 minutes

1 head frisée (6–8 cups), torn into bite-size pieces

2 cups young dandelion greens, torn into bite-size pieces

1 TB. plus 2 TB. extra-virgin olive oil

¼ cup shallot, thinly sliced (about 2 small shallots)

1 TB. Dijon mustard

¼ cup sherry vinegar

½ tsp. kosher salt

¼ tsp. freshly ground black pepper

1. Wash frisée and dandelion greens, spin dry, and return to refrigerator in a large serving bowl.

2. Heat 1 tablespoon olive oil in a small saucepan over medium heat. Add shallots and cook, stirring occasionally, until golden and beginning to crisp, about 5 minutes.

3. Whisk Dijon mustard, vinegar, kosher salt, and pepper into shallots. Bring to a simmer, then whisk in remaining 2 tablespoons olive oil. Remove from heat.

4. Pour warm dressing over greens and toss well. Serve immediately.

THE LOWDOWN

Early spring is the time to head outside to look for young dandelion greens. You want them as tiny as possible—no more than a few inches long. Pull up dandelion greens from your front lawn before they flower, and you'll reap the benefits of a weed-free lawn later in the season, plus you'll enjoy some good eating right away.

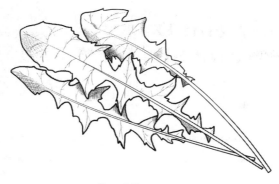

Dandelion greens.

ⓥ Hail Caesar Tuscan Kale Salad

This decadent Caesar salad features a creamy, garlicky dressing, crunchy croutons, and the mild flavor and gorgeous blue-green color of Tuscan kale.

Yield:	Serving size:	Prep time:	Cook time:
10 cups	2 cups	10 minutes	5 minutes

1 bunch Tuscan (lacinato) kale, tough stems removed, torn into bite-size pieces

¼ cup blanched almonds

¼ cup fresh lemon juice (about 2 small lemons)

2 TB. vegan mayonnaise

1 garlic clove, minced, or to taste

1 tsp. vegetarian Worcestershire sauce

1 tsp. Dijon mustard

2 TB. nutritional yeast

1 tsp. *dulse flakes*

½ tsp. freshly ground black pepper

1–2 TB. water, optional

1 recipe *Cheezy Vegan Croutons* (see Chapter 16)

1. Wash kale, spin dry, and return to refrigerator in a large serving bowl.

2. Heat a small sauté pan over medium heat. Add almonds and cook, stirring frequently, until lightly browned at edges. Remove from heat and transfer immediately to a small bowl.

3. In the small bowl of a food processor, combine almonds, lemon juice, vegan mayonnaise, garlic, Worcestershire sauce, Dijon mustard, nutritional yeast, dulse flakes, and black pepper. Pulse until well combined. If mixture looks very thick, add water if necessary.

4. Pour dressing over kale, and toss well. Top with Cheezy Vegan Croutons.

DEFINITION

Dulse is a red seaweed that grows in the Atlantic and Pacific oceans. It adds the fresh, salty flavor of the ocean to foods. Dulse is an excellent source of iodine, phytochemicals, antioxidants, and a wide array of vitamins and minerals. Avoid dulse if you suffer from hyperthyroidism. Dulse is available in flakes as well as its natural dried form, and can be eaten raw, roasted, or pan fried. It is also used as a thickener for soups.

THE LOWDOWN

Blanched almonds have had their skins removed. You can find blanched, sliced almonds in the supermarket. If you prefer to make them yourself, bring a large pot of water to a boil, add raw almonds, and boil 1 minute. Drain, then rub skins off using a large kitchen towel. Rinse and spread on a clean, dry towel for 30 minutes to dry, then proceed with recipe or store in an airtight container.

Ⓥ Ⓡ Health Nut Raw Caesar Salad

This Caesar salad features crunchy curly kale in a raw, oil-free dressing that gets its savory flavor from nuts and seeds. Diced jicama provides a sweet crunch that makes a fun replacement for croutons.

Yield:	Serving size:	Prep time:
10 cups	2 cups	10 minutes plus overnight soak

1 head curly kale, tough stems removed, torn into bite-size pieces

½ cup raw almonds, soaked overnight and drained

2 TB. raw sesame seeds

¼ cup fresh lemon juice (about 2 small lemons)

2 cloves raw garlic, minced (or to taste)

1 tsp. dulse flakes

½ tsp. Bragg Liquid Aminos

2 TB. water

1 cup jicama, peeled and diced into ½-inch pieces

1. Wash kale, spin dry, and return to refrigerator in a large serving bowl.

2. In the small bowl of a food processor, combine almonds, sesame seeds, lemon juice, garlic, dulse flakes, liquid aminos, and water. Pulse until smooth, about 2 minutes.

3. Pour dressing over greens and toss well. Top with jicama cubes, and serve immediately.

Variation: For a classic **Raw Caesar Salad,** replace the kale with romaine lettuce.

THE LOWDOWN

Bragg Liquid Aminos is a protein concentrate derived from soybeans. It contains 16 essential amino acids, and is gluten-free. Bragg Liquid Aminos is appropriate for a raw diet as it is non-GMO; contains no chemicals, artificial colors, or preservatives; and has not been heated.

Grilled Caesar Salad

Romaine lettuce takes on a smoky flavor when quickly grilled. Topped with a cheesy Caesar dressing rich with the nutty flavor of Parmesan cheese and crispy, buttery Parmesan croutons, this special-occasion salad will wow your guests with its rich flavor profile.

Yield:	Serving size:	Prep time:	Cook time:
8 romaine quarters	1 quarter	10 minutes	10 minutes

2 heads romaine lettuce

2 TB. fresh lemon juice (from 1 lemon)

2 TB. mayonnaise

2 TB. apple cider vinegar

1 tsp. Dijon mustard

1 tsp. vegetarian Worcestershire sauce

1 clove plus 1 clove garlic, crushed

¼ tsp. plus ¼ tsp. kosher salt

¼ tsp. plus ¼ tsp. freshly ground black pepper

2 TB. plus 2 TB. extra-virgin olive oil

¼ cup plus ¼ cup finely shredded Parmesan cheese

8 ½-inch slices French bread

¼ cup unsalted butter, melted

1. Heat grill to medium high. Remove tough outer leaves of romaine lettuce, and carefully trim ⅛ inch from root end of lettuce without separating leaves. Cut romaine heads into quarters lengthwise. Wash well, and dry carefully with clean kitchen towels. Set aside.

2. In the small bowl of a food processor, combine lemon juice, mayonnaise, apple cider vinegar, Dijon mustard, Worcestershire sauce, 1 clove garlic, ¼ teaspoon kosher salt, ¼ teaspoon pepper, and 2 tablespoons olive oil. Pulse until smooth, about 2 minutes. Stir in ¼ cup Parmesan cheese, and set aside.

3. Brush bread slices liberally with butter. Brush romaine quarters with 2 tablespoons olive oil, and season with ¼ teaspoon salt and ¼ teaspoon pepper.

4. Grill romaine quarters, turning once or twice, until lightly charred on all sides. Remove to a serving platter. Grill bread slices until toasted. Remove bread from grill, and immediately rub with remaining crushed garlic clove. Sprinkle ¼ cup Parmesan cheese over croutons.

5. Drizzle dressing over romaine quarters. Serve immediately, topped with croutons.

Romaine.

HEADS UP!

Worcestershire sauce usually contains anchovies, so be sure to read the label if you're concerned about keeping your diet vegetarian.

ⓥ Arugula, Grapefruit, and Red Onion Salad

Peppery arugula pairs with bright, citrusy grapefruit and zesty red onion in this refreshing salad.

Yield:	Serving size:	Prep time:
10 cups	2 cups	10 minutes

1 (10 oz.) bag baby arugula (about 8 cups)

2 large grapefruit, cut into segments, reserve juice chilled (see Chapter 16)

1 small red onion, very thinly sliced

1 tsp. white wine vinegar

½ tsp. salt

¼ tsp. freshly ground black pepper

2 TB. extra-virgin olive oil

1. Wash arugula, spin dry, and place in large serving bowl in refrigerator. Chill grapefruit segments.

2. Place sliced onion in a small bowl of ice water. Drain after 10 minutes, and pat dry with paper towels.

3. In a small bowl, combine grapefruit juice, vinegar, salt, and pepper. Whisk in olive oil a few drops at a time.

4. Toss arugula, grapefruit segments, and red onion with dressing. Serve immediately.

Variation: Substitute curly chicory for arugula, and use oranges instead of grapefruit for a fun twist.

THE LOWDOWN

Soaking sliced onion in ice water removes volatile sulphurous compounds—the same ones that make you "cry" when slicing them—which results in a clean, crisp flavor without all the bad breath and digestive unrest that can accompany raw onion consumption.

Arugula, Apple, and Dried Tart Cherry Salad with Goat Cheese

The assertive flavors of arugula stand up to the sweetness of apples and dried tart cherries, while fresh goat cheese adds a tangy note to this salad.

Yield:	Serving size:	Prep time:
10 cups	2 cups	10 minutes

1 (10 oz.) bag baby arugula (about 8 cups)

2 TB. white wine vinegar

½ tsp. kosher salt

¼ tsp. freshly ground black pepper

1 tsp. honey mustard

3 TB. extra-virgin olive oil

2 tart apples, such Granny Smith, peeled and sliced

1 small red onion, very thinly sliced

½ cup dried tart cherries

½ cup crumbled fresh goat cheese

1. Wash arugula, spin dry, and place in large serving bowl in refrigerator.

2. In a small bowl, combine white wine vinegar, salt, pepper, and honey mustard. Whisk in olive oil a few drops at a time.

3. Toss arugula, apple slices, onion, cherries, and goat cheese with dressing. Serve immediately.

THE LOWDOWN

I've included Granny Smith apples in this recipe because they are easy to find at your local supermarket. Try to look for local apples whenever you can. Many varieties of apple are imported from places like New Zealand, which greatly increases your "food miles." Reducing the number of miles that your food travels to get to your plate is what the locavore lifestyle is all about. Educate yourself about the varieties of apples grown in your local area, and know when they are in season. Feel free to substitute your favorites in any of the recipes found throughout this book.

Ⓥ Warm Lentil Salad with Arugula

Warm, comforting lentils pair well with spicy, mature arugula accented with a mustardy vinaigrette and crunchy bell peppers and scallions.

Yield:	Serving size:	Prep time:	Cook time:
8 cups	2 cups	10 minutes	25 minutes

1 cup green lentils (French or DuPuy)	½ tsp. freshly ground black pepper
½ tsp. plus ½ tsp. kosher salt	1 TB. Dijon mustard
1 bunch arugula (about 6 cups), thinly sliced	½ cup extra-virgin olive oil
	1 red bell pepper, julienne cut
2 TB. apple cider vinegar	¼ cup scallions, thinly sliced
2 TB. lemon juice (from 1 lemon)	

1. Bring 8 cups water to a boil in a medium saucepan. Add lentils and ½ teaspoon salt. Cook, stirring occasionally, until lentils are tender, about 25 minutes. Drain and set aside.

2. Wash arugula, spin dry, and place in large serving bowl in refrigerator.

3. In a small bowl, combine vinegar, lemon juice, ½ teaspoon salt, pepper, and Dijon mustard. Slowly whisk in olive oil, a few drops at a time.

4. Toss lentils, bell pepper, scallions, and arugula with dressing, and serve immediately.

THE LOWDOWN

When you slowly whisk oil into the other ingredients in your dressing, you are creating an emulsion. Oil and vinegar do not want to mix. Adding the oil drop by drop helps to suspend the oil in the vinegar in tiny droplets. Adding thickeners such as mustard or honey helps to hold your emulsion together, and also adds flavor. Be sure to add salt to your dressing before you add oil, or it won't dissolve properly.

Ⓥ Wilted Turnip Greens with Apples and Pecans

Turnip greens turn sweet and savory when wilted in a balsamic dressing. Apples and pecans bring a sweet, toasty crunch to this salad.

Yield:	Serving size:	Prep time:	Cook time:
8 cups	2 cups	10 minutes	5 minutes

1 TB. plus 1 TB. extra-virgin olive oil

2 cloves garlic, minced

2 TB. balsamic vinegar

2 bunches turnip greens, tough stems removed, torn into bite-size pieces

½ tsp. kosher salt

¼ tsp. freshly ground black pepper

2 tart apples, such as Granny Smith, peeled and thinly sliced

½ cup pecans, roughly chopped

1. Heat 1 tablespoon olive oil in a medium sauté pan over medium-high heat. Add garlic and cook, stirring constantly, for 1 to 2 minutes, until garlic is just beginning to turn golden. Add balsamic vinegar, and whisk to combine. Whisk in remaining 1 tablespoon olive oil.

2. Add turnip greens to sauté pan along with salt and pepper, and cook, stirring frequently, until greens have wilted, about 3 minutes.

3. Toss turnip greens with apples and pecans, and serve immediately.

Variation: For a heartier salad, peel turnip roots, cut into 1-inch chunks, and toss with 1 tablespoon olive oil. Season with salt and pepper, and roast at 400°F for 20 minutes, stirring a few times. Add roasted turnip to salad along with apples and pecans. Alternately, try this salad with red cabbage in place of turnip greens.

Turnip greens.

Ⓥ Spinach Panzanella

This classic Italian bread salad packs an extra nutritional punch with fresh baby spinach, while red wine vinegar, fresh basil, and salty kalamata olives lend incredible flavor.

Yield:	Serving size:	Prep time:
10 cups	2½ cups	10 minutes

6 ripe plum tomatoes, roughly chopped

1 tsp. salt

2 TB. plus 1 TB. red wine vinegar

½ tsp. freshly ground black pepper

¼ cup extra-virgin olive oil

4 large slices stale Italian bread, cut into 1-inch chunks

½ cup loosely packed fresh basil leaves

6 cups baby spinach

1 cup English seedless cucumber, cut into 1-inch chunks (about ½ cucumber)

½ cup pitted kalamata olives

1. Toss tomatoes with salt, 2 tablespoons red wine vinegar, pepper, and olive oil. Set aside.

2. Sprinkle stale bread chunks with remaining 1 tablespoon red wine vinegar. Stir gently into tomato mixture.

3. Toss basil leaves, baby spinach, cucumber, and kalamata olives in a large bowl. Add tomato/bread mixture, and toss gently to combine. Serve immediately.

Variation: For a more substantial meal, add fresh mozzarella cheese, soy "chicken" strips, or grilled mushrooms.

THE LOWDOWN

Panzanella is best when served in late summer, with the freshest, ripest tomatoes and basil you can find. If you must have this salad out of season, halve tomatoes, drizzle with 1 tablespoon olive oil, and roast for 30 minutes in a 400°F oven before proceeding with the recipe. This will deepen the flavor, improve the texture, and intensify the sweetness of supermarket tomatoes, which tend to be flavorless and mealy.

Ⓥ Escarole, Roasted Pear, and Hazelnut Salad

The slight bitterness of escarole is offset by sweet pears, toasty hazelnuts, and a slightly sweet dressing in this delicious winter salad.

Yield:	Serving size:	Prep time:
10 cups	2½ cups	10 minutes

4 ripe pears, such as Anjou, cored and cut into 8 slices each

1 TB. plus 2 TB. extra-virgin olive oil

½ cup hazelnuts, roughly chopped

¼ cup sherry vinegar

½ tsp. kosher salt

¼ tsp. freshly ground black pepper

¼ cup shallots, finely minced (about 1 large shallot)

1 tsp. agave nectar or raw honey

1 TB. hazelnut oil

1 head escarole, tough outer leaves removed, torn into bite-size pieces

1. Preheat oven to 400°F. Toss pear slices with 1 tablespoon olive oil. Spread evenly on a parchment-lined baking sheet and roast, turning once, for 10 minutes.

2. Place hazelnuts on a separate baking sheet, and toast in oven for 5 minutes, or until lightly browned.

3. In a small bowl, combine vinegar, kosher salt, pepper, shallots, and agave nectar. Whisk to combine. Slowly whisk in hazelnut oil, followed by remaining 2 tablespoons olive oil.

4. Combine escarole and warm pears in a large bowl, and toss gently with dressing to combine. Top salad with toasted hazelnuts, and serve immediately.

HEADS UP!

Nut oils such as hazelnut turn rancid quickly, so store them in the refrigerator to maximize shelf life. If you don't have any hazelnut oil on hand, replace it with an extra tablespoon of olive oil.

Ⓥ Dandelion Greens with Warm Roasted Garlic Dressing

Tender dandelion greens are wilted in a warm dressing, where roasted garlic stands up to the strong flavor of the greens.

Yield:	Serving size:	Prep time:
4 cups	1 cup	10 minutes

8 cups young dandelion greens	¼ tsp. kosher salt
6 cloves roasted garlic (see Chapter 16)	2 TB. extra-virgin olive oil
2 TB. balsamic vinegar	

1. Wash, spin dry, and chill dandelion greens.

2. Place roasted garlic, balsamic vinegar, and kosher salt in a small saucepan. Heat, crushing garlic with a spoon, until warm and smooth. Whisk in olive oil, and heat until very warm. Do not allow mixture to boil.

3. Toss greens with warm dressing. Serve immediately.

Variation: Substitute puntarelle, curly chicory, or escarole if dandelion greens are not available.

Ⓥ Tatsoi and Mizuna Salad with Ginger-Miso Dressing

Wasabi and ginger give subtle heat to this citrusy miso dressing, which dresses tender tatsoi and pepper mizuna to perfection.

Yield:	Serving size:	Prep time:
10 cups	2½ cups	10 minutes

5 cups tatsoi

5 cups young mizuna leaves

2 TB. mellow white miso

1 tsp. *wasabi* powder or paste

3 TB. freshly squeezed orange juice (from ½ orange)

2 TB. fresh ginger, peeled and grated

1 tsp. light sesame oil

2 TB. sunflower oil

1. Wash, spin dry, and chill tatsoi and mizuna.

2. Place miso, wasabi powder, orange juice, ginger, sesame oil, and sunflower oil in small bowl of food processor, and process until smooth and creamy. Alternately, place ingredients in a small jar and shake well until combined.

3. Toss greens with dressing. Serve immediately. Dressing will keep in your refrigerator, in a tightly sealed jar, for 3 days.

DEFINITION

Wasabi is a root that is part of the *Brassica* family, like horseradish and mustard. Wasabi releases its potent heat when grated. While many Japanese restaurants grate wasabi fresh, home cooks will likely want to purchase it in powdered or paste form. Both are available in the Asian grocery section of your supermarket.

ⓥ Fattoush

The crunch of fresh romaine lettuce and crispy, fried pita makes this lemony salad a standout.

Yield:	Serving size:	Prep time:
10 cups	2½ cups	10 minutes

8 cups romaine lettuce

2 TB. plus 2 TB. extra-virgin olive oil

2 loaves pita, torn into small pieces

¼ cup fresh lemon juice (from about 2 lemons)

1 TB. ground sumac

½ tsp. kosher salt

¼ tsp. freshly ground pepper

1 medium cucumber, peeled, seeded, and diced

½ small red onion, thinly sliced, soaked in ice water, and drained

1. Wash, spin dry, and chill romaine lettuce.

2. Heat 2 tablespoons olive oil in a small sauté pan. When oil is hot, add pita and fry until golden brown. Remove and drain on paper towels.

3. Whisk lemon juice with sumac, kosher salt, pepper, and remaining 2 tablespoons of olive oil. Toss dressing with romaine lettuce, fried pita, cucumber, and red onion. Serve immediately.

DEFINITION

Sumac is the ground berries of a decorative bush that grows wild in Italy and the Middle East. It has a lemony, tart flavor and a distinctive dark-red color. Although there is really no flavor substitute for sumac, if you can't find it, add lemon zest mixed with a little salt to your recipe.

Grilled Tri-Color Salad with Parsley-Walnut Pesto

The warm flavors of parsley pesto accent radicchio, Belgian endive, and romaine lettuce, which lose their bitterness when charred on the grill.

Yield:	Serving size:	Prep time:	Cook time:
4 salads	1 wedge of each green	10 minutes	10 minutes

1 small head romaine lettuce, tough outer leaves removed	2 cloves garlic, crushed
2 heads Belgian endive	¼ cup walnuts
1 head radicchio	¼ tsp. kosher salt
1 TB. plus 3 TB. extra-virgin olive oil	¼ tsp. freshly ground pepper
2 cups loosely packed Italian parsley leaves	1–2 TB. water, optional
	2 TB. grated Parmesan cheese, optional

1. Trim ⅛-inch stem end from romaine, radicchio, and endive. Quarter romaine and radicchio, being careful to keep stem end attached. Halve Belgian endive. Brush with 1 tablespoon olive oil and set aside.

2. Heat grill to medium high.

3. Combine parsley, garlic, walnuts, kosher salt, pepper, and remaining 3 table-spoons olive oil in bowl of food processor. Process until smooth, adding 1 to 2 tablespoons warm water if necessary. Stir in Parmesan, if using. Set aside.

4. Grill romaine, radicchio, and endive over direct heat until lightly charred, about 3 minutes per side. Divide among four salad plates, top with pesto, and serve immediately.

Variation: Replace ¼ cup of the parsley with cilantro, and replace walnuts with toasted pumpkin seeds for a pesto with Mexican flair.

Leaf Lettuce and Strawberry Salad with Poppy Dressing

This sweet and sassy salad is a springtime treat!

Yield:	Serving size:	Prep time:
10 cups	2½ cups	10 minutes

8 cups red and/or green leaf lettuce, torn into bite-size pieces

½ cup plain nonfat Greek yogurt

2 TB. apple cider vinegar

1 TB. raw honey or agave nectar

2 TB. poppy seeds

2 cups fresh strawberries, hulled and sliced

½ small red onion, thinly sliced, soaked in ice water, and drained

1. Wash, spin dry, and chill lettuce in a large salad bowl.

2. Whisk yogurt, apple cider vinegar, honey, and poppy seeds in a small bowl.

3. Toss lettuce, strawberries, and red onion with dressing. Serve immediately.

MAKE IT VEGAN

For a vegan version of this poppy dressing, substitute vegan mayonnaise for the yogurt, and sweeten with agave nectar.

Leaf lettuce.

Ⓥ Brussels Sprouts Salad

Brussels sprouts in a salad? Yes! Accented with nutty chick peas and a mustardy vinaigrette, these Brussels sprouts will win you over.

Yield:	Serving size:	Prep time:
6 cups	1½ cups	10 minutes

2 TB. apple cider vinegar

1 TB. fresh lemon juice (from about ½ lemon)

1 TB. agave nectar

1 TB. whole grain Dijon mustard

½ tsp. kosher salt

⅛ tsp. cayenne pepper, or to taste

2 TB. extra-virgin olive oil

4 cups thinly sliced Brussels sprouts

2 cups canned chick peas, rinsed and drained

1. Combine apple cider vinegar, lemon juice, agave nectar, Dijon mustard, kosher salt, and cayenne pepper in a small bowl. Slowly whisk in olive oil.

2. Toss Brussels sprouts and chick peas with dressing. Serve immediately, or refrigerate for up to 4 hours.

Variation: If raw Brussels sprouts don't appeal to you, blanch in boiling, salted water for 2 minutes, then chill and proceed with recipe.

THE LOWDOWN

To easily make paper-thin slices, a *mandoline* is a helpful. This French-style slicer with a sharp, adjustable blade can be pricey, but similar, more affordable slicers can be found in the housewares department of your local Asian grocery store.

Ⓥ Ⓡ Everything in the Whole Wide Refrigerator Salad

When I was growing up, my mom worked and went to school, so she'd often throw dinner together out of what was in the refrigerator. This crunchy, flavorful dinner salad is bursting with the flavors of fresh veggies, while Green Goddess dressing lends its creamy, herbal goodness. This one's for you, Mom!

Yield:	Serving size:	Prep time:
16 cups	4 cups	10 minutes

10 cups mixed salad greens, such as leaf lettuce, romaine, mesclun mix, or spinach

½ cup raw cashews, soaked overnight and drained

½ cup ripe Hass avocado (1 small avocado)

2 TB. apple cider vinegar

1 TB. fresh lemon juice (from ½ lemon)

1 tsp. Bragg Liquid Aminos

1 clove garlic, crushed

2 TB. fresh Italian parsley, stems removed, roughly chopped

2 TB. chives, sliced

2 TB. fresh tarragon, roughly chopped, or 1 tsp. dried

¼ cup lightly packed fresh basil leaves

2 TB. flax oil

1 red bell pepper, seeded and thinly sliced

1 small cucumber, peeled, seeded, and thinly sliced

1 cup cherry tomatoes, halved

1 cup carrots, peeled and chopped

1 cup broccoli florets, cut into bite-size pieces

1 cup cauliflower florets, cut into bite-size pieces

½ small red onion, thinly sliced, soaked in ice water and drained

¼ cup sunflower seeds

1. Wash salad greens, spin dry, and chill in refrigerator.

2. Combine cashews, avocado, vinegar, lemon juice, Bragg Liquid Aminos, garlic, parsley, chives, tarragon, basil leaves, and flax oil in bowl of food processor. Process until dressing is smooth.

3. Toss lettuce, bell pepper, cucumber, tomatoes, carrots, broccoli, cauliflower, red onion, and sunflower seeds with dressing. Serve immediately.

THE LOWDOWN

Green Goddess dressing is a 1970s classic. This slimmed-down version eliminates unhealthy ingredients such as mayonnaise and added salt, and gives it a healthy, raw makeover. Try it as a dip for fresh veggies, a spread for crackers, or even on a baked potato.

Appetizers and Snacks

In This Chapter

- Creating party pleasers
- Making quick, nutritious snacks

Having a party? You'll need some crowd-pleasing finger foods. Just because it's party food, that doesn't mean it needs to be unhealthy. Greens have their place at the table no matter what the occasion may be, from a savory bite passed on an elegant silver tray, to homey and delicious dumplings eaten in messy splendor at the kitchen table.

Chips and dip achieve a new, healthy level with two kinds of kale chips, plus hot and cold dips that bring greens into the snacking arena.

Perhaps you need a quick snack for the family to eat on the run. You'll find those here, too. So roll up your sleeves, invite some friends over, and get cooking!

Spanakopita

Spinach and feta cheese are wrapped in buttery phyllo in these triangles of delicious Greek goodness.

Yield:	Serving size:	Prep time:	Cook time:
36 triangles	4 triangles	45 minutes	20 minutes

1½ lb. spinach, tough stems trimmed

2 TB. extra-virgin olive oil

½ cup white onion, finely chopped (1 small onion)

½ cup scallions, sliced, white and green parts

2 cloves garlic, finely chopped

1 cup feta, crumbled

¼ cup ricotta

½ tsp. freshly grated nutmeg

1 TB. fresh dill, finely chopped

2 TB. fresh Italian parsley, finely chopped

½ tsp. freshly ground black pepper

2 TB. lemon juice (from ½ lemon)

½ package phyllo sheets, thawed

½ cup unsalted butter, melted (1 stick)

1. Preheat oven to 375°F. In a steamer basket, steam spinach over 1 inch of water for 2 minutes. Drain in a colander and cool. Using your hands, press to squeeze all water from spinach. Chop spinach into small pieces.

2. Heat olive oil in a medium sauté pan over medium-high heat. Add onion and cook until softened, about 8 minutes, stirring frequently. Add scallions and garlic, and cook 2 minutes more, stirring often.

3. Mix feta, ricotta, nutmeg, dill, parsley, and black pepper in a large mixing bowl. Add onion mixture, spinach, and lemon juice. Stir well.

4. Cover phyllo sheets with a damp kitchen towel to keep them from drying out while you are working. Lay one sheet phyllo on work surface and brush with melted butter. Place another phyllo sheet on top of the first, and brush with butter again. Cut phyllo stack lengthwise into four pieces with a sharp knife.

5. Place a heaping teaspoon of filling at the top corner of one phyllo strip. Fold the corner inward to create a triangle, and then continue to fold into triangles, as though you are folding a flag. Moisten the final edge of phyllo with butter, and seal. Repeat process until all phyllo and filling have been used.

6. Place spanakopita 1 inch apart on a parchment-lined baking sheet, and bake for 15 to 20 minutes, or until crisp and golden.

To freeze: Making spanakopita can be time-consuming, especially for beginners, but their incomparable flavor is worth the effort. To make in advance, prepare spanakopita through step 5, then freeze in a single layer on a baking sheet. Transfer to a well-sealed plastic freezer bag to store for up to 3 months. Bake frozen spanakopita at 350°F for about 30 minutes.

THE LOWDOWN

You can easily substitute frozen spinach in any recipe that calls for fresh spinach to be steamed, drained, and squeezed dry. One package of frozen spinach equals 1½ to 2 pounds of fresh greens. Just defrost, drain, and squeeze dry. Baby spinach and tender young bunches of spinach are interchangeable when cooked fresh, but when using bagged mature spinach, add an extra ½ pound of greens, since you'll lose more weight when removing large, tough, mature stems. Weigh your produce at the grocery store if you don't have a kitchen scale. You'll be starting with a large volume of fresh greens, to yield a relatively small amount of cooked greens, so don't be surprised by the amount of spinach in these recipes.

Ⓥ Spinach Pies

These lemony spinach pies are traditionally enjoyed in Lebanon during the Lenten season, but you'll love the combination of spinach and flaky puff pastry any time of the year.

Yield:	Serving size:	Prep time:	Cook time:
24 pies	2 pies	30 minutes	25 minutes

1½ lbs. baby spinach

3 TB. extra-virgin olive oil

1 cup yellow onion, finely chopped

½ cup pine nuts

1 clove garlic, minced

½ tsp. kosher salt

½ tsp. freshly ground black pepper

1 tsp. ground sumac

1 (17.5-oz.) package puff pastry, defrosted

1 TB. nigella seeds, optional

1. Preheat oven to 375°F. In a steamer basket, steam spinach over 1 inch of water for 2 minutes. Drain in a colander and cool slightly. When spinach has cooled, press to squeeze all water from spinach. Chop spinach into small pieces.

2. Heat 3 tablespoons olive oil in a medium sauté pan over medium-high heat. Add onion and cook until softened, about 8 minutes, stirring frequently. Add pine nuts and garlic, and cook 2 minutes more, stirring often.

3. In a large mixing bowl, stir onion mixture into spinach. Add salt, black pepper, and sumac. Set aside.

4. Cover puff pastry with a damp kitchen towel to keep it fresh while you are working. Flour your work surface and rolling pin well. Roll puff pastry, one sheet at a time, into a thin rectangle, about the thickness of a piece of cardboard. Using a 4-inch round cutter, cut pastry into 12 rounds.

5. Place a tablespoon of filling in the middle of each round. Lift two sides of the circle and pinch the edges together, then lift the third side, and pinch together to make a three-sided pie. Repeat with remaining rounds.

6. Roll second sheet of pastry, cut, and repeat as above.

7. Place pies 2 inches apart on a parchment-lined baking sheet, sprinkle with nigella seeds (if using), and bake for 25 minutes, or until golden. Serve hot or at room temperature.

To freeze: Prepare spinach pies through step 6, then freeze in a single layer on a baking sheet. Transfer to a well-sealed plastic freezer bag to store for up to 3 months. Bake frozen spinach pies at 375°F for about 25 minutes.

Ⓥ Crispy Baked Kale Chips

These simple kale chips are so good, even small children will devour them without realizing that they're eating their veggies. Salty, crisp, and savory, their potato chip–like goodness is everything you want in a chip.

Yield:	Serving size:	Prep time:	Cook time:
6 cups	1 cup	5 minutes	20 minutes

6 cups lacinato or curly kale, tough stems removed, torn into large pieces

2 tsp. extra-virgin olive oil

½ tsp. kosher salt

1. Preheat oven to 275°F. Toss kale with olive oil and salt, and spread on parchment-lined baking sheets, ensuring that kale chips do not touch one another.

2. Bake for 20 minutes, or until dry and crisp.

3. Serve immediately, or store in an airtight container for up to 3 days.

> **HEADS UP!**
>
> It's difficult to say how many bunches of kale you will need for your chips, as curly and lacinato kale have very different yields, and merchants package their kale in different-sized bunches. Trim and wash your kale, then measure. Experiment with varieties to see which make your favorite chips.

V R Cheezy Vegan Raw Kale Chips

You'll need a dehydrator to make this raw, vegan answer to nacho cheese chips. These spicy, cheesy-tasting chips are so savory and delicious, you'll have a hard time believing that they're actually good for you! Curly kale is the best choice for these chips, as you'll want to capture as much flavorful topping as possible.

Yield:	Serving size:	Prep time:	Cook time:
6 cups	1 cup	10 minutes plus overnight soaking time	About 8 hours

6 cups curly kale, tough stems removed, torn into large pieces

½ cup raw cashews, soaked overnight, liquid discarded

¼ cup pumpkin seeds, soaked for 2–4 hours, liquid discarded

¼ cup raw sesame seeds, soaked for 2–4 hours, liquid discarded

¼ cup nutritional yeast

2 TB. lemon juice (from 1 lemon)

2 TB. Bragg Liquid Aminos

2 TB. filtered water

1 tsp. Anaheim chile powder

1 tsp. smoked paprika

½ tsp. kosher salt

½ tsp. freshly ground black pepper

1. Wash kale, and spin in salad spinner until completely dry. Set aside in a large mixing bowl.

2. In the large bowl of a food processor, combine cashews, pumpkin seeds, sesame seeds, nutritional yeast, lemon juice, liquid aminos, water, Anaheim chile powder, smoked paprika, kosher salt, and black pepper. Run processor until mixture is smooth and well combined.

3. Pour cashew mixture over kale, and mix well with your hands, rubbing the topping in to coat evenly.

4. Set dehydrator to approximately 100°F. Spread kale evenly on dehydrator trays. Dehydrate for 8 to 10 hours, until crisp and dry, but still somewhat pliable.

5. Serve immediately, or store at room temperature in an airtight container for up to 7 days.

Variations: You can change this recipe up a couple of ways. Eliminate the Anaheim chile powder and smoked paprika for each variation. For **Indian-Spiced Cheezy Vegan Raw Kale Chips,** add 1 teaspoon cumin, 1 teaspoon Madras curry powder, and 1 teaspoon turmeric. For **Middle Eastern–Style Cheezy Vegan Raw Kale Chips,** add 1 teaspoon cumin, $\frac{1}{2}$ teaspoon ground sumac, and 1 teaspoon coriander. For **Chinese-Style Cheezy Vegan Raw Kale Chips,** add 2 teaspoons Chinese five-spice powder and 1 tablespoon Asian-style hot sauce (such as Sriracha). For **Japanese-Style Cheezy Vegan Raw Kale Chips,** add 2 teaspoons wasabi powder and 1 tablespoon dark sesame oil.

THE LOWDOWN

Pound for pound, making these chips at home will be a huge cost savings, even if you have to go out and purchase a dehydrator. You'll pay about $8 for 3 to 4 ounces of vegan kale chips at your local specialty market. That's $30 to $40 per pound, and many don't even feature organic ingredients! Making your own kale chips is easy and economical, and your house will smell mouth-wateringly amazing while they're dehydrating.

Spicy Spinach Yogurt Dip

Hollow out a loaf of pumpernickel bread for this crunchy, creamy, spicy take on a 1970s classic, or serve a bowl of dip with raw veggies or pita chips. Lemony spinach, crunchy water chestnuts, and healthy Greek yogurt slim down an old favorite without skimping on taste.

Yield:	Serving size:	Prep time:	Cook time:
4 cups	¼ cup	15 minutes plus 2 hours chilling time	None

1 (12-oz.) package frozen spinach, thawed, drained, squeezed dry, chopped

2 cups nonfat Greek yogurt

½ cup water chestnuts, drained and finely chopped

½ cup thinly sliced scallions, white and green parts

1 clove garlic, smashed and finely chopped

1 TB. lemon zest

2 TB. lemon juice (from ½ lemon)

¼ tsp. cayenne pepper

1 tsp. hot pepper sauce, such as Tabasco

1 TB. prepared horseradish

½ tsp. kosher salt

½ tsp. freshly ground black pepper

1. Combine spinach, Greek yogurt, water chestnuts, scallions, garlic, lemon zest, lemon juice, cayenne pepper, hot pepper sauce, horseradish, salt, and black pepper in a medium mixing bowl.

2. Chill for 2 hours, or up to 2 days, in refrigerator.

MAKE IT VEGAN

To make a vegan spinach dip, omit Greek yogurt, and substitute 1½ cups tofu sour cream and ½ cup vegan mayonnaise. Since the salt content of vegan mayonnaise may vary, add salt at the end, ¼ tsp. at a time. Taste and adjust to your liking. Chill as directed.

THE LOWDOWN

To chop garlic finely, use the side of your chef's knife to crush each clove. Remove papery skin, then chop finely. Alternately, peeled cloves can be run through a garlic press.

Ⓥ Stuffed Mushrooms with Amaranth and Walnuts

Earthy mushrooms are baked with a flavorful filling of sautéed amaranth, toasted walnuts, and crispy bread crumbs for a perfect autumn or winter first course.

Yield:	Serving size:	Prep time:	Cook time:
12 mushroom caps	3 mushroom caps	20 minutes	30 minutes

12 jumbo stuffing mushrooms

¼ cup extra-virgin olive oil, divided

½ cup walnuts, toasted and chopped

¼ cup thinly sliced, peeled shallot (about 2 shallots)

2 cloves garlic, smashed and finely chopped

½ lb. young amaranth leaves, tough stems removed

½ tsp. kosher salt

½ tsp. black pepper

¼ cup herb-seasoned panko bread crumbs

¼ cup dry white wine, such as sauvignon blanc

1. Preheat oven to 400°F. With a damp cloth, clean any dirt from mushrooms. Carefully remove stems from mushroom caps. Chop stems, and set aside in a small bowl.

2. Oil a baking dish large enough to accommodate the mushroom caps. Place mushroom caps in baking dish, and drizzle with 1 tablespoon olive oil.

3. Heat 2 tablespoons olive oil in a large sauté pan over medium-high heat. Add shallots and cook, stirring frequently, until softened, about 5 minutes. Add garlic and mushroom stems, and continue to cook for another 5 to 7 minutes, stirring frequently. Add amaranth, salt, and black pepper, and cook for 2 to 3 minutes more, until amaranth has wilted and most of the liquid in the pan has evaporated.

4. Lightly spoon mushroom mixture evenly among mushroom caps. In a small bowl, combine panko bread crumbs with 1 tablespoon olive oil. Sprinkle evenly over mushrooms. Carefully pour white wine into bottom of baking dish.

5. Bake for 30 minutes. Serve hot or at room temperature.

Ⓥ Napa Cabbage Summer Rolls

Rice paper wrappers surround a flavorful filling of Napa cabbage, crunchy veggies, and bean threads in this summery, low-fat appetizer.

Yield:	Serving size:	Prep time:	Cook time:
12 summer rolls	2 summer rolls	20 minutes, plus 20 minutes chilling time	None

12 8-inch rice paper wrappers

1 (3-oz.) package dried bean thread noodles

½ cup carrot, *julienne* cut

½ cup zucchini, julienne cut

3 large scallions, julienne cut

1 cup Napa cabbage, thinly sliced

2 TB. cilantro leaves

2 TB. basil leaves, torn into small pieces

2 TB. low-sodium soy sauce

2 TB. rice wine vinegar

1 TB. dark sesame oil

1 tsp. Thai chile paste

1 clove garlic, smashed and finely chopped

1. Dip rice paper wrappers in a large bowl of warm water, one at a time. Drain on clean kitchen towels. Do not stack, or they will stick together.

2. In a large bowl, cover bean threads with boiling water, and soak for 10 minutes. Drain and cut into small pieces.

3. In a medium bowl, combine carrot, zucchini, scallions, Napa cabbage, cilantro, and basil. Toss well.

4. Evenly divide vegetable mixture and bean threads among rice paper rounds, placing filling along lower third of wrapper, about 1 inch from edge. Fold the bottom edge over the filling, then fold each side in, and roll tightly (as you would a burrito). Press to seal tightly.

5. Place summer rolls on a large plate, cover with plastic wrap, and refrigerate for 20 minutes, or overnight. Meanwhile, make dipping sauce. Stir soy sauce, rice wine vinegar, dark sesame oil, Thai chile paste, and garlic together in a small bowl.

6. Serve summer rolls with small bowls of dipping sauce.

Napa cabbage.

THE LOWDOWN

Summer rolls aren't just for enjoying in the spring and summer. Vary this recipe throughout the year with locally available vegetables. In autumn, try adding julienned apples and lightly steamed butternut squash. In winter, sweet potatoes can be julienne cut and lightly roasted, with shredded kale standing in for Napa cabbage.

DEFINITION

The **julienne** cut, also known as matchstick, is easy to do. Cut your vegetable into lengthwise strips about 1/8-inch thick, then slice these strips lengthwise into 1/8-inch-wide slices. This will provide long, thin "matchsticks" of veggies, perfect for an elegant sauté, or for rolling up inside summer rolls or sushi.

Amaranth, Artichoke, and Caramelized Leek Dip

Get ready to dig into this warm, gooey delight with the flavors of garlicky sautéed amaranth, marinated artichoke hearts, and sweet caramelized leeks, plus bubbly cheddar and Parmesan cheese. Serve this addictive dip with raw veggies, pita chips, or tortilla chips.

Yield:	Serving size:	Prep time:	Cook time:
4 cups	¼ cup	20 minutes	25 minutes

3 TB. extra-virgin olive oil

2 cups leeks, white and light green parts, thinly sliced

2 cloves garlic, smashed and finely chopped

6 cups tender young amaranth leaves, stems removed

1 (6-oz.) jar marinated artichoke hearts, drained and chopped

1 cup mayonnaise

1 cup grated sharp cheddar cheese

½ cup grated Parmesan cheese

¼ tsp. cayenne pepper, or to taste

¼ tsp. kosher salt

½ tsp. freshly ground black pepper

¼ tsp. sweet paprika

1. Preheat oven to 400°F. Heat olive oil in a large sauté pan over medium heat. Add leeks and cook, stirring frequently for 2 minutes. Reduce heat to low, and continue to cook leeks until very soft and golden brown, stirring occasionally, for about 20 minutes.

2. Increase heat to high, add garlic, and cook, stirring constantly, for 1 minute. Add amaranth and continue to cook, stirring often, until amaranth has wilted and liquid has evaporated. Remove from heat and stir in artichoke hearts. Cool slightly.

3. In a large bowl, combine mayonnaise, sharp cheddar, ¼ cup Parmesan, cayenne pepper, kosher salt, and black pepper. Mix well, and stir in amaranth mixture.

4. Grease an 8-inch ovenproof baking dish. Spread dip in dish, and sprinkle remaining ¼ cup Parmesan and sweet paprika evenly over the top.

5. Bake, uncovered, for 25 minutes, or until golden and bubbling. Serve immediately.

> **MAKE IT VEGAN**
>
> It's easy to make this dip vegan! Substitute vegan mayonnaise for traditional mayo, and replace cheddar and Parmesan cheese with 1¼ cups meltable vegan shredded cheese, such as Daiya, mixed with 2 tablespoons nutritional yeast. Stir 1 cup "cheese" mixture into dip, and sprinkle remaining mixture on top. Bake as directed. If you don't like vegan "cheese," eliminate the cheese entirely, and double the leeks.

Ⓥ Savoy Cabbage "Sushi" Rolls

Roll 'em up! Pretty and pliable Savoy cabbage provides an easy and inexpensive wrapper for these "mock maki," filled with brown rice, avocado, and crunchy cucumber and carrot.

Yield:	Serving size:	Prep time:	Cook time:
8 rolls	2 rolls	30 minutes	None

8 large Savoy cabbage leaves

2 cups sushi rice, cooked according to package instructions

2 avocados, each cut lengthwise into 12 slices

1 cup carrot, julienne cut

1 cup cucumber, julienne cut

4 scallions, julienne cut

Wasabi paste and low-sodium soy sauce for dipping

1. Trim tough end of cabbage leaves where the leaf meets the stem, and cut edges of leaves to make an approximate rectangle shape. Bring a large pot of water to a boil, and blanch cabbage leaves, one at a time. Cool quickly in ice water, then lay on clean kitchen towels to drain.

2. Wrap a bamboo sushi mat in plastic wrap. Working one at a time, place a cabbage leaf on the sushi mat (long sides horizontal), and press ¼ cup sushi rice along the lower third of the leaf. Along the center of the rice, arrange 2 avocado strips, and ⅛ of carrot, cucumber, and scallions. Lift edge of mat up and over, bringing the lower edge of the cabbage leaf over the filling. Use the mat to roll over, and press back to create a long, rounded roll. Lay on a serving plate and set aside. Repeat.

3. Slice rolls with a very sharp knife, and serve with wasabi and low-sodium soy sauce for dipping.

Ⓥ Samosas with Mustard Greens

These tasty samosa pastries are a delectable treat!

Yield:	Serving size:	Prep time:	Cook time:
24 samosas	4 samosas	30 minutes	20 minutes

2 TB. sunflower oil

2 cloves garlic, smashed and finely chopped

½ tsp. grated ginger

2 TB. curry powder

6 cups mustard greens

2 TB. water

½ cup small English peas, fresh or frozen

2 large russet potatoes, peeled, boiled, and mashed

1 TB. cilantro, finely chopped

¼ tsp. kosher salt, or to taste

½ package puff pastry (1 sheet)

½ cup bottled chutney, such as Major Grey's

1. Preheat oven to 375°F. Heat sunflower oil in a medium sauté pan over medium-high heat. Add garlic, grated ginger, and curry powder, and cook, stirring constantly, for 1 minute. Add mustard greens and water. Cook, stirring occasionally, until greens have wilted and water has evaporated. Cool slightly, then chop greens into small pieces.

2. Combine peas, mashed potatoes, cilantro, kosher salt, and mustard greens mixture in a large mixing bowl. Mix well.

3. On a well-floured work surface, roll puff pastry into a thin sheet. Using a 4-inch round cutter, cut 12 circles of dough. Roll each circle to 5 inches, then cut in half to make half moon shapes.

4. Working with one piece of pastry at a time, roll the half moon into a small cone in your palm. Fill the cone with a heaping teaspoon of filling, then pinch the top to seal into a small triangle. Place samosa on a parchment or foil-lined baking sheet, and repeat.

5. Bake samosas for 20 minutes, or until puffed and golden. Serve immediately, with chutney for dipping.

THE LOWDOWN

Substitute any spicy green for the mustard greens, such as arugula or turnip greens. Try mashed sweet potato in place of russet potatoes, and finely diced carrot or parsnip in place of peas. Work with in-season produce to make these samosas a seasonal sensation at any time of the year.

ⓥ ⓡ Colorful Collard Veggie Wraps

Fill a lunchbox or party tray with these bright, crunchy, raw wraps with an Asian flair.

Yield:	Serving size:	Prep time:	Cook time:
6 wraps	1 wrap	20 minutes	None

6 large collard leaves, tough ribs removed

½ tsp. sea salt

2 TB. sesame butter

1 TB. Bragg Liquid Aminos

2 TB. fresh lemon juice (from ½ lemon)

1 tsp. grated fresh ginger

1 clove garlic, smashed and finely chopped

1 cup shredded carrot

1 cup shredded red cabbage

1 cup English cucumber, julienne cut

1 cup red bell pepper, julienne cut

1 cup snow peas, tough strings removed, julienne cut

1 cup yellow squash, julienne cut

1. Rub collard leaves with salt, and place in colander for 10 minutes to soften. Rinse well and drain on clean kitchen towels.

2. Stir sesame butter, liquid aminos, lemon juice, ginger, and garlic together in a small bowl.

3. In a large mixing bowl, combine carrot, red cabbage, cucumber, bell pepper, snow peas, and yellow squash. Mix gently with your hands.

4. Working with one collard leaf at a time, overlap leaf to fill empty space where rib has been removed. Place 1 cup vegetable mixture on the lower third of the leaf. Drizzle with 1 teaspoon sesame mixture. Fold bottom of leaf over filling, then fold in sides. Roll tightly into a cylinder. Place on a plate, and repeat with remaining collard leaves, sauce, and filling.

5. Serve immediately, or refrigerate overnight. To serve as hors d'oeuvres, slice each roll into four even pieces, and secure with toothpicks.

> **THE LOWDOWN**
>
> Sesame butter is similar to tahini, but it is unprocessed. Look for it in your local natural food store or co-op. To make your own sesame butter, process 1 cup raw sesame seeds in your food processor with 1 tablespoon light sesame oil. Store in the refrigerator in a sealed glass jar for up to 2 weeks.

Ⓥ Broccoli, Radicchio, and Belgian Endive Fritto Misto

Fill a lunchbox or party tray with these bright, crunchy, raw wraps with an Asian flair.

Yield:	Serving size:	Prep time:	Cook time:
4 servings	20 minutes	10 minutes	None

6 cups safflower oil, for frying

1 cup all-purpose flour

2 tsp. baking powder

2 tsp. kosher salt

½ cup dry white wine, such as pinot grigio

½ cup cold filtered water

3 TB. extra-virgin olive oil

4 cups broccoli, tough stems peeled and trimmed, cut into ¼-inch-thick slices

2 heads Treviso radicchio, stem end intact, cut lengthwise into 4 pieces

4 heads Belgian endive, stem end intact, cut lengthwise in half

Lemon wedges, for serving

1. In a large stock pot, heat cooking oil to 370°F over medium heat. Use a deep-fat-frying thermometer to ensure that oil is at the correct temperature. Heat oven to 300°F, and place a large, oven-proof serving platter lined with a clean kitchen towel in oven.

2. While oil is heating, whisk together all-purpose flour, baking powder, 1 teaspoon kosher salt, white wine, filtered water, and olive oil.

3. Working a few pieces at a time, dip the pieces of broccoli, radicchio, and endive in batter, and fry until golden, about 3 to 4 minutes. Remove from oil with a long-handled mesh spoon (available at Asian grocery stores), and keep warm on platter in oven. Repeat until all vegetables are fried.

4. Sprinkle fritto misto with remaining 1 teaspoon kosher salt, garnish with lemon wedges, and serve immediately.

HEADS UP!

Deep fat frying results in crisp, delicious food, but you'll want to observe some simple safety rules. Hot oil and water do not mix, so make sure your vegetables are dry before battering them. Keep your distance when frying, and use a long-handled mesh spoon to remove food from oil. Keep an eye on the thermometer, and regulate heat carefully. Keep a fire extinguisher in your kitchen, and know how to use it. When you're done frying, cool oil completely, and dispose of it in an old coffee or tomato-sauce can.

Ⓥ *Bruschetta* with Greens and Roasted Garlic

Lemony, savory greens top delectable slices of grilled Italian bread, rubbed with roasted garlic and plenty of extra-virgin olive oil. Pass the napkins!

Yield:	Serving size:	Prep time:	Cook time:
12 slices	2 slices	15 minutes	10 minutes

4 TB. extra-virgin olive oil

2 cloves garlic, smashed and finely chopped

½ tsp. crushed red pepper flakes, or to taste

8 cups escarole, torn into small pieces

4 cups dandelion greens or puntarelle, torn into small pieces

2 TB. fresh lemon juice, from ½ lemon

½ tsp. kosher salt

½ tsp. freshly ground black pepper

12 large slices Italian bread

1 head roasted garlic (see Chapter 16)

1. Heat 2 tablespoons olive oil in a large sauté pan over medium-high heat. Add chopped garlic and cook for 1 minute, stirring constantly. Add crushed red pepper flakes and cook for 30 seconds more. Add escarole and dandelion greens all at once, then add lemon juice, salt, and black pepper. Reduce heat to medium low and cook, stirring frequently, until greens are very soft. Add a few tablespoons of water if greens begin to stick to pan.

2. Heat grill or broiler to high. Squeeze roasted garlic from papery skin into a small bowl, and mash into a paste with remaining 2 tablespoons of olive oil. Toast bread on grill grates or under broiler. Spread roasted garlic mixture evenly on bread slices, and top with warm greens.

DEFINITION

Bruschetta (pronounced broos-KETT-a), simply means bread that has been toasted over coals. Topped with the savory garlic and greens mixture above, it's a perfect accompaniment to creamy winter vegetable soups. In summer, mix fresh tomatoes, basil, garlic, and chopped red onion for a fresh and delicious bruschetta topping.

Ⓥ Ⓡ Beet Carpaccio with Baby Arugula

Paper-thin raw beet slices stand in for sliced beef in this earthy, peppery take on carpaccio that's a perfect first course for a special dinner.

Yield:	Serving size:	Prep time:	Cook time:
4 servings	1 cup	15 minutes	None

2 large red beets, peeled and scrubbed

2 TB. fresh lemon juice (from ½ lemon)

1 tsp. dry mustard

1 tsp. agave nectar

2 TB. extra-virgin cold-pressed olive oil

2 cups baby arugula

½ cup chopped almonds

1 large apple, such as Gala, unpeeled, sliced, and julienne cut

¼ tsp. sea salt, or to taste

1. Using a mandoline, slice beets into paper-thin slices. Arrange beets in a circular pattern to cover the bottom of four chilled serving plates.

2. In a small bowl, mix lemon juice, dry mustard, agave nectar, and extra-virgin olive oil. Toss baby arugula with half of dressing and divide evenly, spooning onto center of each circle of beets. Top arugula with almonds and apples, and drizzle with remaining dressing. Sprinkle with a little sea salt, and serve immediately.

Sensational Soups

Who doesn't love soup? In Part 4, take a trip around the world without leaving your kitchen. From light, raw preparations that are ready in minutes to savory, hot bowls of goodness, soup really is good food.

The soups in the following chapters run the gamut from chilled gazpacho to creamy vegetable soups, brothy bowls of comfort, hearty chilis, and filling stews, all of which nourish your body and soul.

Light Soups

In This Chapter

- Creamy vegetable soups
- Light, brothy soups
- Raw soups

Who doesn't love soup? Served hot or cold, the light and refreshing delights in this chapter offer something for everyone. On a hot day, keep your kitchen cool with raw offerings found in this chapter such as Spinach Gazpacho, Raw Broccoli Soup, or perhaps some Tomato and Kale Soup. Vegans and calorie counters will delight in the many light dishes, such as Miso Soup with Asian Greens. Those seeking comfort on a chilly day with want to snuggle up with a hot mug of sweet and creamy Belgian Endive, Pear, and Celery Root Soup.

Most of the soups in this chapter are ready in under an hour, so you won't need to work all day to enjoy the soothing flavors and textures of these delicious recipes!

Fava Bean Soup with Puntarelle

This traditional Roman dish features creamy, slightly sweet fava beans with the contrasting flavor and texture of garlicky, bitter puntarelle.

Yield:	Serving size:	Prep time:	Cook time:
8–10 cups	1 cup	15 minutes plus overnight soaking	1½–2 hours

4 cups dried, peeled fava beans, soaked overnight

3 TB. extra-virgin olive oil

1 cup yellow onion, finely chopped (1 small onion)

1 cup leeks, sliced, white and light green parts only

½ cup carrot, peeled and finely chopped

½ cup celery, finely chopped

3 cloves garlic, smashed and finely chopped

1 bay leaf

2 qt. light vegetable stock

1 tsp. kosher salt, or to taste

½ tsp. freshly ground black pepper

2 TB. fresh lemon juice (from ½ lemon)

6 cups puntarelle, sliced into thin ribbons

½ cup Pecorino Romano cheese, grated (optional)

1. Drain soaked fava beans and rinse well. Heat a large stockpot over medium heat, and add 1 tablespoon olive oil. Add onion, leeks, carrot, and celery, and cook, stirring frequently, for 5 minutes. Add 1 clove garlic and bay leaf, and cook 1 minute more.

2. Add fava beans and vegetable stock, bring to a boil, and reduce heat to a low simmer. Cover pot and cook, stirring occasionally, until fava beans are tender, about 1½ hours.

3. Cool soup slightly, and purée in batches in blender (or use a handheld immersion blender) until smooth. Fill blender only halfway with hot soup, do not fit cover on tightly, and place a folded kitchen towel over the top of the blender to prevent soup from overflowing. Be extremely careful when puréeing hot soups.

4. Rinse stockpot clean and return soup to pot. Season with salt, freshly ground pepper, and lemon juice. Allow soup to rest for at least 10 minutes to allow flavor to develop.

5. Heat 2 tablespoons olive oil in a medium sauté pan over medium-high heat, and add 2 cloves garlic. Cook for 1 minute, stirring constantly, then add puntarelle all at once. Cook for 5 minutes more, stirring often, until puntarelle has softened.

6. Stir puntarelle into soup, and taste. Adjust salt and pepper if necessary.

7. Serve in large bowls, and top each serving with a spoonful of Pecorino Romano cheese (if using).

Variation: You can substitute tender young dandelion greens to make **Fava Bean Soup with Dandelion,** if true puntarelle is not available.

To freeze: Prepare soup through step 6, but omit black pepper. Do not add Pecorino Romano cheese if freezing. Cool soup completely, and pour into freezer-safe jars or containers, leaving 1 inch headspace at the top of the container to allow for expansion during freezing process. Store in freezer for up to 3 months. Defrost, season with black pepper, and serve.

HEADS UP!

Be sure to look for dried fava beans that are peeled for this recipe. The skin of the fava bean is bitter and time-consuming to remove. This soup can also be made with fresh fava beans. You'll need to purchase about four large bags of beans to yield 4 cups of fava beans. Pop beans out of pod, blanch for 1 to 2 minutes, and then peel skin from each bean. When using fresh fava beans, you will significantly reduce cooking time, so check often after about 40 minutes.

MAKE IT VEGAN

To make this recipe vegan, simply omit Pecorino Romano cheese. To add a savory interest to soup, top with Cheezy Toasted Bread Crumbs (see Chapter 16).

🅥 Miso Soup with Asian Greens

Enjoy this light, nourishing soup with the savory flavor of miso and the brightness of lightly cooked Asian greens.

Yield:	Serving size:	Prep time:	Cook time:
8 cups	2 cups	5 minutes	30 minutes

8 cups filtered water

½ cup yellow onion, sliced

½ cup carrot, sliced

1 4-inch piece *kombu*

6 cups mixed Asian greens (such as mizuna, baby bok choy, and mustard greens), sliced into ribbons

½ cup mellow white miso

1 TB. low-sodium soy sauce, or to taste

1. Place water, onion, carrot, and kombu in a medium soup pot. Bring to a boil, reduce heat to medium, and simmer for 15 minutes. Strain solids, rinse pot clean, and return broth to pot.

2. Return broth to a boil, and add mixed Asian greens. Cook over medium-high heat until greens are tender, about 5 minutes. Remove from heat.

3. In a small bowl, stir miso together with ¼ cup of hot broth. Add miso to soup, stir well, and season to taste with soy sauce. Serve immediately.

To freeze: Prepare soup through step 2. Cool completely, and pour into freezer-safe jars or containers, leaving 1 inch headspace. When ready to serve, defrost soup, and complete step 3. Do not freeze or boil miso, as its flavor and beneficial enzymes will be destroyed.

DEFINITION

Kombu is a dark-colored kelp of the *Laminaria* family. Its leaves are dried and used primarily in Japanese cooking. Kombu has detoxifying properties and aids digestion. It is rich in vitamins and trace minerals. You can find kombu in the Asian aisle of your grocery store.

Mizuna.

Ⓥ Lettuce Soup

Lettuce soup has a delicate, slightly sweet flavor. It's a great way to get rid of wilted lettuce, or the tough outer leaves and ribs of varieties such as romaine—use any type, or combine several to create your favorite flavor combination.

Yield:	Serving size:	Prep time:	Cook time:
6–8 cups	1 cup	5 minutes	20 minutes

2 TB. extra-virgin olive oil

1 cup leeks, thinly sliced, white and light green parts only

1 cup yellow onion, thinly sliced (about 1 small onion)

½ cup celery, thinly sliced

1 clove garlic, smashed and finely chopped

1 TB. fresh tarragon, finely chopped

1 TB. fresh Italian parsley, finely chopped

1 tsp. fresh thyme leaves, finely chopped

6 cups filtered water

2 medium russet potatoes, peeled and cut into ¼-inch dice

6 cups lettuce, roughly chopped

½ tsp. kosher salt, or to taste

1 TB. fresh lemon juice

1. In a medium stockpot, heat olive oil over medium heat. Add leeks, onion, and celery. Sauté vegetables until softened and translucent, about 5 to 7 minutes, stirring often. Add garlic, tarragon, parsley, and thyme, and cook for 1 minute more.

2. Add water and potatoes, and bring to a boil over high heat. Immediately reduce heat to a low simmer, and cook until potatoes are tender, about 10 minutes. Add lettuce, and cook until lettuce has softened (cooking time will depend on the type and freshness of the lettuce you are using, about 5 to 7 minutes).

3. Cool soup slightly, and purée in batches in blender. Return to a clean pot, and season with salt and lemon juice. Serve immediately, or chill to serve cold.

Variations: Enjoy all these soup variations!

Chilled Watercress Soup: Omit tarragon and thyme. Use watercress in place of lettuce, and increase lemon juice to 2 tablespoons. Purée, season, and chill for at least 4 hours. Serve in small cups.

Cream of Spinach Soup: Omit tarragon. Add ½ tsp. freshly ground nutmeg along with parsley and thyme. Stir in ¼ cup tofu sour cream after puréeing. Serve hot with freshly ground black pepper if desired.

Sorrel Soup: Omit tarragon, thyme, and lemon juice. Cook sorrel until it has turned dark green in color. Stir in ¼ cup tofu sour cream after puréeing. Serve hot or cold.

Ⓥ Ⓡ Spinach *Gazpacho*

Bright-green spinach gazpacho is a refreshing liquid salad. Enjoy a bowl of this bright, chilled refresher as a summer first course, or pass in demitasse cups at your next garden party.

Yield:	Serving size:	Prep time:	Cook time:
5 cups	1 cup	15 minutes	None

2 cups cucumber, seeded and roughly chopped (1 large cucumber)

1 cup green bell pepper, cored, seeded, and roughly chopped (1 pepper)

2 cups yellow grape tomatoes

1 cup white onion, roughly chopped

1 clove garlic, chopped

1 tsp. kosher salt

2 TB. apple cider vinegar

¼ cup blanched, sliced almonds

1 tsp. sweet paprika

½ tsp. freshly ground black pepper

¾ cup filtered water

2 TB. lemon juice (from ½ lemon)

1. Combine cucumber, bell pepper, grape tomatoes, onion, garlic, salt, vinegar, almonds, paprika, black pepper, water, and lemon juice in blender or food processor. You will likely have to work in batches, but don't worry about combining everything in each batch, as you'll stir it all together at the end.

2. Chill mixture in refrigerator for 4 hours, or overnight.

To freeze: Prepare recipe through step 2. Pour into freezer-safe jars or containers with 1 inch headspace, and freeze. Defrost in refrigerator overnight before serving. Do not defrost soups to be served cold at room temperature, as dangerous organisms can multiply under these conditions.

DEFINITION

Gazpacho is native to the Andalucía region of Spain, and is traditionally tomato based. If you're allergic to almonds, try substituting a 1-inch slice of French bread fried in 1 tablespoon olive oil. Experiment with your gazpacho recipes by adding melon, avocado, or different herbs.

Turnip Soup with Turnip Greens

Enjoy this earthy soup on a cold winter's night. The flavor of turnips is sweetened and lightened aromatic vegetables and a touch of cream.

Yield:	Serving size:	Prep time:	Cook time:
8 cups	2 cups	15 minutes	30 minutes

1 bunch turnips with greens (about 3–4 4-inch turnips)

2 TB. unsalted butter

1 cup yellow onion, thinly sliced

½ cup shallot, thinly sliced (about 2 shallots)

1 carrot, peeled and thinly sliced

¼ cup celery, thinly sliced

1 clove garlic, smashed and finely chopped

8 cups light vegetable stock

½ tsp. kosher salt

½ tsp. freshly ground black pepper

½ cup light cream

¼ tsp. freshly grated nutmeg

1 TB. fresh lemon juice, or to taste

1. Separate turnips from greens. Wash greens well in several changes of cold water, remove tough stems, and slice into ribbons. Scrub and peel turnips, and cut into ½" dice.

2. Heat butter in a medium stockpot over medium-high heat. Add onion, shallot, carrot, celery, and garlic. Cook, stirring often, until vegetables are translucent and soft, about 5 to 7 minutes. Add turnips and vegetable stock, bring to a boil, and reduce heat to a medium. Cook until turnips are tender, about 10 minutes.

3. Purée soup in blender or using handheld immersion blender, and return to pot. Bring soup back to a boil, add greens, and cook until greens are tender, about 3 minutes.

4. Stir in salt, black pepper, light cream, and nutmeg. Return to a simmer and cook for 1 to 2 minutes. Taste soup, and add lemon juice a little bit at a time until the taste is pleasing to your palate. Serve immediately.

To freeze: Prepare soup through step 3. Chill and transfer to freezer-safe jars or containers, leaving 1 inch headspace. When ready to serve, defrost soup, bring to a boil, and complete step 4.

MAKE IT VEGAN

Use extra-virgin olive oil in place of butter. Replace light cream with ¼ cup cold rice milk stirred into 1 teaspoon cornstarch. Cook soup for 5 minutes after addition of cornstarch/rice milk mixture, then add lemon juice as directed.

Ⓥ Ⓡ Amaranth and Avocado Soup

Amaranth gets in touch with its Mexican roots in this savory and delicious raw soup. If you have a Vita-Mix blender, you can purée it for a few extra minutes to serve warm. Otherwise, use very warm (not boiling!) water to create a warm, but still raw, creation.

Yield:	Serving size:	Prep time:	Cook time:
4 cups	1 cup	10 minutes	None

2 cups amaranth, well washed, tough stems removed

1 cup Hass avocado (1–2 avocados)

1 yellow bell pepper, cored, seeded, and chopped

½ cup white onion

1 clove garlic, smashed and finely chopped

2 TB. fresh lime juice (from 1 lime)

½ tsp. ground cumin seed

¼ tsp. cayenne pepper, or to taste

2 TB. cilantro leaves

1 tsp. Bragg Liquid Aminos

3 cups very warm, filtered water

1. Combine amaranth, avocado, bell pepper, onion, garlic, lime juice, cumin, cayenne pepper, cilantro, liquid aminos, and warm water in blender. Blend on high until very smooth.

2. Garnish each bowl with cilantro leaves. Serve immediately.

HEADS UP!

It might seem like a good idea to get warm water right from the tap for this recipe, but think again. If your home was built prior to the mid-1970s, there's a good chance that your pipes can leach lead into your hot water. Unless you have a filtered instant-hot tap, it's best to heat filtered water on the stove or in your electric tea kettle when you need hot water for cooking or drinking.

Ⓥ Pickled Mustard Greens Soup with Cellophane Noodles and Tofu

Enjoy a big bowl of this tangy, spicy, Asian-inspired noodle soup, which is excellent if you feel a cough or cold coming on.

Yield:	Serving size:	Prep time:	Cook time:
12 cups	2 cups	10 minutes	20 minutes

1 (3-oz.) package *glass noodles*

1 tsp. dark sesame oil

1 TB. safflower oil

2 cups yellow onion, thinly sliced

1 cup (2–3 medium) carrots (about 1 ¼ cups), peeled, halved, and thinly sliced

1 cup celery, thinly sliced

3 cloves garlic, smashed and finely chopped

2 tsp. freshly grated ginger

¼ cup crushed red pepper flakes, or to taste

8 cups light vegetable stock

2 cups pickled mustard greens (see Chapter 15)

1 tsp. lime zest (from 1 small lime)

1 TB. fresh lime juice (from 1 small lime)

1. In a large bowl, cover noodles with boiling water, and soak for 10 minutes. Drain well, and toss with dark sesame oil. Set aside.

2. In a large stockpot, heat safflower oil over medium-high heat. Add onion, carrots, and celery, and cook, stirring frequently, for 3 minutes. Add garlic, ginger, and crushed red pepper, and cook 1 minute more.

3. Add vegetable stock, bring to a boil, and reduce heat to medium. Cook until vegetables are tender, about 10 minutes. Stir in mustard greens, lime zest, and lime juice.

4. When ready to serve, divide noodles evenly among six bowls, ladle hot soup over each serving, and enjoy immediately.

To freeze: Eliminate step 1. Prepare soup through step 3, eliminating lime zest and juice. Cool, then transfer to freezer-safe jars or containers with 1 inch headspace. When ready to serve, prepare noodles as directed in step 1, bring defrosted soup to a boil, and add lime zest and juice. Ladle hot broth over noodles and serve immediately.

DEFINITION

Glass noodles, or cellophane noodles, are made from mung bean starch, and are shiny and clear when soaked in hot water. They are often packaged as "dried bean threads". If you can't find them, you can substitute rice vermicelli (made from rice starch), or even cooked angel hair pasta.

Ⓥ Ⓡ Raw Kale and Tomato Soup

Fresh tomatoes, garlic, basil, and kale star in this summery raw soup with a kick from a touch of red cherry pepper.

Yield:	Serving size:	Prep time:	Cook time:
4 cups	1 cup	10 minutes	None

6 large beefsteak tomatoes, peeled and seeded

1 tsp. extra-virgin cold-pressed olive oil

10 kale leaves, tough ribs removed, torn into small pieces

1 clove garlic, smashed and finely chopped

1 hot cherry pepper, cored and seeded, roughly chopped

2 cups warm filtered water (not boiling)

½ tsp. fine sea salt

½ tsp. freshly ground black pepper

6 fresh basil leaves, plus additional leaves for garnish

1. Combine tomatoes, olive oil, kale, garlic, cherry pepper, water, sea salt, black pepper, and basil in blender or food processor. Blend on high until smooth.

2. Serve immediately, garnished with additional basil leaves.

THE LOWDOWN

Not all olive oils are suitable for a raw diet. The only way to be sure your olive oil has not been heated above 115°F is to contact the company and ask. Raw foodists believe that heating food in excess of 115°F destroys essential enzymes and nutrients. The best olive oils are labeled "first cold pressing," which indicates that the oil is from the purest first pressing of olives. Oils that are not labeled cold-pressed have likely been heated during a second or even third pressing to extract as much oil from the olives as possible. Whatever you believe regarding raw food philosophy, olive oils that have been heated are more likely to be bitter tasting. You really do get what you pay for!

Spinach and Arborio Rice Soup

Curl up with this creamy, comforting spinach soup with a hint of lemon and nutty Parmesan. Substitute baby spinach if you're in a hurry.

Yield:	Serving size:	Prep time:	Cook time:
8 cups	2 cups	5 minutes	25 minutes

1 TB. extra-virgin olive oil	6 cups light vegetable stock
2 cups leeks, white and light green parts, thinly sliced	4 cups spinach, tough stems removed, sliced into thin ribbons
½ cup carrot, peeled and finely chopped	1 tsp. lemon zest
½ cup celery, finely chopped	1 TB. fresh lemon juice
½ cup arborio rice	½ cup freshly grated Parmesan cheese
1 tsp. kosher salt	½ tsp. freshly ground black pepper

1. Heat olive oil in a medium stockpot over medium-high heat. Add leeks, carrot, and celery. Cook, stirring frequently, until vegetables have softened, about 5 minutes.

2. Increase heat to high. Add arborio rice, salt, and vegetable stock. Bring to a boil, then reduce heat to medium and cook until rice is tender, about 15 minutes. Add spinach and lemon zest. Cook until spinach has softened, about 2 minutes.

3. Remove from heat, and stir in lemon juice, Parmesan cheese, and black pepper. Serve immediately.

MAKE IT VEGAN

Eliminate Parmesan cheese, and substitute *Cheezy Toasted Bread Crumbs* (see Chapter 16).

Belgian Endive, Pear, and Celery Root Soup

The sweetness of pears takes the bitter edge away from Belgian endive, as the perfume of fresh celery root adds an earthy goodness to this deliciously different soup that's perfect for a special occasion.

Yield:	Serving size:	Prep time:	Cook time:
10 cups	2 cups	10 minutes	30 minutes

2 TB. unsalted butter

1 cup leeks, white and light green parts, thinly sliced

½ cup celery, thinly sliced

1 ripe pear, peeled, cored, and cut into chunks

1 medium celery root, peeled and cut into 1-inch dice (about 2 cups)

6 cups light vegetable stock

2 cups Belgian endive, trimmed of base and outer leaves, cut into thin ribbons

½ cup light cream

1 tsp. kosher salt

½ tsp. freshly ground black pepper

¼ cup dry white wine, such as sauvignon blanc

1 tsp. fresh lemon juice

1. Heat butter in a medium stockpot over medium heat. Add leeks and celery. Cook, stirring often, for 5 to 7 minutes, or until leeks are softened and translucent.

2. Add pear, celery root, vegetable stock, and Belgian endive. Cook for 15 minutes more, stirring frequently, until vegetables are soft. Remove from heat, and stir in cream, salt, and black pepper.

3. Purée soup using a handheld immersion blender, or in batches in a blender.

4. Rinse pot clean, return soup, and bring to a simmer. Add wine, and simmer 5 minutes more. Add lemon juice, and serve immediately.

THE LOWDOWN

It's difficult to find locally grown Belgian endive (and expensive, too). Try this recipe with the tender, white inner leaves of frisée, which you can easily find at a farmers market, or even grow yourself.

Belgian endive.

ⓥ ⓡ Broccoli Soup

The creamy taste and texture of this soup may surprise you, as the almonds, sunflower seeds, and spices temper the flavor of raw broccoli.

Yield:	Serving size:	Prep time:	Cook time:
4 cups	1 cup	20 minutes	None

2 cups raw broccoli florets, cut into bite-sized pieces

1 cup raw broccoli stems, peeled and sliced

½ cup raw almonds

½ cup raw sunflower seeds

1 tsp. Bragg Liquid Aminos

2 TB. fresh lemon juice (from ½ lemon)

1 clove garlic, smashed and finely chopped

1 yellow bell pepper, cored, seeded, and roughly chopped

1 cup warm filtered water (not boiling)

¼ tsp. ground cumin seeds

¼ tsp. cayenne pepper

1 TB. nutritional yeast

1. Combine 1½ cup broccoli florets, broccoli stems, almonds, sunflower seeds, liquid aminos, lemon juice, garlic, bell pepper, water, cumin, cayenne pepper, and nutritional yeast in blender. Blend on high until very smooth.

2. Divide evenly among four bowls, and garnish with remaining ½ cup broccoli florets. Serve immediately.

HEADS UP!

If you're allergic to nuts and/or seeds, you can still enjoy this recipe. Simply substitute 1 cup ripe avocado for the almonds and sunflower seeds.

Ⓥ Potato, Leek, and Watercress Soup

The French classic slims down in this luscious vegan version, with a peppery kick from the addition of watercress. Serve this delicious soup hot in early spring, and chilled in the summer months.

Yield:	Serving size:	Prep time:	Cook time:
8 cups	2 cups	15 minutes	40 minutes

2 TB. extra-virgin olive oil

2 cups leeks, white and light green parts, thinly sliced

½ cup shallot, thinly sliced

1 cup yellow onion, thinly sliced

3 large russet potatoes, peeled and cut into ½-inch cubes

6 cups filtered water

1 tsp. sea salt, or to taste

6 cups watercress, sliced into thin ribbons

1 TB. fresh lemon juice

½ tsp. freshly ground black pepper

1. Place olive oil in a large stockpot at medium-high heat. Add leeks, shallot, and onion. Sauté, stirring frequently, until leek mixture is very soft and translucent, about 10 minutes.

2. Add potatoes, water, and sea salt. Bring to a boil, then reduce heat to medium and simmer until potatoes are tender, about 20 minutes.

3. Stir in watercress, and cook for 1 to 2 minutes more, until watercress is tender.

4. Remove from heat, add lemon juice and black pepper, and taste to see if more salt is needed. Serve hot or cold.

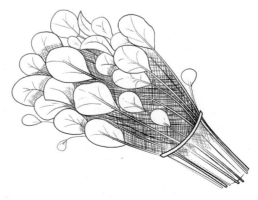

Watercress.

THE LOWDOWN

Potato-based soups are delicious and comforting, so it's tempting to try to freeze them. Unfortunately, potatoes turn mealy and develop an unpleasant texture when frozen, so it's best to enjoy this soup fresh. All soups do benefit from a night in the fridge to allow flavors to marry, though, so feel free to make a day in advance and warm up before serving.

Hearty Soups and Stews

In This Chapter

- Hearty bean soups
- Cold-weather warmers
- Comfort food classics

Nothing satisfies like a steaming bowl of soup, stew, or chili. In this chapter, we'll explore hearty offerings from many cultures, such as kitchari (India), caldo (Portugal), ribollita (Italy), and collard and black-eyed pea soup (the American South), as well as soul-satisfying delights from Mexico, Thailand, the American Southwest, eastern Europe, and France. What do all these dishes have in common? Delicious, nutritious greens, of course. So put on your apron, and get ready to travel the world!

Ⓥ Ribollita

Ribollita, a traditional dish of Tuscany, literally means "reboiled." This thick, nourishing soup is chock-full of lacinato kale, Swiss chard, aromatic vegetables, and white beans.

Yield:	Serving size:	Prep time:	Cook time:
12 cups	2 cups	15 minutes plus over-night soaking time	1½–2 hours

1½ cups dried cannellini beans, soaked overnight

1 shallot, peeled and halved

4 garlic cloves, smashed and finely chopped

1 small sprig fresh rosemary (or ½ tsp. dried)

1 small sprig fresh sage (or ½ tsp. dried)

3 TB. extra-virgin olive oil, plus more for serving

2 cups yellow onion, diced

1 cup carrot, peeled and diced

1 cup celery, diced

2 bunches lacinato kale

1 bunch Swiss chard

1 bay leaf

2 quarts light vegetable stock

1 tsp. kosher salt, or to taste

½ tsp. freshly ground black pepper

6 1-inch-thick slices stale country bread

1. Drain beans and rinse well. Place them in a medium saucepan with enough water to cover by 1 inch. Add shallot, 1 clove garlic, rosemary, and sage. Bring to a boil, reduce heat to medium low, and cook, uncovered, until tender. Depending on the age of the beans, this will take about 1 to 1½ hours. When beans are cooked, you should have tender beans, along with 3 to 4 cups cooking liquid. Do not drain—remove shallot, garlic, and herb branches. Set aside.

2. Heat a large stockpot over medium heat, and add olive oil. Add onion, carrot, and celery, and cook, stirring frequently, for 5 minutes. Add 3 garlic cloves and cook 1 minute more.

3. Increase heat to high. Add lacinato kale and Swiss chard, and cook, stirring frequently, for 5 minutes, or until greens are wilted. Add vegetable stock, beans and cooking liquid, bay leaf, salt, and black pepper, and cook until greens are tender, about 20 minutes more.

4. Remove bay leaf. Add bread to soup, return to a boil, and cook, stirring to break up bread, for 10 minutes more. Ladle into bowls, and drizzle each portion with a little extra-virgin olive oil. Serve immediately.

To freeze: Prepare soup through step 3, but omit black pepper. Cool soup completely, and pour into freezer-safe jars or containers, leaving 1 inch headspace at the top of the container to allow for expansion during freezing process. Store in freezer for up to 3 months. Defrost, bring to a boil, and add bread as directed in step 4. Season with black pepper, and serve.

THE LOWDOWN

Fresh cranberry beans make a fantastic substitute for dried white beans in this recipe. Look for them at your local farmers market in the fall, usually beginning in early October. If you have a dehydrator, you can dry your own fresh cranberry beans and use them throughout the winter as well.

Ⓥ Hearty Collard and Black-Eyed Pea Soup

This spicy bowl of collard greens and black-eyed peas is smoky, a little hot, and very satisfying.

Yield:	Serving size:	Prep time:	Cook time:
12 cups	2 cups	10 minutes	30 minutes

3 TB. extra-virgin olive oil

2 cups leeks, thinly sliced

1 cup carrot, peeled, halved, and sliced

2 cups celery, thinly sliced

3 cloves garlic

1 large bunch collard greens, stems removed, sliced into ribbons

½ tsp. chili powder

½ tsp. smoked paprika

½ tsp. dried oregano

½ tsp. Cajun spice

¼ cup dry white wine, such as sauvignon blanc

1 (14-oz.) can fire-roasted tomatoes

8 cups vegetable stock

2 cans black-eyed peas, drained and rinsed

2 TB. fresh lemon juice (from ½ lemon)

1 TB. Louisiana hot pepper sauce (such as Crystal)

1 tsp. kosher salt

½ tsp. black pepper

¼ cup fresh Italian parsley, finely chopped

1. Heat olive oil in a large stockpot over medium heat. Add leeks, carrot, and celery, and cook, stirring, until leeks are translucent, about 5 minutes. Add garlic, and cook 1 minute more.

2. Increase heat to high. Add collard greens, chili powder, smoked paprika, oregano, and Cajun spice. Cook, stirring frequently, until greens have wilted, about 5 minutes.

3. Add wine, tomatoes, and vegetable stock. Heat to a boil, reduce to a simmer, and cook until vegetables are tender, about 15 minutes more.

4. Add black-eyed peas, lemon juice, hot pepper sauce, salt, and black pepper. Cook until beans are heated through. Add parsley and serve immediately.

To freeze: Prepare soup through step 4. Cool completely, then ladle into freezer-safe jars or containers, leaving 1 inch headspace. Freeze for up to 3 months.

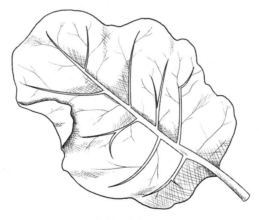

Collard Greens.

THE LOWDOWN

Black-eyed peas have long been considered a symbol of good luck in the American South, but evidence points to ancient Jewish Rosh Hashana celebrations as the birthplace of this idea. Others say that the tradition started when Northern soldiers destroyed crops, but left "field peas" behind as something fit only for animals to eat, and so the tradition was born. It is customary to eat black-eyed peas along with collard greens on New Year's Day to invite prosperity in the coming year. Although pork is usually included in this dish as well, smoked paprika, chili powder, and Cajun spice bring a smoky flavor to this vegetarian version of a classic.

Ⓥ Vegetable Barley Soup

Take comfort in a hot and hearty bowl of chunky veggies, cabbage, kale, and nutty barley in a flavorful tomato broth.

Yield:	Serving size:	Prep time:	Cook time:
12 cups	2 cups	15 minutes	45 minutes

2 TB. extra-virgin olive oil

1 cup leeks, thinly sliced, white and light green parts only

1 cup white onion, diced

1 cup carrot, peeled, halved, and diced

1 cup celery, diced

½ cup parsnip, peeled, halved, and chopped

½ tsp. ground allspice

1 tsp. fresh thyme leaves, chopped (or ½ tsp. dried thyme)

½ small head green or red cabbage, shredded (about 4 cups)

1 head curly kale, tough stems removed, shredded (about 6–8 cups)

1 tsp. kosher salt, or to taste

½ cup pearled barley, rinsed and drained

8 cups light vegetable stock

1 (28-oz.) can peeled plum tomatoes with liquid, lightly crushed or chopped

½ tsp. freshly ground black pepper

2 TB. chopped fresh dill

1 TB. balsamic vinegar

1. In a large stockpot, heat olive oil over medium heat. Add leeks, onion, carrot, celery, and parsnip. Sauté vegetables until leeks and onions are translucent, about 5 minutes, stirring often. Add allspice and thyme, and cook for 30 seconds more.

2. Add cabbage and kale, and cook, stirring, until wilted, about 5 minutes. Add salt, barley, vegetable stock, and plum tomatoes. Bring to a boil, and immediately reduce heat to a simmer. Cook until barley and cabbage are tender to the bite, about 30 minutes.

3. Remove from heat, and add black pepper, fresh dill, and balsamic vinegar. Serve immediately.

Variation: For **Chunky Vegetable Soup,** omit barley and plum tomatoes. Add 2 cloves garlic, 1 cup diced fennel, and 1 peeled and diced celery root to the sautéed vegetable mixture, then add stock along with a 14-ounce can of diced fire-roasted tomatoes and 8 ounces of baby red potatoes, halved. Cook until vegetables are tender.

To freeze: Prepare soup through step 3. Cool completely, then ladle into freezer-safe jars or containers, leaving 1 inch headspace. Freeze for up to 3 months.

HEADS UP!

When freezing soups, stews, and casseroles, it's important to know that the flavor or many herbs and spices is changed during the freezing process. Some people don't really notice this difference, while others find it objectionable. If you value convenience, and want to pull a ready-to-eat meal out of the freezer on a busy day, by all means prepare the recipes as directed, adding spices during the cooking process. If you find that the flavors of certain spices are not pleasing to you after freezing, consider leaving them out when preparing food to be frozen. Attach an index card or strip of masking tape to the container with a list of ingredients to be added, and you'll have perfect results every time.

Ⓥ Amaranth and Black Bean Chili

This chili has just the right amount of spice from dried chiles, cumin, chili powder, and garlic. Black beans, corn, kabocha squash, and amaranth add a Southwestern flair, while a little tequila adds a kick. This chili is the perfect use for more mature amaranth leaves, as their texture will stand up to the firm bite of corn and beans.

Yield:	Serving size:	Prep time:	Cook time:
12 cups	2 cups	15 minutes	30 minutes

2 dried Anaheim chile peppers

2 TB. extra-virgin olive oil

2 large yellow onions, diced

1 medium green bell pepper, cored, seeded, and diced

1 medium yellow bell pepper, cored, seeded, and diced

2 cloves garlic, smashed and finely chopped

1 tsp. ground cumin

1 TB. chili powder

¼ cup tequila

4 cups vegetable stock

2 cups Kabocha squash, peeled, seeded, and diced (about ½ squash)

1½ cups corn kernels, fresh or frozen

2 (14-oz.) cans black beans, drained and rinsed

6 cups amaranth leaves, tough stems removed, sliced into ribbons

1 TB. fresh lime juice (from 1 lime)

1. Place Anaheim chile peppers in a heatproof bowl. Cover with boiling water, and let stand until softened, about 10 minutes. Drain, core, seed, and chop peppers.

2. Heat olive oil in a large stockpot over medium-high heat. Add onions and bell peppers, and cook, stirring often, until vegetables are soft, about 10 minutes.

3. Add chopped chile peppers, garlic, cumin, and chili powder, and cook for 5 minutes more. Stir in tequila, and cook until liquid has nearly evaporated.

4. Add vegetable stock and Kabocha squash. Reduce heat to medium, and cook until squash is tender, about 25 minutes. Add corn, black beans, and amaranth leaves. Cook until amaranth is tender, about 5 minutes more. Remove from heat, stir in lime juice, and serve immediately.

To freeze: Prepare recipe through step 3. Pour into freezer-safe jars or containers with 1 inch headspace, and freeze for up to 3 months.

HEADS UP!

Chile peppers contain capsaicin, the active metabolite that makes them hot. Capsaicin can burn your skin and eyes as well as your tongue, so be sure to wear gloves when handling hot peppers, and wash hands well afterward. Capsaicin levels are highest in the inner membrane of the pepper, known as the pith, so removing the white ribs that run along the inside of the pepper will reduce the heat of a pepper. Heat is determined using the Scoville scale, which measures the amount of capsaicin present. Anaheim chiles (as well as poblanos) are at the lower end of the Scoville scale, with 1,500 to 2,000 Scoville units, while habanero chiles can have as much as 350,000 to 580,000 Scoville units of heat. The spiciest known chile is the Trinidad Moruga Scorpion chile, with a heart-stopping 1,500,000 to 2,000,000 Scoville units of scorching heat. Consume at your own risk!

ⓥ Miso Udon Bowl with Baby Bok Choy

Miso soup joins stir-fried baby bok choy and udon noodles, a chewy Japanese wheat noodle, for a fast and healthy one-pot meal that will warm you from the inside out.

Yield:	Serving size:	Prep time:	Cook time:
12 cups	3 cups	10 minutes	30 minutes

8 cups filtered water

½ cup yellow onion, sliced

½ cup carrot, sliced

1 4-inch piece kombu

1 TB. light sesame oil

4 cups baby bok choy, halved if very small, quartered or sliced if larger

1 (8-oz.) package fresh udon

¼ package firm silken tofu, cut into ½-inch cubes

½ cup mellow white miso

1 TB. low-sodium soy sauce, or to taste

½ cup sliced scallions, green parts only

1. Place water, onion, carrot, and kombu in a medium soup pot. Bring to a boil, reduce heat to medium, and simmer for 15 minutes. Strain solids, pressing to remove all liquid, and set broth aside.

2. In a wok or wide stockpot, heat sesame oil over medium-high heat. Add bok choy, and stir-fry for 3 minutes. Carefully add hot stock, udon noodles, and tofu, and cook until bok choy and noodles are tender, about 10 minutes.

3. In a small bowl, stir miso together with ¼ cup of hot broth. Add miso to soup, stir well, and season to taste with soy sauce. Ladle into bowls and top with scallions. Serve immediately.

Variation: For **Nabeyaki Udon,** eliminate tofu. Stir-fry 8 ounces thinly sliced fresh shiitake mushrooms and 1 cup thinly sliced carrot with bok choy. When soup is nearly done, carefully break four eggs, one at a time, into a small bowl, and tip gently into soup. Cook without stirring until egg whites have set.

THE LOWDOWN

Udon noodles are a thick, chewy Japanese noodle made of wheat flour. They are available in fresh, dried, and instant form. You can substitute any of these in this recipe. Just be sure to follow the cooking instructions on the package, as cooking times will vary.

Ⓥ *Caldo Verde* (Portuguese Kale and Potato Soup)

Roasted garlic mellows the flavors of this smoky, filling potato and kale soup from Portugal.

Yield:	Serving size:	Prep time:	Cook time:
10 cups	2 cups	10 minutes	30 minutes

1 large bunch curly kale	1 head roasted garlic (see Chapter 16)
1 large bunch collard greens	4 large Yukon Gold potatoes, peeled and diced
¼ cup extra-virgin olive oil, plus more for serving	8 cups vegetable stock
1 cup soy chorizo, removed from casing and crumbled	½ tsp. kosher salt, or to taste
1 cup yellow onion, diced	½ tsp. freshly ground black pepper

1. Remove tough stems from kale and collards. Cut leaves in half lengthwise, then stack, roll, and cut crosswise into the thinnest ribbons you can manage (this is called a chiffonade cut).

2. Heat olive oil in a large stockpot over medium-high heat. Add chorizo and cook, stirring frequently for 5 minutes. Add onions and cook until soft and translucent, about 5 minutes more.

3. Stir in roasted garlic, potatoes, and vegetable stock. Cook over medium heat, stirring occasionally, until potatoes have softened, about 15 minutes. Season with salt. Be sure to taste soup for seasoning, as different brands of chorizo will have different levels of saltiness.

4. Cool slightly, then purée using a handheld immersion blender, or in blender or food processor. Wipe pot clean, and return soup to pot.

5. Return soup to a boil. Add greens all at once and cook for 5 minutes. Add black pepper and taste one more time to adjust seasoning if necessary. Ladle into bowls, drizzle with extra-virgin olive oil, and serve immediately.

Variation: If you can't find soy chorizo, or prefer to keep soy out of your diet, you can leave out the chorizo, sauté 1 teaspoon smoked paprika with the onions, and add an additional potato.

> **DEFINITION**
>
> **Caldo Verde,** which means "green broth," is a simple peasant fare from the Minho province of Portugal that has evolved into what many would say is the Portuguese national dish. In its simplest form, it consists of *couve gallego* (a type of kale rarely seen outside of Portugal), potatoes, a little garlic, and water. In thrifty peasant fashion, a single slice of chorizo might be served as an extravagance. The elevation of this dish has resulted in more luscious versions, brimming with chorizo, onions, and good olive oil. It is traditionally served with *broa,* a type of Portuguese corn bread. However you make it, as the Portuguese say, "Bom Apetite!"

Broccoli Cheddar Soup

Cheesy, creamy broccoli and cheddar soup is the perfect lunch or supper for a snowy day. Cayenne pepper and dry mustard add a flavorful kick to warm you up.

Yield:	Serving size:	Prep time:	Cook time:
10 cups	2 cups	10 minutes	30 minutes

2 bunches broccoli

2 TB. all-purpose flour

4 TB. unsalted butter, at room temperature

1 cup yellow onion, diced

½ cup celery, diced

½ cup carrot, peeled and diced

1 clove garlic, smashed and finely chopped

6 cups vegetable stock

1 cup heavy cream

½ tsp. kosher salt, or to taste

½ tsp. freshly ground black pepper

½ tsp. dry mustard

¼ tsp. cayenne pepper, or to taste

1 cup sharp cheddar cheese, shredded

¼ cup beer, such as lager

1. Separate broccoli florets from stems. Chop florets into bite-sized pieces, blanch quickly in boiling water, and set aside. Peel stems, trim away tough areas, and cut into small dice.

2. Using your fingers, rub flour into 2 tablespoons butter to form a smooth paste *(beurre manie).* Set aside.

3. Heat remaining 2 tablespoons butter in a large stockpot over medium heat. When butter is sizzling, add onion, celery, carrot, garlic, and broccoli stems. Cook, stirring frequently, until vegetables have softened and onions are translucent, about 5 to 7 minutes.

4. Add stock, bring to a boil, and reduce heat to medium. Cook, stirring occasionally, until broccoli stems are tender, about 15 minutes. Stir in heavy cream, return to a low boil, and whisk in flour/butter mixture. Add broccoli florets and salt, and cook until florets are tender and soup has thickened, about 5 minutes.

5. Reduce heat to low, and add black pepper, dry mustard, and cayenne pepper. Add cheddar cheese a little at a time, stirring constantly to mix well. When cheese has melted, stir in beer, remove from heat, and serve immediately.

DEFINITION

Beurre manie is French for "kneaded butter." Equal parts of flour and butter are rubbed together by hand, forming a smooth paste in which the flour particles are coated with butter. When whisked into a soup or sauce, the butter melts, releasing the flour particles without forming clumps.

Ⓥ Lentil and Spinach Soup

Earthy lentils and tender spinach make a satisfying, nutritious soup in an herb-scented vegetable and tomato broth.

Yield:	Serving size:	Prep time:	Cook time:
12 cups	2 cups	10 minutes	45 minutes

2 cups lentils

2 TB. extra-virgin olive oil

1 cup yellow onion, finely diced

½ cup celery, finely diced

½ cup carrot, peeled and finely diced

2 cloves garlic, smashed and finely chopped

1 tsp. fresh thyme leaves, chopped

1 tsp. fresh rosemary, chopped

1 (14-oz.) can diced tomatoes

10 cups vegetable stock

½ cup dry white wine, such as sauvignon blanc

1 tsp. kosher salt, or to taste

½ tsp. freshly ground black pepper

¼ cup finely chopped *fines herbes*

1 TB. fresh lemon juice

1. Pour lentils into a bowl, and carefully pick over for soil or small pieces of stone. Rinse well, and set aside.

2. Heat olive oil in a large stockpot. Add onion, celery, and carrot, and cook, stirring frequently, until onion is translucent, about 5 minutes. Add garlic, thyme, and rosemary, and cook 1 minute more.

3. Add diced tomatoes and vegetable stock, and bring to a boil. Stir in lentils and white wine, and reduce heat to medium low. Cover and cook until lentils are tender, 20 to 30 minutes, stirring occasionally. Add salt after lentils have been cooking for 15 minutes.

4. Remove from heat, season with black pepper, fines herbes, and lemon juice. Serve immediately, or refrigerate for up to 3 days.

> **DEFINITION**
>
> **Fines herbes** is a blend of fresh herbs used in French cooking. It traditionally contains parsley, chives, chervil, and tarragon. Make fines herbes by chopping herbs very finely, then stir together. Add to food at the end of the cooking process to keep flavors bright and fresh. Fines herbes can be used to season soups, vinaigrettes, omelettes, potato dishes, and sauces. Marjoram is sometimes added as well. Although you can use dried herbs in a pinch, using fresh herbs will provide the best flavor.

Ⓥ Borscht with Cabbage, Beet Greens, and Potatoes

This homey soup of root vegetables and cabbage is simple peasant fare at its finest.

Yield:	Serving size:	Prep time:	Cook time:
10 cups	2 cups	15 minutes	25 minutes

1 bunch beets with beet greens (about 1 lb.)

2 large carrots

2 TB. safflower oil

2 cups yellow onion, thinly sliced

1 tsp. kosher salt

6 cups vegetable stock, hot

½ head green cabbage, quartered and sliced into thin ribbons

2 large Yukon Gold potatoes, julienne cut

1 TB. fresh lemon juice

Tofu sour cream, for serving (optional)

1. Separate beets from beet greens. Wash greens well in several changes of cold water, slice into thin ribbons, and set aside. Scrub and peel beets and carrots. Shred beets and carrots using the large holes on a box grater, or with the shredding blade of your food processor.

2. Heat safflower oil over medium heat. Add onion and salt, and cook, stirring often, until translucent, about 5 minutes. Add shredded beet and carrot, and cook 5 minutes more, stirring frequently.

3. Add hot vegetable stock, cabbage, and potatoes to pot, bring to a boil, and reduce to a simmer. Cook until vegetables are tender, about 30 minutes.

4. Remove from heat and stir in lemon juice. Serve immediately, topped with a spoonful of tofu sour cream for each serving, if desired.

THE LOWDOWN

Borscht is a wonderful winter comfort food. Vary the recipe by adding root vegetables such as rutabaga, parsnip, celery root, or turnips in place of, or in addition to, the carrots and potatoes. For a more sophisticated version fit for royalty, replace the onions with leeks, purée soup, and add a sprinkle of chives and a spoonful of vegan caviar.

Ⓥ Thai Coconut Soup with Rice Noodles and Watercress

What's better than a big bowl of spicy coconut broth, brimming with rice noodles and veggies? Alter the heat of this tangy, spicy soup by adding more ginger and Thai chile paste to the mix!

Yield:	Serving size:	Prep time:	Cook time:
8 cups	2 cups	10 minutes	15 minutes

2 bulbs lemongrass

1 TB. safflower oil

1 TB. freshly grated ginger

2 cloves garlic, finely chopped

1 TB. Thai chile paste, or to taste

½ cup leeks, julienne cut

½ cup carrots, julienne cut

1 cup baby bella mushrooms, thinly sliced

6 cups vegetable stock

1 (14-oz.) can coconut milk

4 oz. thin Thai rice noodles (about ¼ package)

6 cups watercress, sliced into ribbons

1 TB. fresh lime juice

1. Trim tough stems and root end of lemongrass until you are left with the lower 2½ inches of the bulb. Smash it with the flat side of your knife, peel off the woody outer layers, and chop finely.

2. Heat safflower oil in a large stockpot over medium heat. Add lemongrass, ginger, garlic, and Thai chile paste, and sauté for 2 minutes, stirring constantly. Add leeks, carrots, and mushrooms. Stir for 2 more minutes, then add vegetables stock and coconut milk.

3. Bring soup to a boil, then add rice noodles and watercress, reduce heat to medium, and cook just until noodles are tender (about 4 minutes for very thin noodles).

4. Remove from heat, stir in lime juice, and serve immediately.

HEADS UP!

Don't waste the woody parts of the lemongrass that you trim away! Use them to make stock for future pots of spicy Asian soups, or steep them in boiling water with ginger for a fantastic-tasting, healing tea. Lemongrass can be hard to find, so when you see it at the market, buy a bunch and freeze it. Just wrap tightly in plastic wrap, cover with tightly sealed heavy duty aluminum foil, and freeze for up to 6 months.

ⓥ Sweet Potato and Butter Bean Stew with Mustard Greens

Spicy, slightly bitter mustard greens are in perfect harmony with dark-orange sweet potatoes and tender butter beans in this robust stew.

Yield:	Serving size:	Prep time:	Cook time:
4 cups	1 cup	20 minutes	None

1 lb. mustard greens

2 TB. safflower oil

2 cups yellow onion, thinly sliced

2 cloves garlic, smashed and finely chopped

1 tsp. smoked paprika

½ tsp. dried oregano

½ tsp. dried thyme

¼ tsp. crushed red pepper flakes

6 cups vegetable stock

½ tsp. kosher salt

2 large sweet potatoes, peeled and cut into ½-inch dice

2 (14-oz.) cans butter beans, drained and rinsed

½ tsp. freshly ground pepper

1. Trim tough stems from mustard greens. Blanch in boiling water for 3 minutes, cool quickly in an ice bath, drain, and cut into bite-sized pieces. Set aside.

2. Heat safflower oil over medium-high heat. Add onions and sauté until translucent, about 5 minutes. Add garlic, smoked paprika, oregano, thyme, and crushed red pepper flakes, and cook, stirring constantly, for 1 minute more.

3. Add vegetable stock, salt, and sweet potato. Bring to a boil, reduce to a simmer, and cook for 15 minutes, stirring occasionally. Add mustard greens and butter beans, and cook until sweet potato and greens are tender, about 10 minutes more. Season with black pepper, and serve immediately.

Variation: For a curried version of this soup, replace smoked paprika, dried oregano, and dried thyme with 1 tablespoon curry powder, and substitute chickpeas for butter beans.

Ⓥ Tortilla Soup with Swiss Chard

A smoky, spicy red broth is filled with chunky veggies, plenty of garlicky Swiss chard, and corn tortilla strips.

Yield:	Serving size:	Prep time:	Cook time:
10 cups	2 cups	15 minutes	40 minutes

4 TB. extra-virgin olive oil

2 cups white onion, finely diced

2 medium poblano peppers, cored, seeded, and finely diced

1 red bell pepper, cored, seeded, and finely diced

1 canned chipotle chile in adobo, finely diced

¼ cup celery, finely diced

½ cup carrot, halved and sliced

½ head roasted garlic (see Chapter 16)

¼ cup cilantro

½ tsp. dried oregano

½ tsp. kosher salt

8 cups vegetable stock

2 cloves garlic, smashed and finely chopped

1 large bunch Swiss chard, tough stems removed, chiffonade cut

2 medium zucchini, halved and sliced

6 corn tortillas

2 TB. safflower oil

1 TB. lime juice

½ tsp. freshly ground black pepper

1 medium avocado, cut into small dice

1. Heat 2 tablespoons olive oil in a large stockpot. Add onion, poblano pepper, bell pepper, chipotle chile, celery, and carrot, and cook until onion is translucent, stirring frequently, about 5 minutes.

2. Add roasted garlic, 2 tablespoons cilantro, oregano, and salt, and stir for 1 minute more. Add stock and bring to a boil. Reduce heat to low and simmer for 10 minutes.

3. Heat remaining 2 tablespoons olive oil in a wide sauté pan, add chopped garlic, and stir for 1 minute. Add Swiss chard, and sauté until softened, about 5 minutes. Stir chard and zucchini into soup, and simmer until tender, about 10 minutes more.

4. Slice tortillas into thin strips. Wipe sauté pan clean, and heat safflower oil. Fry tortilla strips until crisp, and drain on paper towels.

5. Season soup with lime juice and black pepper. Ladle into bowls, and serve garnished with diced avocado, remaining 2 TB. cilantro, and plenty of fried tortilla strips.

To freeze: Prepare recipe through step 3. Pour into freezer-safe jars or containers with 1 inch headspace, and freeze for up to 3 months. Defrost in refrigerator, heat, and season to taste with freshly ground black pepper. Fry tortillas and add to soup before serving.

THE LOWDOWN

What about salt? When should you salt your food during the cooking process? And how is it measured? Often, beginning cooks prefer to measure their salt, and add it when specified in the recipe. As you become more experienced, you may wish to salt your food to taste. Salting during the cooking process helps to draw out the flavors of the food. Experiment with measuring out your salt at the beginning of the recipe, and then adding a little pinch every time you add a new ingredient to the pan, especially when sautéing. This will help to build flavor as you cook, and you may find that you need less salt. Tasting your food as you're cooking is the only way to know you're seasoning it correctly—this is why we say "season to taste." Kosher salt is easy to pinch when cooking, as its large, flaky grains are easy to grab. Just remember that it measures at twice the volume of sea salt or table salt, so ½ teaspoon of kosher salt = ¼ teaspoon of sea salt or table salt.

Ⓥ Kitchari

This thick stew of mung beans, rice, and vegetables is fragrant with coconut, ginger, and Indian spices.

Yield:	Serving size:	Prep time:	Cook time:
10 cups	2 cups	15 minutes	40 minutes

2 TB. safflower oil

2 cups yellow onion, finely diced

2 cloves garlic, smashed and finely chopped

2 TB. grated ginger

2 TB. cilantro, finely chopped

1 TB. turmeric

1 TB. curry powder

1 tsp. ground cumin

½ tsp. cinnamon

½ tsp. ground cardamom

¼ tsp. ground cloves

½ tsp. freshly ground black pepper

½ tsp. sea salt

¼ cup dried, unsweetened coconut

3 cups whole mung beans, washed and soaked overnight

1½ cups brown basmati rice

6 cups mustard greens, blanched and chopped

1 TB. fresh lemon juice

1. Heat safflower oil over medium heat. Add onions and cook until softened and translucent, about 5 minutes.

2. Add garlic, ginger, cilantro, turmeric, curry powder, cumin, cinnamon, cardamom, cloves, black pepper, and salt. Stir for 2 minutes more.

3. Add coconut, mung beans, and basmati rice to pot with filtered water to cover by 3 inches. Bring to a boil, reduce heat to a simmer, and cook, stirring occasionally, until rice and beans are soft. Stir in mustard greens and cook 5 minutes more.

4. Remove from heat, add lemon juice, and serve immediately.

To freeze: Prepare recipe through step 4. Pour into freezer-safe jars or containers with 1 inch headspace, and freeze for up to 3 months.

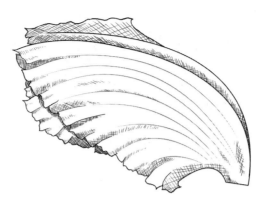

Mustard greens.

THE LOWDOWN

Kitchari is a traditional Ayurvedic healing food. It is easily digested, and is usually cooked until all ingredients are very soft. Anti-inflammatory spices combine with the healing properties of garlic, ginger, and onions, making kitchari the perfect food to consume when you feel a cold coming on. Kitchari is often consumed as part of a fast in yogic traditions. Monodiet fasting, in which one easily digested and nutritious food is consumed at every meal for a period of about a week, is healthier than juice or water fasting, and can provide a metabolic "break" for your body. Try kitchari during the change of seasons, when colds and flu are most likely to strike.

The Main Event

Your dinner table will never be the same. Learn to properly cook pasta, rice, and grains. Vegans, vegetarians, and those looking for a healthier lifestyle will delight in the variety of dinnertime options, including pasta dishes, casseroles, and main courses fit for company. Greens are not just a side dish—give them a starring role on your plate!

Pasta, Rice, and Grains

In This Chapter

- Perfect pastas
- Hearty rice creations
- Great grain dishes

Greens and whole grains are the perfect combination to satisfy your appetite and nourish your body. Pasta, rice, and grains combine with greens to make fantastic and filling one-pot meals. This chapter presents plenty of delicious meals that will keep your family and friends coming back for seconds.

Cooking Perfect Pasta

The secret to perfectly cooked pasta is plenty of water and salt. Fill a large pot with cold water, bring to a boil, and add salt (it doesn't matter what kind). Your goal is to make the cooking water taste like seawater. Don't be afraid of the salt, as most of it will not be absorbed into your pasta. Improperly salted pasta will taste flat no matter how flavorful the sauce.

HEADS UP!

It might seem like a good idea to add salt before you boil water for pasta, but don't do it. Adding salt before boiling can "pit" your stainless steel cookware, eroding the surface layers of metal. Wait until water is boiling, then add salt, to ensure a long life for your precious pots! Start with 1/2 teaspoon of kosher salt per quart of water, and adjust according to your taste.

Be sure to bring water to a full, rolling boil before adding your pasta. Adding pasta when you just see a few bubbles will result in a gummy, sticky mass of noodles. Wait until you have vigorous bubbles rolling toward the middle of the pot, then add pasta all at once. Stir continuously until water returns to a boil, then regulate heat to keep at a moderate boil.

Do not add oil to the cooking water! Although oil will keep your pasta from sticking together, it will also prevent it from absorbing sauce and flavor, yielding a slippery bowl of flavorless food.

Stir pasta frequently, and taste often. Most people prefer their pasta cooked al dente, which means firm to the tooth. Although your pasta package may be printed with instructions, these are a general guideline, not a hard and fast rule. Taste when you near the end of the cooking time, and drain when it's cooked the way you like it.

Rules for Rice

Despite what you may have heard, it's not that difficult to cook perfect, fluffy rice every time. Unlike pasta cookery, which simply requires ample water, rice requires a measuring cup, correctly sized cookware with a tight-fitting lid, and a little patience.

Follow these tips, and you'll have perfect rice, every time:

- Measure rice with a dry measuring cup, and water with a liquid measure. Improper measurements are the number-one cause of poorly cooked rice.

- Rinse your rice. Rinsing will wash away impurities, as well as excess starch, resulting in a fluffy pot of rice with distinct grains.

- Keep a lid on it! Tightly cover your rice, and resist the urge to peek under the lid until you're near the end of the suggested cooking time. You will know your rice is ready when water has been absorbed, and steam holes can be observed in the rice.

- Some longer-cooking varieties of rice benefit from shortening the cooking time, and allowing the rice to stand, covered, for 5 to 10 minutes before serving.

- Check package instructions. Different varieties of rice require different ratios of rice to water, and cooking times vary widely, from 15 minutes for white basmati, to up to 45 minutes for most brown rice varieties.

- Add salt at the beginning of the cooking process, so it is absorbed into the rice along with the water.

- A little fat, in the form of butter or olive oil, will add flavor and separate the grains of rice as they cook. Add fat when you add rice and salt.

To cook a perfect pot of basmati rice, rinse 1 level measuring cup of rice, drain, and place in a small saucepan with 1¾ cups filtered water. Add 1 teaspoon salt, and 1 teaspoon butter or oil. Bring to a boil, stir once, and reduce heat to the lowest setting. Cook without stirring or removing cover for 15 minutes. Turn off heat, let stand for 2 minutes, then fluff with a fork and serve.

The Goodness of Grains

Enliven your meals and surprise your palate by exploring the world of grains. Millet, farro, oats, buckwheat groats, amaranth, barley, bulgur, corn grits, wheatberries, and quinoa are examples of delicious, healthy grains that can add variety and nutrition to your diet.

Those following a gluten-free diet will be thrilled with the variety of delicious, hearty grains. You won't miss wheat when you're dining on millet, corn, quinoa, buckwheat, amaranth, or millet.

THE LOWDOWN

Amaranth is a high-protein, gluten-free seed derived from the same plant as amaranth leaves. Although it is treated as a grain, it is not technically part of that family of grasses, as its plants bear leaves and fruit (the edible seed that emerges from the flower). Amaranth is easily grown in most climates (see Chapter 4 for growing tips). To harvest amaranth seeds, wait until 3 to 7 days after the first frost. Pick flower heats, rub through a screen to release dry seeds, and blow away any remaining bits of the flower using your hair dryer or an air compressor. Dry amaranth seeds in your dehydrator to ensure that they do not mold during storage, and store in an airtight container, such as a glass jar.

ⓥ Whole-Wheat Spaghetti with Amaranth, Chickpeas, and Tomatoes

The nutty flavor of whole-wheat spaghetti pairs perfectly with chickpeas, amaranth, and fresh tomatoes in this deliciously different pasta dish.

Yield:	Serving size:	Prep time:	Cook time:
12 cups	2 cups	10 minutes	20 minutes

1–2 TB. kosher salt

16 oz. whole-wheat spaghetti

2 TB. extra virgin olive oil

2 cloves garlic, thinly sliced

1 pint cherry tomatoes, quartered

½ tsp. crushed red pepper flakes

½ tsp. kosher salt

½ tsp. freshly ground black pepper

1 lb. amaranth, washed in several changes of cold water, thick stems removed, thinly sliced

2 (15.5-oz.) cans of chickpeas, drained and rinsed

1 TB. lemon zest

2 TB. fresh lemon juice

½ cup Italian parsley, finely chopped

1. Bring water to a rolling boil, season with salt, and cook spaghetti until al dente. It should finish cooking just as your sauce is ready. If not, reserve ½ cup of the cooking water, then drain well and set aside.

2. Meanwhile, heat olive oil in a wide sauté pan over medium-high heat. Add garlic and cook, stirring frequently, until it just begins to turn golden, about 1 to 2 minutes.

3. Add cherry tomatoes, crushed red pepper, salt, and freshly ground pepper. Cook for 1 to 2 minutes, until tomatoes just begin to soften. Add amaranth, toss well, and cook for another minute or two, until spinach is wilted.

4. Add chickpeas, lemon zest, lemon juice, and chopped parsley. Stir and toss mixture together until heated through, about 1 more minute. Add pasta and toss well to combine. If it looks very dry, add a little bit of the pasta cooking water.

5. Remove from heat, and serve immediately.

THE LOWDOWN

Fresh cranberry beans make a fantastic substitute for dried white beans in this recipe. Look for them at your local farmers market in the fall, usually beginning in early October. If you have a dehydrator, you can dry your own fresh cranberry beans and use them throughout the winter as well.

Ⓥ Tabbouleh-Stuffed Belgian Endive

Belgian endive makes the perfect serving vehicle for tabbouleh. This classic grain dish features the nutty flavor of bulgur paired with parsley, lemon juice, olive oil, scallions, and plenty of fresh tomatoes.

Yield:	Serving size:	Prep time:	Cook time:
12 stuffed leaves	3 stuffed leaves	25 minutes	None

½ cup fine bulgur

4 TB. extra-virgin olive oil

4 cups curly parsley, finely chopped

4 ripe plum tomatoes, cored and seeded, cut into very small dice

1 cup scallions, white and green parts, thinly sliced

½ tsp. kosher salt

½ tsp. freshly ground pepper

¼ cup fresh lemon juice

12 large Belgian endive leaves

1. Place bulgur in a medium bowl, and stir in 1 tablespoon olive oil. Mix well. Pour hot (not boiling) water over bulgur, stir, and cover with plastic wrap. Set aside for 15 minutes.

2. When bulgur has absorbed water, drain in a fine mesh sieve to remove any excess liquid. Toss drained bulgur with 3 tablespoons olive oil, parsley, tomatoes, scallions, salt, pepper, and lemon juice. Taste and adjust seasonings to your liking.

3. Distribute tabbouleh equally between Belgian endive leaves. Serve immediately.

Make ahead: Tabbouleh may be refrigerated overnight. Fill Belgian endive leaves immediately before serving.

HEADS UP!

Tabbouleh is traditionally made with curly parsley, and you'll need plenty of it to make it authentic. Wash parsley well and spin dry in salad spinner before chopping to ensure that leaves stay fresh, not mushy. Enjoy tabbouleh warm, cold, or at room temperature.

Mexican-Style Rice, Beans, and Greens

Convenient, quick, and delicious, this one-dish supper combines quick-cooking basmati rice, black beans, and garlicky sautéed greens with a tomato and chile kick.

Yield:	Serving size:	Prep time:	Cook time:
6 cups	1½ cups	10 minutes	20 minutes

2 cups basmati rice

2 tsp. kosher salt

1 tsp. plus 2 TB. extra-virgin olive oil

1 cup white onion, diced

2 cloves garlic, smashed and finely chopped

8 cups mixed mild-tasting greens, such as spinach, amaranth, kale, or Swiss chard

1 12 oz. can black beans, rinsed and drained

1 4 oz. can diced tomatoes with green chiles

½ tsp. freshly ground black pepper

½ tsp. dried oregano

½ cup scallions, green and white parts, thinly sliced

1 cup cheddar cheese, shredded

4 TB. sour cream

1. In a small saucepan with a tight-fitting lid, stir together 3½ cups water, basmati rice, 1 teaspoon kosher salt, and 1 teaspoon olive oil. Bring to a boil, reduce heat to the lowest setting, and cover. Cook for 15 minutes. Remove from heat, and let stand 2 minutes. Fluff with fork.

2. While rice is cooking, heat 2 tablespoons olive oil in a large sauté pan. Add onion, and cook until translucent, about 5 minutes. Add garlic, and cook 1 minute more.

3. Add greens and remaining 1 teaspoon salt. Cook, stirring frequently, for 5 minutes, or until greens are wilted and tender.

4. Stir in black beans, canned tomatoes, black pepper, and oregano. Cook for 5 minutes more.

5. Divide rice evenly among bowls, top with greens mixture, and garnish each serving with 2 tablespoons scallions, 2 tablespoons shredded cheddar and 1 tablespoon sour cream.

To freeze: Rice can easily be cooked in advance and steamed in your microwave. Cook rice as usual. Cool completely. Portion into desired servings in freezer-safe zip top bags, and freeze. When ready to serve, place rice in a microwave safe bowl with a teaspoon of water, cover tightly with plastic wrap, and microwave for 1 to 2 minutes. Fluff rice and serve. Rice may be frozen for up to 6 months. To freeze bean mixture, cook through step 4, cool completely, and ladle into freezer-safe jars or containers. Freeze for up to 3 months.

MAKE IT VEGAN

The ready availability of quality vegan cheese and sour cream substitutes makes it easy for everyone to enjoy this dish. Try pepper jack–flavored shreds, and stir a little lime zest into your tofu sour cream for a real treat.

Ⓥ Farro with Tuscan Kale, Walnuts, and Cranberries

Nutty farro is enlivened with kale, walnuts, and the acidic bite of dried cranberries.

Yield:	Serving size:	Prep time:	Cook time:
12 cups	2 cups	15 minutes, plus over-night soaking	35 minutes

1 cup farro, well rinsed

1 tsp. kosher salt

3 TB. olive oil

1 large bunch scallions, sliced, white and light-green parts separated from dark green parts

¼ cup dry white wine

2 cups well-flavored vegetable stock, kept at a simmer

8 cups Tuscan kale, tough stems removed, thinly sliced

½ cup unsweetened dried cranberries

½ cup toasted, chopped walnuts

Salt and pepper to taste

1. Rinse farro well, pick over for impurities, and soak overnight in plenty of cold water.

2. Place farro in a medium saucepan with salt and enough water to cover by ½ inch. Bring to a boil over high heat, and cook for 20 minutes. Drain well and set aside.

3. Heat olive oil in a large saucepan over medium-high heat, and add white and light-green parts of scallions. Sauté for 2 minutes, then add farro and white wine. Cook, stirring constantly, until wine has evaporated.

4. Working ½ cup at a time, add the hot stock, stirring frequently. With the last ½ cup of stock, add the dark-green scallion, kale, and dried cranberries. When nearly all of the stock has been absorbed, remove from heat, and stir in chopped walnuts. Taste, and adjust salt and pepper if necessary.

Whole-Wheat Penne with Arugula Pesto and Fresh Tomatoes

Use the tiniest leaves of baby arugula for a pleasing bite to offset the acidity of fresh tomatoes in this perfect spring pasta dish.

Yield:	Serving size:	Prep time:	Cook time:
10 cups	2 cups	10 minutes	15 minutes

¼ cup pine nuts	½ cup extra-virgin olive oil
1–2 TB. plus ½ tsp. kosher salt	1 TB. lemon zest
1 lb. whole-wheat penne	½ tsp. freshly ground black pepper
4 cups loosely packed baby arugula leaves	½ cup freshly grated Parmesan cheese (optional)
2 cloves garlic, smashed and chopped	4 large plum tomatoes, cored, seeded, and finely chopped

1. Heat a small, nonreactive sauté pan over medium heat. Add pine nuts and toast, shaking pan frequently, until golden all over, about 5 minutes.

2. Bring a large pot of water to a boil for pasta. Season with 1 to 2 tablespoons kosher salt, and cook penne according to package directions. Prepare pesto while pasta is cooking.

3. Combine toasted pine nuts, arugula, garlic, lemon zest, black pepper, and ½ teaspoon salt in bowl of food processor. Turn machine on, and slowly drizzle in olive oil until well combined. If pesto appears too thick, blend in a spoonful or two of pasta water to thin.

4. Place pesto in a large serving bowl, and stir in grated Parmesan, if using. Drain pasta and add to pesto. Stir in tomatoes. Serve immediately.

Variation: For **Whole-Wheat Penne with Broccoli Pesto and Fresh Tomatoes,** replace pine nuts with almonds, and substitute 3 cups steamed broccoli for arugula.

Arugula.

THE LOWDOWN

During the winter months, when local tomatoes are out of season, try this recipe with sun-dried tomatoes. True sun-dried tomatoes are sold dry, not packed in oil. Rehydrate sun-dried tomatoes by pouring very hot (not boiling water) over tomatoes to cover. Remove from water when softened, chop finely, and add to pasta.

Mafaldine with Spinach, Broccoli, and Ricotta

Enjoy the delicious flavors of vegetable lasagna without turning the oven on. Curly mafaldine noodles resemble a hybrid of lasagna and fettuccine.

Yield:	Serving size:	Prep time:	Cook time:
12 cups	2 cups	20 minutes	20 minutes

1 TB. kosher salt

1 large head broccoli

1 lb. mafaldine pasta

3 TB. extra-virgin olive oil

3 cloves garlic, very thinly sliced

8 cups baby spinach

4 cups tomato sauce (see Chapter 16)

1 cup ricotta cheese

½ cup Parmesan cheese, grated

1. Bring a large pot of water to a rolling boil, and season with salt. Separate broccoli into florets. Trim and peel stems, and cut into ½-inch slices. Cook broccoli stems and florets for 5 minutes, remove from water with slotted spoon, and set aside.

2. Return water to a rolling boil, and cook pasta according to package directions.

3. While pasta is cooking, heat olive oil in a large sauté pan over medium-high heat. Add garlic, and stir for 1 to 2 minutes, until garlic is golden but not brown. Add broccoli, and stir for 5 minutes more. Add spinach, and cook until wilted, about 2 minutes. Stir in tomato sauce, and bring to a simmer.

4. Drain mafaldine, and add to simmering sauce. Toss well, and stir in ricotta and Parmesan. Remove from heat, and serve immediately.

MAKE IT VEGAN

It's easy to make your own vegan ricotta cheese. Crumble half a package of firm silken tofu into small pieces, using your fingers. Stir in 1 cup plain vegan yogurt and 1 tablespoon lemon juice. Refrigerate for 30 minutes. Use vegan ricotta in this recipe and others to approximate the flavor and texture of creamy ricotta cheese. Add ½ cup *Cheezy Toasted Bread Crumbs* (see Chapter 16) in place of Parmesan cheese.

Ⓥ "No Noodle" Spinach and Eggplant Lasagna

Roasted eggplant slices stand in for pasta in this slimmed-down vegan take on lasagna.

Yield:	Serving size:	Prep time:	Cook time:
1 9×13-inch casserole	⅛ of casserole	30 minutes	45 minutes

2 medium eggplants

1 TB. plus 1 tsp. kosher salt

4 TB. extra-virgin olive oil

1 TB. nutritional yeast

¼ cup fresh basil leaves, chiffonade cut

2 TB. Italian parsley, finely chopped

2 cups vegan mozzarella

Double recipe vegan ricotta (see sidebar above)

3 cloves garlic, smashed and finely chopped

2 lbs. fresh spinach, tough stems removed, torn

4 cups tomato sauce (see Chapter 16)

1. Heat oven to 375°F. Slice eggplant into ¼-inch rounds, leaving skin intact. Sprinkle slices evenly with 1 tablespoon kosher salt, layer in a colander, and drain in sink for 20 minutes. Rinse eggplant slices, and pat dry with paper towels.

2. Brush eggplant slices evenly with 2 tablespoons olive oil. Lay slices on parchment-lined baking sheets, and roast until golden and tender. Set aside to cool.

3. Stir nutritional yeast, basil, parsley, and 1 cup vegan mozzarella into ricotta. Set aside.

4. In a large sauté pan, heat remaining 2 tablespoons olive oil over medium-high heat. Add garlic and cook, stirring constantly, until golden, about 1 minute. Add spinach and remaining 1 teaspoon salt, and cook, stirring often, until spinach is tender and has released all of its liquid.

5. Oil a 9×13-inch casserole dish. Spread 1 cup of tomato sauce on the bottom of the dish, and cover with an even layer of eggplant. Top eggplant with a third of the ricotta mixture and then a third of spinach. Add another cup of tomato sauce and repeat layers, ending with a layer of eggplant topped with tomato sauce. Top casserole with 1 cup vegan mozzarella, and cover tightly with aluminum foil. Bake for 35 minutes, or until hot and bubbly. Serve immediately.

THE LOWDOWN

While many believe that the bitterness common in eggplant is located in the skin, it is actually the seeds that are to blame. Look for a smaller eggplant, and buy a male specimen whenever possible, as the female eggplant has more seeds. A female eggplant has a deep, oblong-shaped indentation at the bottom, while a male eggplant has a shallow, rounded dimple.

Mexican *Fideos* with Swiss Chard

Fideos is a thick, brothy pasta dish, cooked in a spicy red broth.

Yield:	Serving size:	Prep time:	Cook time:
8 cups	2 cups	15 minutes	20 minutes

1 dried guajillo chile, soaked in hot water for 10 minutes

4 cups vegetable stock

1 (14.5-oz.) can diced fire-roasted tomatoes with green chiles

2 TB. extra-virgin olive oil

8 oz. fideos noodles (or vermicelli), broken into large pieces

2 cloves garlic, smashed and finely chopped

2 bunches Swiss chard, tough stems removed, chiffonade cut

1 bay leaf

½ tsp. dried oregano

½ tsp. ground cumin

½ tsp. kosher salt

½ tsp. freshly ground black pepper

¼ cup crumbled Oaxaca cheese

2 TB. chopped cilantro

¼ cup tofu sour cream

1 tsp. lime zest

1 tsp. fresh lime juice

1. Drain guajillo chile, and discard soaking water. Place guajillo chile, vegetable stock, and fire-roasted tomatoes in blender, and blend until nearly smooth.

2. Heat olive oil in a large sauté pan over medium heat. Add noodles and cook, stirring constantly, until golden. Quickly remove noodles with a slotted spoon and drain on paper towels.

3. Add garlic to pan, and cook, stirring constantly, for 1 minute. Add Swiss chard, bay leaf, oregano, cumin, salt, and black pepper, and cook for 2 minutes. Return noodles to pan, and pour stock over. Bring to a boil, and reduce heat to a simmer. Cook, covered, until most of liquid is absorbed, about 15 minutes.

4. While fideos is cooking, make crema. Stir together cilantro, tofu sour cream, lime zest, and lime juice.

5. Ladle fideos into bowls, and top each serving with a spoonful of crema and Oaxaca cheese. Serve immediately.

DEFINITION

Fideos (pronounced FEE-day-wah) can be found in the Latin section of your grocery store. These noodles, similar to capellini, are often packaged in little "nests," which are broken apart by hand before cooking. If you can't find true fideos, vermicelli is an acceptable substitute.

Lemony Spinach Risotto

Spinach and the bright flavor of lemon accent this creamy risotto.

Yield:	Serving size:	Prep time:	Cook time:
8 cups	2 cups	15 minutes	30 minutes

8 cups vegetable stock

1 TB. extra-virgin olive oil

2 small shallots, finely chopped

2 cups arborio or carnaroli rice

½ cup dry white wine, such as pinot grigio, warmed slightly

½ tsp. kosher salt

8 cups baby spinach

1 tsp. lemon zest

2 TB. unsalted butter

½ cup Parmesan cheese

1. Bring vegetable stock to a simmer in a small saucepan. In a medium saucepan, heat olive oil over medium heat. Add shallots and cook until translucent, about 5 minutes, stirring often. Remove shallots with a slotted spoon, and set aside.

2. Add rice and continue to cook, stirring constantly, until rice is translucent and lightly toasted (do not let rice brown), about 8 minutes. Return shallots to pan.

3. Add white wine and salt, and cook, stirring constantly, until wine is absorbed.

4. Add stock slowly, ½ cup at a time, stirring constantly, adding more each time stock is absorbed. With the last ½ cup of stock, add spinach and lemon zest. When nearly all stock has been absorbed and rice is cooked, remove from heat and stir in butter and Parmesan. Serve immediately.

THE LOWDOWN

Risotto is a delicious rice dish made with short-grain Italian rice. Toasting the rice in hot fat, combined with the gradual addition of stock, slowly releases the starches in the rice, resulting in a creamy texture. Risotto should be cooked al dente, so taste it often to make sure it isn't becoming mushy or overcooked. Remember that your risotto will continue to cook and absorb liquid after you remove it from the heat, so work quickly and have your guests at the table. A proper risotto should flow when spooned onto the plate, not stick together in a clump. Practice makes perfect risotto, so keep trying if you don't get it exactly right the first time.

Polenta with Balsamic-Glazed Radicchio and Fennel

Creamy polenta is the perfect match for the sweet and slightly bitter flavors of balsamic-glazed radicchio and fennel.

Yield:	Serving size:	Prep time:	Cook time:
8 cups	2 cups	10 minutes	45 minutes

5 cups vegetable stock

1¼ cups fine-grain yellow polenta

1½ tsp. kosher salt

1 clove garlic, smashed and finely chopped

2 TB. extra-virgin olive oil

2 heads Treviso radicchio, trimmed and cut into 8 wedges each

2 bulbs fennel, trimmed and cut into 8 wedges each

½ cup balsamic vinegar

½ cup Italian fontina cheese, coarsely grated

½ cup Parmesan cheese, grated

1. Heat oven to 400°F. Bring vegetable stock to a boil in a medium saucepan, then slowly add polenta in a thin stream, stirring constantly. Stir in 1 teaspoon salt, and stir continuously until mixture returns to a boil. Reduce heat to a simmer, and cook until liquid is absorbed and polenta is soft, about 30 minutes, stirring almost constantly.

2. While polenta is cooking, gently toss radicchio and fennel with olive oil, garlic, and ½ teaspoon salt. Spread evenly on a large baking sheet and roast, stirring occasionally, until tender, about 20 minutes.

3. Bring balsamic vinegar to a boil in a small saucepan over high heat, and boil until liquid is reduced by half and syrupy. Pour balsamic syrup over radicchio and fennel, and roast for 5 minutes more.

4. Stir fontina and Parmesan into polenta. Spoon onto serving plates, and top with radicchio and fennel. Serve immediately.

HEADS UP!

Polenta needs three things—patience, plenty of liquid, and lots of stirring. It's tempting to use quick-cooking polenta or to skimp on the stirring, but both of these actions will result in an inferior product. Polenta, also known as cornmeal mush, develops its creamy texture through gelatinization of starches. Using a coarse-grained meal, such as stone-ground grits, will give a very different result than true Italian polenta, which is fine grained and very creamy. Try polenta topped with tomato sauce or sautéed broccoli rabe.

Radicchio.

Ⓥ Paella with Fennel, Kale, and Marcona Almonds

This dish of flavorful Calasparra rice, saffron, salty marcona almonds, and tender kale will be a revelation for your taste buds. Pour the sangria and invite some friends for this classic Spanish party dish.

Yield:	Serving size:	Prep time:	Cook time:
8 cups	2 cups	10 minutes	45 minutes

½ tsp. saffron threads

6½ cups light vegetable stock

¼ cup extra-virgin olive oil

3 medium yellow onions, finely chopped

1 bulb fennel, trimmed and finely chopped

1 tsp. kosher salt

½ tsp. freshly ground black pepper

5 cloves garlic, minced

2 tsp. dried oregano

1 TB. smoked paprika

1 bay leaf

2 TB. salt-packed capers, rinsed and drained

½ cup pimiento-stuffed Spanish green olives, sliced

3 cups Calasparra rice (or arborio)

¾ cup white wine

Juice of 1 lemon

8 cups curly kale, tough stems removed, chiffonade cut

½ cup finely chopped flat-leaf parsley

4 piquillo peppers, sliced; or 2 bell peppers, roasted, peeled, and sliced

½ cup marcona almonds, roughly chopped

1. Pound the saffron threads in a mortar and pestle, or crush between your fingertips. Add to stock and bring to a simmer in a small saucepan. Keep warm until needed.

2. Heat olive oil in a paella pan or a large sauté pan over medium-high heat. Add onions and fennel. Cook until soft and translucent, stirring often, about 10 minutes.

3. Add salt, pepper, garlic, oregano, paprika, bay leaf, capers, and olives, and cook for another 3 minutes or so.

4. Add rice and cook, stirring constantly, until grains are evenly covered with oil, about 3 more minutes.

5. Add the wine and lemon juice, and stir briskly to deglaze the bottom of the pan. Add kale, and cook for 3 minutes more, stirring constantly.

6. Spread the rice evenly over the bottom of the pan, and then add the stock all at once.

7. Bring to a boil over high heat and cook *without stirring* for about 5 minutes. Cover with a tight-fitting lid and reduce heat to medium-low.

8. Cook for 20 minutes without stirring.

9. Remove from heat. Garnish with parsley, piquillo peppers, and marcona almonds. Serve immediately, in the pan in which paella was cooked.

HEADS UP!

Paella is the quintessential Spanish rice dish made with saffron and short-grained rice. The secret to really delicious, authentic paella is to form a crust on the bottom of the pan. Allowing the rice to cook without stirring will create this flavorful crust, but be sure to moderate the heat so as not to allow the rice to burn. Paella is traditionally made in a wide, shallow steel pan with handles, but it's not necessary to buy specialty equipment if you have a large sauté pan with a lid.

Ⓥ Sesame Noodles with Wilted Tatsoi

The nutty flavor of sesame butter is gently spiced with chile oil, garlic, ginger, and scallions in this chewy noodle dish accented with mildly spicy tatsoi.

Yield:	Serving size:	Prep time:	Cook time:
10 cups	1 cup	15 minutes	40 minutes

2 tsp. kosher salt	2 TB. fresh ginger, grated
12 oz. whole-wheat spaghetti, broken in half	1 clove garlic, smashed and chopped
½ cup sesame butter	1 tsp. chile oil or Thai chile paste
¼ cup low-sodium soy sauce	6 cups tatsoi
2 TB. rice wine vinegar	1 cup sliced scallions, white and green parts
¼ cup hot water	2 TB. sesame seeds

1. Bring a large pot of water to a boil, and add salt. Cook pasta, stirring frequently, according to package directions.

2. While pasta is cooking, combine sesame butter, soy sauce, 2 tablespoons rice wine vinegar, hot water, ginger, garlic, and chile oil in food processor or blender. Process until smooth.

3. Drain pasta, and immediately toss with sesame dressing, tatsoi, scallions, and sesame seeds. Serve hot or cold.

Variation: For **Peanut Noodles with Wilted Tatsoi,** replace sesame butter with smooth peanut butter, and stir in ¼ cup chopped roasted peanuts in place of sesame seeds.

Ⓥ *Quinoa* with Pickled Mustard Greens

Nutty, chewy quinoa is delicious when combined with fragrant spices and pickled greens in this protein-rich dish inspired by Indian cuisine.

Yield:	Serving size:	Prep time:	Cook time:
6 cups	1 cup	10 minutes	40 minutes

2 cups quinoa	¼ tsp. ground cardamom
2 TB. coconut oil	½ tsp. freshly ground black pepper
1 cup yellow onion, finely diced	½ tsp. sea salt
1 clove garlic, smashed and finely chopped	4 cups vegetable stock
1 TB. grated ginger	1 cup pickled mustard greens, or other pickled greens (see Chapter 15)
1 tsp. curry powder	

1. Heat a nonreactive sauté pan over medium heat, and add quinoa. Stir quinoa constantly until lightly toasted, about 5 minutes. Remove from heat, rinse quinoa well, and set aside to drain.

2. Heat coconut oil in a medium saucepan over medium heat. Add onions and cook until softened and translucent, about 5 minutes. Add garlic and cook 1 minute more.

3. Add quinoa to pan and cook for 2 minutes, stirring often. Add ginger, curry powder, cardamom, black pepper, salt, and vegetable stock. Stir well, and bring to a boil over high heat.

4. Cover, reduce heat to low, and cook for 25 minutes. Stir in pickled greens, and serve immediately.

DEFINITION

Quinoa is not a grain at all, but the seed of a plant that is related to beets, chard, and spinach. Quinoa is rich in protein, particularly the amino acid lysine, making it an excellent addition to vegan and vegetarian diets. Its carbohydrates are released slowly, which helps regulate blood sugar and hunger. The flavor and texture of quinoa is best when it is toasted and then rinsed well before cooking.

Kale and Winter Squash–Stuffed Shells

Enjoy this deliciously different take on stuffed pasta shells. Savory kale and sweet winter squash filling and a creamy béchamel sauce make this the perfect dish to welcome autumn.

Yield:	Serving size:	Prep time:	Cook time:
12 shells	3 shells	10 minutes	40 minutes

12 large pasta shells

1 small yellow onion

2 cups winter squash, such as butternut, peeled and cut into 1-inch cubes

3 TB. extra-virgin olive oil

½ tsp. kosher salt

½ tsp. freshly ground black pepper

2 cloves garlic, smashed and chopped

2 bunches Tuscan kale, tough ribs removed, chiffonade cut

6 fresh sage leaves, finely chopped (or ½ tsp. dried sage)

2 TB. unsalted butter

2 TB. all-purpose flour

2 cups whole milk, heated

1 whole clove

1 bay leaf

¼ tsp. freshly grated nutmeg

1 cup Parmesan cheese, grated

1. Cook pasta shells according to package directions. Drain and set aside. Heat oven to 400°F. Cut onion in half and peel. Set half of onion aside for béchamel sauce, and cut remaining half in a small dice.

2. Toss squash cubes with 1 tablespoon olive oil, ¼ teaspoon salt, and ¼ teaspoon pepper. Spread evenly on a baking sheet lined with parchment paper, and roast for 15 to 20 minutes, or until tender and golden. Set aside to cool.

3. Heat 2 tablespoons olive oil in a large sauté pan over medium-high heat. Add diced onion and cook until translucent, stirring often, about 5 minutes. Add garlic and stir until golden, about 2 minutes. Add kale, ¼ teaspoon salt, and ¼ teaspoon pepper. Cook until kale is tender, about 8 minutes, stirring frequently.

4. Using a potato masher, gently mash squash. Stir in kale mixture and sage, and combine well. Distribute filling evenly between shells. Butter a baking dish just large enough to hold shells (about 9×9 inches), arrange shells in dish, and set aside.

5. Heat a small saucepan over medium-high heat, then add butter. When butter is melted and sizzling, add flour all at once, and whisk constantly to create a roux, about 3 minutes. The roux should smell toasty and be a pale golden color. Whisk in hot milk all at once. Press clove into reserved onion half, and add to sauce along with bay leaf and nutmeg. Reduce heat to a simmer, and cook until sauce is thickened, about 10 minutes. Strain to remove solids.

6. Pour sauce over stuffed shells, then top with Parmesan cheese. Cover and bake until hot and bubbly, about 30 minutes. Serve immediately.

THE LOWDOWN

In this recipe you are making a blonde roux. A roux is simply equal measures of cooked fat and flour, used to thicken soups, sauces, and stews. Roux can be cooked to varying degrees, resulting in different flavors. For the béchamel sauce in this recipe, the roux is cooked just enough to eliminate the unpleasant flavor and gritty texture of uncooked flour. In some Cajun and Creole dishes, roux is cooked for up to 30 minutes (or, in traditional Southern lore, long enough to drink two beers), and used to thicken and flavor dishes such as gumbo and etoufee. Roux can be cooked and then frozen, allowing you to quickly thicken a soup or sauce without fuss.

Ⓥ Kenyan Rice Pilau with Kachumbari

Fragrant spiced rice pilaf is topped with a cool, crunchy cabbage salad in this classic Kenyan celebration dish.

Yield:	Serving size:	Prep time:	Cook time:
8 cups rice, plus 4 cups kachumbari	2 cups rice, 1 cup kachumbari	30 minutes	30 minutes

2 cups finely shredded cabbage

2 plum tomatoes, seeded and thinly sliced

1 small cucumber, seeded and thinly sliced

1 small yellow onion, halved and thinly sliced

1 small hot chile pepper (such as serrano), seeded and thinly sliced

2 TB. apple cider vinegar

¼ cup cilantro, finely chopped

1 tsp. kosher salt

2 tsp. cumin seeds

1 tsp. cardamom seeds

3 whole cloves

½ tsp. ground cinnamon

½ tsp. freshly ground black pepper

½ tsp. ground piri piri chiles (or cayenne)

1 TB. coconut oil

2 cloves garlic, smashed and finely chopped

1 TB. freshly grated ginger

1 TB. tomato paste

2 cups basmati rice

6 cups vegetable stock, heated

1 can black-eyed peas, rinsed and drained

1. To make kambuchari, in a medium bowl, stir cabbage, tomatoes, cucumber, ½ of onion, chile pepper, apple cider vinegar, cilantro, and ½ teaspoon salt. Set aside for 30 minutes.

2. Heat a small, nonreactive sauté pan over medium-high heat. Add cumin seeds, cardamom seeds, and cloves, and dry toast, stirring constantly, until fragrant, about 5 minutes. Place toasted spices in a coffee grinder with cinnamon, black pepper, and ground chiles. Grind into a fine powder. Set aside.

3. Heat coconut oil over medium heat in a medium saucepan. Add remaining onion and cook until translucent, about 5 minutes, stirring often. Add garlic, ginger, and spice mixture, and stir for 1 minute more. Add tomato paste and remaining ½ teaspoon of salt, mix well, then add rice and cook, stirring constantly until lightly toasted, about 5 minutes.

4. Add hot vegetable stock to rice mixture and bring to a boil. Stir well, cover, and reduce heat to a low simmer. Cook for 15 to 20 minutes, or until rice has absorbed liquid. Stir in black-eyed peas.

5. Spoon rice pilau into bowls, and top with kachumbari.

DEFINITION

Pilau is a rice pilaf, often served at Kenyan weddings, that illustrates the fusion of African and Indian flavors in East African cooking. It is traditionally served with curried meat dishes, or with kachumbari, a type of coleslaw. The combination of hot, fragrant rice and cool, crunchy salad makes a pleasingly spicy dish.

Ⓥ Swiss Chard and Mascarpone Ravioli

Swiss chard, garlic, and mascarpone cheese make a delicious ravioli filling. Using wonton wrappers means you won't spend the whole day in the kitchen!

Yield:	Serving size:	Prep time:	Cook time:
24 ravioli	6 ravioli	30 minutes	7–8 minutes

1 TB. extra-virgin olive oil

1 clove garlic, smashed and finely chopped

6 cups Swiss chard, leaves only

¼ tsp. kosher salt

1 cup mascarpone cheese

½ cup Parmesan cheese, grated

Pinch of nutmeg

49 wonton wrappers (1 package)

2 cups tomato sauce (see Chapter 16)

Cheezy Toasted Bread Crumbs (see Chapter 16)

1. Heat olive oil over medium heat in a medium sauté pan. Add garlic and stir for 1 minute. Add Swiss chard and salt, and cook until chard has softened, about 5 minutes.

2. Combine Swiss chard mixture, mascarpone, Parmesan, and nutmeg in food processor. Process until smooth.

3. Working a few at a time, spoon 1 tablespoon filling onto wonton wrappers, moisten edges with a little water, using your fingertip, and press to seal. Be sure to press air out of ravioli, away from center filling, and seal completely to avoid leaking during cooking process. Repeat until you have made 24 ravioli.

4. Cook ravioli in boiling water for 7 to 8 minutes, or until tender and heated through. Serve immediately with tomato sauce and Cheezy Toasted Bread Crumbs.

Ⓥ Amaranth and Rice-Stuffed Tomatoes

Juicy beefsteak tomatoes are stuffed with amaranth and arborio rice and combined with traditional southern Italian flavors in this delicious entrée.

Yield:	Serving size:	Prep time:	Cook time:
6 tomatoes	1 tomato	20 minutes	45 minutes

¾ cup arborio rice

1 tsp. kosher salt

3 TB. olive oil

1 cup red onion, finely chopped

2 cloves garlic, thinly sliced

1 pound amaranth leaves, chiffonade cut

6 large beefsteak tomatoes

½ tsp. freshly ground black pepper

½ cup vegan mozzarella, diced or shredded

2 TB. Italian parsley, finely chopped

8 fresh basil leaves, chiffonade cut

Cheezy Toasted Bread Crumbs (see Chapter 16)

1. Preheat oven to 400 degrees. Bring 2½ cups filtered water to a boil, add arborio rice and ½ teaspoon salt, and cook for exactly 10 minutes. Drain immediately and set aside in a large bowl to cool.

2. Heat olive oil in a wide sauté pan over medium heat. Add red onion and cook, stirring frequently, until translucent, about 5 minutes. Add garlic and cook for 1 minute more.

3. Add amaranth and remaining ½ teaspoon salt to onion mixture, and stir until tender, about 3 minutes.

4. Oil a wide, 2-quart baking dish large enough to accommodate tomatoes. Place a fine mesh strainer over a bowl. Cut the core from the top of each tomato, then scoop the pulp and seeds from each tomato into the strainer, using a melon baller or sharp spoon. Leave the outer flesh and skin of the tomato intact. Press down on the seeds and pulp in the strainer to extract as much liquid as possible. Discard remaining pulp in strainer, and reserve the liquid left in the bowl. Place the scooped-out tomatoes into the prepared baking dish.

5. Combine rice, amaranth mixture, vegan mozzarella, parsley, black pepper, and basil. Lightly spoon the filling into the tomatoes, filling each to the top. Pour the reserved tomato juice over and around the tomatoes.

6. Cover the baking dish tightly with aluminum foil and bake for 25 minutes, or until liquid is hot and bubbling. Remove foil and bake for another 5 minutes. Serve hot or at room temperature, topped with Cheezy Toasted Bread Crumbs.

Variation: Try this filling in stuffed peppers. Make filling as directed, and stuff six cored bell peppers. Place stuffed peppers in a Dutch oven with 2 cups tomato sauce and ½ cup white wine. Cook, covered, over medium heat for 35 minutes or until peppers are tender.

Ⓥ Bok Choy Fried Rice

Crunchy bok choy is a great addition to gingery, slightly spicy fried rice.

Yield:	Serving size:	Prep time:	Cook time:
8 cups	2 cups	10 minutes	10 minutes

1 TB. safflower oil	4 cups cold, cooked brown rice
2 cloves garlic, smashed and finely chopped	1 tsp. low-sodium soy sauce
1 TB. freshly grated ginger	1 tsp. Asian hot sauce, such as Sriracha
1 cup yellow onion, thinly sliced	½ cup scallions, green parts only, thinly sliced
2 cups bok choy, thinly sliced	½ cup roasted almonds, roughly chopped
1 cup fresh shiitake mushrooms, thinly sliced	
1 cup peas, fresh or frozen	

1. Heat safflower oil in a wok or large sauté pan over high heat. Add garlic and ginger, and stir for 1 minute. Add onion, and cook for 1 minute more.

2. Push onion mixture to the side of the wok, and add bok choy. Stir-fry for 2 minutes, then push to the side and add mushrooms. Stir for 3 minutes, then add peas. Stir 1 minute more and push to the side.

3. Add rice, soy sauce, and hot sauce to wok, and stir-fry until heated through. Stir vegetables into rice, and cook 1 minute more. Serve immediately, topped with scallions and almonds.

Entrées

In This Chapter

- Hearty main courses
- Creative casseroles
- Perfect pizzas, burgers, and more

When most people think of sitting down to dinner, an entrée is expected. In this chapter, we'll look at composed dishes with a central protein that provide comforting familiarity to those accustomed to a meal centered around meat, such as "Chicken-Fried" Seitan. We'll also explore pot pies, enchiladas, burgers, pizzas, and other entrées that will bring creativity, fun, and flavor to your dinner table.

Rethink the Main Event

When many people think of a traditional dinner plate, there is meat at the center, with a few veggies as side dishes. Making vegetables such as nutritious greens more than an afterthought revolutionizes dinnertime. Think outside the box when planning meals—a hearty stir-fry, pot pie, or casserole can provide all of your nutritional needs along with plenty of fiber and nutrients. Think of the meals in this chapter as a starting point, but remember that you can create a nourishing, hearty meal using combinations of all of the foods in this book. The main course does not have to be "the main event," but the dishes in this chapter are designed to provide a complete meal. If you plan to add a salad, soup, or side dish, consider a smaller entrée portion.

Ⓥ Bok Choy, Tofu, and Shiitake Stir-Fry

Crunchy bok choy joins nutritious tofu and flavorful shiitake mushrooms in a ginger-and-garlic-laced sauce. Serve over jasmine or basmati rice for a satisfying supper.

Yield:	Serving size:	Prep time:	Cook time:
8 cups	2 cups	10 minutes	8 minutes

1 TB. minced fresh ginger

3 TB. minced fresh garlic

1 tsp. lemon juice

3 TB. grapeseed oil

1 tsp. dark sesame oil

¼ tsp. kosher salt

¼ tsp. freshly ground black pepper

1 large head bok choy, leaves and stalks thinly sliced

4 tsp. low-sodium soy sauce

2 cups snow peas

2 red bell peppers, thinly sliced

½ lb. firm silken tofu, cut into 1-inch cubes

1. In a small bowl, combine ginger, garlic, lemon juice, 1 tablespoon grapeseed oil, sesame oil, salt, and pepper. Set aside.

2. Heat wok over medium-high heat. Add remaining 2 tablespoons of grapeseed oil. Add garlic mixture and cook, stirring constantly, until fragrant, about 30 seconds. Add bok choy and cook, stirring constantly, for 2 minutes. Add soy sauce, snow peas, and peppers, and cook for 1 minute more.

3. Push vegetables to the side of the wok and add tofu. Cook, stirring constantly, until lightly browned. Add ginger-and-garlic mixture, stir vegetables back together with tofu and sauce, and cook until heated through. Serve immediately.

THE LOWDOWN

A successful stir-fry depends on having a pan with enough surface area to stay very hot in the center, where ingredients are cooked individually. A round-bottomed wok allows you to push cooked ingredients to the side, where they will be held warm while the next ingredient cooks. If you don't have a wok, use your largest flat-bottomed sauté pan, and remove vegetables with a slotted spoon before adding tofu.

Ⓥ Pan-Seared Bok Choy with Oyster Mushroom Miso Gravy

Pan-seared young bok choy is smothered in a show-stopping gravy made with sautéed oyster mushrooms and savory white miso. Serve with mashed potatoes for a fun twist on a traditional meal.

Yield:	Serving size:	Prep time:	Cook time:
8 bok choy halves with 4 cups mushroom gravy	2 bok choy halves with 1 cup mushroom gravy	15 minutes	25 minutes

4 young whole bok choy (about 6 inches long)

2 TB. grapeseed oil

2 TB. shallot, finely chopped (about 1 large shallot)

2 cloves garlic, smashed and finely chopped

1 (8 oz.) can oyster mushrooms, thinly sliced

1 TB. all-purpose flour

2 TB. mellow white miso

2 cups vegetable stock, heated

1 TB. Italian parsley, finely chopped

1 tsp. fresh tarragon, finely chopped

½ tsp. freshly ground pepper

1. Cut bok choy in half lengthwise. Steam until crisp-tender, about 5 minutes. Set aside.

2. Heat 1 tablespoon grapeseed oil over medium-high heat in cast-iron frying pan or heavy-bottomed sauté pan. Add bok choy, and cook without stirring until seared to a golden brown, about 3 to 5 minutes. Remove bok choy from pan; keep warm.

3. Heat remaining tablespoon grapeseed oil in same sauté pan. Add shallot and cook, stirring frequently, until softened, about 5 minutes. Add garlic and stir 1 minute more. Add oyster mushrooms, and cook, stirring occasionally, until golden and sizzling, about 7 minutes. Add flour and stir for 1 minute.

4. Stir miso into hot vegetable stock, then add to mushroom mixture. Stir well, and cook until thickened and bubbling, about 5 minutes. Stir in parsley, tarragon, and black pepper.

5. Place two bok choy halves on each plate, and top with oyster mushroom gravy. Serve immediately.

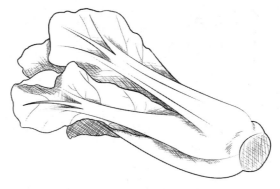

Bok choy.

Kale and Mushroom Pot Pie

Store-bought puff pastry makes this savory, herb-infused pot pie a quick and hearty dinner for a chilly winter night.

Yield:	Serving size:	Prep time:	Cook time:
1 9–inch-square casserole	⅙ of casserole	10 minutes	40 minutes

- 2 TB. canola oil
- ½ cup yellow onion (about 1 small onion, finely chopped
- 2 TB. shallot (about 1 large shallot), finely chopped
- 2 cloves garlic, smashed and finely chopped
- ½ cup carrot, finely chopped
- ½ cup celery, finely chopped
- 1 TB. fresh sage, finely chopped
- 1 TB. Italian parsley, finely chopped
- 1 tsp. freshly thyme leaves, finely chopped
- 1 tsp. rosemary leaves, finely chopped
- 1 (8-oz.) package fresh cremini mushrooms, quartered

- 1 large bunch Tuscan kale, tough ends of stems trimmed, thinly sliced
- 2 TB. all-purpose flour
- 4 cups vegetable stock
- 2 large Yukon gold potatoes, peeled and cut into ½-inch dice
- 1 tsp. Bragg Liquid Aminos
- ½ tsp. freshly ground black pepper
- 2 cups small English peas, fresh or frozen
- 1 sheet frozen commercial puff pastry (such as Pepperidge Farm)
- 2 TB. soy or rice milk

1. Heat oven to 400°F. Heat canola oil in a large sauté pan over medium-high heat. Add onion and shallot, and cook, stirring often, until softened and beginning to turn a light golden color, about 10 minutes. Add garlic, carrot, celery, sage, parsley, thyme, and rosemary, and stir for 2 minutes more.

2. Increase heat to high, and add mushrooms to onion mixture. Cook, stirring often, until mushrooms begin to color, about 10 minutes. Add kale and cook for 3 minutes more, stirring once. Add flour and cook for 1 additional minute, stirring constantly.

3. Stir hot stock into mushroom and kale mixture, then add potatoes, liquid aminos, and pepper. Bring to a boil, and reduce heat to a simmer. Cook until potatoes are tender and sauce has thickened, about 10 minutes. Stir in peas and remove from heat.

4. Oil a 9-inch-square ovenproof baking dish. Pour vegetable mixture into dish and set aside.

5. Cut puff pastry to fit the baking dish with a 1-inch overhang. Crimp edges of pastry, and cut several slits to allow steam to escape.

6. Brush top of pastry with soy or rice milk, and bake until pastry is golden brown and filling is bubbling hot, about 25 minutes. Serve immediately.

To freeze: Prepare through step 5. Wrap in freezer wrap or aluminum foil, then securely wrap with several layers of plastic wrap. Secure with tape. Freeze for up to 3 months. Do not defrost. Bake frozen casserole in 375°F oven for 1 hour, or until pastry is golden brown and filling is bubbling hot.

THE LOWDOWN

Vary your pot pie recipe using seasonal ingredients. Seek out mushroom that are local to your area, such as shiitake or hen of the woods, or ask about foraged varieties at your farmers market. Try substituting the oyster mushroom miso gravy from the previous recipe for the sauce used here. In late summer, replace kale with zucchini or lightly steamed broccoli, and stir 2 cups vegan cheese substitute in with peas.

ⓥ Amaranth and Corn Tamales with Tomatillo Salsa

Tamales are a fun party food! Masa dough is stuffed with a savory amaranth and sweet corn filling, then wrapped in corn husks and steam-baked in the oven. These delicious morsels are served with a spicy tomatillo salsa that will make you say, "Olé!"

Yield:	Serving size:	Prep time:	Cook time:
24 tamales	4 tamales	40 minutes	35 minutes

24 dried corn husks

2 TB. extra-virgin olive oil

½ cup white onion, finely chopped

4 cloves garlic, smashed and finely chopped

2 large bunches amaranth, stems trimmed, thinly sliced (about 12 cups)

1½ tsp. kosher salt

½ tsp. freshly ground black pepper

2 TB. fresh cilantro, finely chopped

2 cups sweet corn kernels, fresh or frozen

4 cups *masa harina*

2 tsp. baking powder

½ cup corn oil

½ cup coconut oil, melted

3 cups vegetable stock

Tomatillo salsa (see Chapter 16)

1. Tear off a thin strip of each corn husk to use as a tie. Soak corn husks and strips in a large bowl of warm water to soften. Heat oven to 400°F.

2. Heat olive oil in a large sauté pan over medium-high heat. Add onion and cook, stirring often, until softened, about 5 minutes. Add garlic and cook for 1 minute more. Add amaranth, ½ teaspoon salt, and pepper, and cook until amaranth is tender and liquid has evaporated, about 5 to 7 minutes. Stir in cilantro and corn, and set aside.

3. In a large bowl, mix masa harina, baking powder, and remaining 1 teaspoon salt. Stir in corn oil and coconut oil, and mix well. Stir in vegetable stock, and stir until a soft dough is formed.

4. Working one at a time, lay a corn husk on a clean work surface. Spread masa dough into a 3-inch square, about ½ inch thick. Spoon about 1½ tablespoons of amaranth filling down the center of the dough. To wrap tamales, bring one side of corn husk up to fold dough over filling, then release corn husk and repeat

with other side. Fold first side back over toward the center, then tuck the top flap down. Fold second side into center, and fold bottom flap up. You should have a tight, square bundle. Secure with a reserved corn husk strip, and repeat.

5. Place tamales on a rack inside a large roasting pan. Carefully pour 2 inches boiling water under tamales. Cover with a tight-fitting lid, or several layers of heavy aluminum foil, and bake for 35 minutes. Serve tamales hot or warm, with tomatillo salsa.

> **DEFINITION**
>
> **Masa harina** is a flour that is made from field corn (maize) that has been treated with slaked lime to loosen the kernel, soften the corn, and make the nutrients more accessible to your digestive system. The wet, soaked corn is ground into a dough, which is then dried to make masa harina. Fresh masa dough, which has not been dried, can be found in Mexican specialty markets, but masa harina can be found in the Mexican aisle of most grocery stores.

Ⓥ Shepherd's Pie

Chard and kale join mushrooms to make sure you won't miss the meat in this vegan take on traditional shepherd's pie. Worcestershire sauce and ketchup are essential for authentic flavor in this saucy stew tucked beneath a layer of luscious mashed potatoes.

Yield:	Serving size:	Prep time:	Cook time:
1 9×13-inch casserole	2-inch slice	25 minutes	45 minutes

2 TB. extra-virgin olive oil

1 cup yellow onion, finely chopped

1 cup carrot, finely chopped

1 cup celery, finely chopped

2 cloves garlic, smashed and finely chopped

1 lb. white button mushrooms, finely chopped

1 large bunch Tuscan kale, tough stems trimmed, chiffonade cut

1 large bunch Swiss chard, tough stems trimmed, chiffonade cut

½ tsp. kosher salt

½ tsp. freshly ground black pepper

2 TB. vegan Worcestershire sauce

1 TB. prepared ketchup

1 cup red wine (such as merlot)

1 cup vegetable stock

6 cups hot mashed potatoes

1. Preheat oven to 400°F. Heat olive oil in a large sauté pan over medium-high heat. Add onion, carrot, and celery, and cook until softened and beginning to brown, about 10 minutes, stirring frequently. Add garlic and cook for 1 minute more.

2. Add mushrooms to onion mixture and cook, stirring frequently, until mushrooms have released their liquid and begun to brown. Stir in kale, Swiss chard, salt, and pepper, and cook until tender, about 5 minutes more. Add Worcestershire sauce, ketchup, red wine, and vegetable stock. Stir well, and remove from heat.

3. Grease a 9×13-inch casserole. Pour mushroom mixture into casserole, and carefully spoon mashed potatoes over the top. Spread potatoes gently to combine.

4. Bake casserole for 45 minutes, or until potatoes have turned golden brown and stew beneath is bubbling hot.

THE LOWDOWN

Shepherd's pie is a traditional Irish recipe, normally made with lamb. In England, it is made with beef and called cottage pie. Both feature a tomato-and-Worcestershire-based sauce and plenty of golden potatoes on top. Try varying your mashed potato recipe to change up this dish—caramelized leeks or onions, cheese, or horseradish would all be delicious additions!

Ⓥ Barbecue Tempeh Sandwich with Spicy Mustard Greens

Tempeh marinated in your favorite barbecue sauce makes an amazing sandwich when topped with spicy mustard greens and a quick remoulade sauce. Serve on a crusty Portuguese-style roll to soak up the sauce and "pot liquor" from the greens.

Yield:	Serving size:	Prep time:	Cook time:
4 sandwiches	1 sandwich	15 minutes	15 minutes

2 (8-oz.) packages tempeh

1½ cups barbecue sauce

2 TB. grapeseed oil

2 cloves garlic, smashed and finely chopped

¼ tsp. crushed red pepper flakes

Pinch of cayenne pepper

8 cups mustard greens, tough stems trimmed, roughly chopped

1 tsp. kosher salt

1 TB. apple cider vinegar

¼ cup vegan mayonnaise

1 TB. shallot, finely chopped (about 1 shallot)

1 tsp. lemon zest

1 tsp. capers, finely chopped

2 TB. gherkin or cornichon pickles, finely chopped (about 5 small pickles)

½ tsp. freshly ground black pepper

1 tsp. Louisiana hot sauce (such as Crystal)

4 crusty sandwich rolls (such as Portuguese rolls), split\

1. Slice tempeh into ¼-inch strips, and gently toss with barbecue sauce to coat. Set aside to marinate for 15 minutes.

2. Heat a medium sauté pan over medium-high heat. Add grapeseed oil and garlic. Cook, stirring frequently, for 1 minute. Add crushed red pepper flakes and cayenne, and stir for 30 seconds more. Add mustard greens and ¾ teaspoon salt. Cook, stirring occasionally, until greens are crisp-tender, about 8 minutes.

3. Stir vegan mayonnaise, shallot, lemon zest, capers, pickles, black pepper, ¼ tsp. salt, and hot sauce together in a small bowl. Set aside.

4. Remove cooked greens to a small bowl. Wipe sauté pan clean, heat over medium-high heat, and add tempeh strips. Cook until browned on each side, turning carefully.

5. Spread each roll with a generous amount of remoulade sauce. Top with tempeh, then divide mustard greens evenly among sandwiches. Serve immediately, with plenty of napkins.

HEADS UP!

Tempeh burns easily when coated with sticky, sweet barbecue sauce. Try a nonstick pan, and be sure to stay near the stove. Turn carefully with a heatproof spatula, and remove when lightly browned and sizzling. Be sure to give the tempeh a full 15 minutes to marinate and soak up the sauce, or place in the fridge before you leave for work in the morning to have it ready to hit the pan as soon as you walk through the door.

Ⓥ "Chicken-Fried" Seitan with Braised Collards

Crispy, savory seitan nuggets are fried up "chicken style" with cornmeal and spices, and served on a bed of tender braised collard greens.

Yield:	Serving size:	Prep time:	Cook time:
4 servings	4 oz. seitan, 2 cups greens	10 minutes	45 minutes

2 TB. extra-virgin olive oil

1 red onion, halved and thinly sliced

4 cloves garlic, smashed and finely chopped

¼ tsp. crushed red pepper flakes

2 bunches collard greens, tough stems trimmed, chiffonade cut (about 14 cups)

2 tsp. kosher salt

1 cup apple cider

1 TB. apple cider vinegar

1 cup fine cornmeal

2 tsp. sweet paprika

2 tsp. Creole spice (such as Tony Chacere's)

1 tsp. freshly ground black pepper

¼ tsp. cayenne pepper, or to taste

2 (8-oz.) packages seitan strips

½ cup safflower oil

1. Heat olive oil over medium-high heat in a large saucepan with a tight-fitting lid. Add onion and cook until softened, about 5 minutes, stirring occasionally. Add garlic and crushed red pepper flakes, and cook, stirring constantly, for 1 minute more.

2. Add collard greens and salt to onion mixture and cook, stirring frequently, for 5 minutes, until greens begin to wilt. Add apple cider and apple cider vinegar, and bring to a boil. Cover, reduce heat to low, and cook for 30 minutes, stirring occasionally.

3. Meanwhile, combine cornmeal, sweet paprika, Creole spice, black pepper, and cayenne pepper in a paper bag. Add seitan, and shake well to coat.

4. Remove lid from collard greens, increase heat to medium, and continue to cook until liquid has nearly evaporated and greens are tender, about 10 minutes more.

5. Heat safflower oil in a large frying pan, preferably cast iron. When a pinch of flour sizzles when added to the pan, add seitan, working in batches if necessary. Fry until crispy and golden, stirring every minute or so, for about 5 minutes. Drain on paper towels.

6. Divide greens evenly among four plates, and top each serving with seitan. Serve immediately.

THE LOWDOWN

The braising method in this recipe can be used with any liquid and any greens. Just sauté the onions and garlic, season as desired, and add greens and enough liquid to cook them gently. Keep the heat as low as possible, and cook until greens are meltingly tender. Replace the apple cider with dark beer, vegetable stock, or a combination of vegetable stock and white wine. Serve with cornbread, biscuits, or crusty rolls for dipping in the delicious sauce!

Cauliflower "Mac and Cheese" with Kale

Cauliflower and kale replace pasta in this zesty casserole, which features plenty of smoky, creamy cheese sauce and a crispy bread-crumb topping.

Yield:	Serving size:	Prep time:	Cook time:
8 cups	2 cups	15 minutes	20 minutes

2 TB. extra-virgin olive oil

2 cloves garlic, smashed and finely chopped

2 TB. all-purpose flour

3 cups milk, heated

1 bay leaf

1 canned chipotle chile in adobo, finely chopped

½ tsp. kosher salt

½ tsp. freshly ground black pepper

¼ tsp. freshly grated nutmeg

1 medium head cauliflower, cut into florets

1 large bunch kale, tough stems removed, roughly chopped

2 cups shredded Monterey Jack cheese

2 cups shredded sharp cheddar cheese

1 cup panko bread crumbs

2 TB. melted butter

1. Preheat oven to 400°F. Heat olive oil in a medium saucepan over medium heat. Add garlic and cook, stirring frequently, for 1 minute. Add flour and stir to combine well. Cook, stirring constantly, until flour is a light golden color (blonde roux). Slowly whisk in hot milk, and add bay leaf, chipotle, salt, black pepper, and nutmeg. Bring sauce to a boil, then reduce to a simmer. Cook, stirring frequently, until sauce has thickened enough to coat the back of a spoon, about 15 minutes.

2. Meanwhile, bring a pot of salted water to a boil. Blanch cauliflower for 8 minutes, or until crisp tender, then blanch kale in same water for 2 minutes. Drain thoroughly.

3. Working a handful at a time, whisk cheese into sauce, mixing until each addition is completely melted before adding more.

4. Stir kale and cauliflower into cheese sauce.

5. Oil an ovenproof baking dish large enough to accommodate cauliflower mixture. Pour cauliflower into baking dish. In a small bowl, stir together panko and melted butter. Spread panko mixture on top of casserole, and bake for 20 minutes, or until topping is golden brown. Serve immediately.

Kale and Potato Enchiladas Verde

Corn tortillas are fried, then stuffed with a cheesy potato and kale filling and smothered in a garlicky roasted tomatillo and pumpkin seed salsa.

Yield:	Serving size:	Prep time:	Cook time:
12 enchiladas	3 enchiladas	15 minutes	20 minutes

1 pound tomatillos, husks removed, scrubbed

3 fresh poblano chiles, seeded and roughly chopped1 large white onion, roughly chopped

4 cloves garlic, peeled and smashed

2 TB. extra-virgin olive oil

2 medium Yukon gold potatoes, peeled and diced

1 tsp. kosher salt

1 large bunch kale, tough stems removed, roughly chopped

1 cup vegetable stock

¼ cup pumpkin seeds, toasted and ground in mortar and pestle or food processor

¼ cup fresh cilantro, finely chopped

2 TB. lime juice

1 tsp. sugar

2 TB. grapeseed oil

12 corn tortillas

1 cup queso fresco or Monterey Jack cheese

1. Preheat broiler. Cut tomatillos in half, and spread on a foil-lined baking sheet. Toss with poblano chiles, onion, garlic, and 1 tablespoon olive oil. Broil for 10 minutes, stirring frequently, until vegetables have softened and tomatillos are lightly charred. Transfer to blender or food processor, and blend until smooth.

2. Place potatoes and salt in a saucepan with water to cover by ½ inch, and bring to a boil. Reduce heat to medium, and cook for 10 minutes, then add kale and continue to cook until potatoes and kale are tender. Drain thoroughly, then mash. Set aside, covered to keep warm.

3. Heat remaining 1 tablespoon olive oil in a medium saucepan. Add tomatillo mixture, and fry until reduced to the consistency of tomato paste. Stir in vegetable

stock and ground pumpkin seeds, bring to a boil, and cook until reduced by half. Stir in cilantro, lime juice, and sugar. Set aside, covered to keep warm.

4. In a small fry pan, heat grapeseed oil. Working one at a time, fry tortillas for 30 seconds on each side. Keep tortillas warm and covered once cooked.

5. To assemble enchiladas, spoon 2 tablespoons potato mixture and 1 tablespoon cheese into center of each tortilla, and roll up. Place on a large, rimmed platter. When all tortillas are rolled, smother in tomatillo salsa and serve immediately.

> **THE LOWDOWN**
>
> The tomatillo salsa in this recipe is known in Mexico as pipian. It is a form of mole flavored with pumpkin seeds. Try this delicious, addictive sauce over steamed vegetables, or stir it into rice and beans or black bean soup.

Pizza Bianco with Spinach

Creamy ricotta, mozzarella cheese, and garlicky sautéed spinach top a tender pizza crust in this classic white pizza.

Yield:	Serving size:	Prep time:	Cook time:
1 12-inch pizza	¼ of pizza	10 minutes	25 minutes

2 TB. extra-virgin olive oil

3 cloves garlic, thinly sliced

¼ tsp. crushed red pepper flakes

1 pound baby spinach

½ tsp. kosher salt

½ tsp. freshly ground black pepper

1 lb. pizza dough (see Chapter 16)

1 cup ricotta cheese

1 cup fresh mozzarella cheese, squeezed to release extra moisture, cut into ½-inch cubes

1. Heat oven to 500°F. Heat olive oil in a large sauté pan over medium-high heat. Add garlic and cook, stirring constantly, until golden, about 2 minutes. Add crushed red pepper, spinach, and salt. Cook, stirring frequently, until spinach has wilted and liquid has evaporated, about 4 minutes. Stir in black pepper.

2. Using your hands or a rolling pin, stretch pizza dough on a well-floured surface to a 12-inch round. Transfer to an oiled baking sheet. Spread ricotta evenly over dough. Top with spinach mixture, then evenly sprinkle mozzarella cubes over pizza.

3. Bake pizza, turning once to ensure even cooking, until crust is golden brown and cheese is melted and bubbly, about 12 minutes. Allow pizza to rest for 5 minutes, then slice and serve.

MAKE IT VEGAN

Use vegan ricotta cheese (see Chapter 12), and replace mozzarella with a nondairy tapioca-based mozzarella. Bake as directed.

Ⓥ Green Pizza

This deliciously different vegan pizza is baked with a simple topping of olive oil and nutritional yeast, then smothered in delicious broccoli and spinach sautéed in plenty of garlic and oil.

Yield:	Serving size:	Prep time:	Cook time:
1 12-inch pizza	¼ of pizza	10 minutes	15 minutes

1 lb. pizza dough (see Chapter 16)

3 TB. extra-virgin olive oil

1 TB. nutritional yeast

4 cloves garlic, thinly sliced

1 head broccoli, blanched and cooled

1 pound baby spinach

1 tsp. kosher salt

½ tsp. freshly ground black pepper

1. Heat oven to 500°F. Using your hands or a rolling pin, stretch dough on a well-floured surface to form a 12-inch round. Transfer to an oiled baking pan. Mix 1 tablespoon olive oil and nutritional yeast in a small bowl, then brush evenly over surface of dough. Bake until crust is puffed and golden, about 12 minutes.

2. Meanwhile, heat remaining 2 tablespoons olive oil in a large sauté pan over medium-high heat. Add garlic and cook, stirring constantly, until golden. Add broccoli, spinach, and salt. Cook, stirring frequently, until spinach has wilted and vegetables are tender, about 5 minutes. Season with black pepper.

3. Spoon broccoli mixture evenly over baked pizza dough, slice, and serve hot or at room temperature.

Variation: Replace spinach and broccoli with 2 large bunches broccoli rabe. Top with toasted pine nuts.

ⓥ Swiss Chard Tortilla Lasagna

Layers of corn tortillas are smothered in sautéed Swiss chard, fire-roasted tomatoes, black beans, and a cheesy, spicy chile sauce in this fun twist on traditional lasagna.

Yield:	Serving size:	Prep time:	Cook time:
1 9×13-inch casserole	⅛ of casserole	20 minutes	50 minutes

¼ cup extra-virgin olive oil	3 cups rice or soy milk
4 cloves garlic, thinly sliced	4 cups vegan Monterey Jack–style cheese
2 bunches Swiss chard, tough stems trimmed, chiffonade cut	1 can diced green chiles (such as Ortega brand)
½ tsp. kosher salt	½ tsp. cayenne pepper, or to taste
½ tsp. black pepper	15 corn tortillas
1 (28-oz.) can fire-roasted tomatoes	2 cans black beans, rinsed and drained
2 TB. all-purpose flour	
2 TB. nutritional yeast	

1. Preheat oven to 375°F. Heat 2 tablespoons olive oil in a large sauté pan over medium-high heat. Add garlic and cook until golden, about 2 minutes. Add Swiss chard and salt, and cook, stirring frequently, until tender, about 5 minutes. Add black pepper and fire-roasted tomatoes. Increase heat to high, bring to a boil, then reduce heat and simmer 10 minutes.

2. Heat remaining 2 tablespoons olive oil over medium heat in a medium saucepan. Add flour all at once and whisk vigorously to combine. Cook for 2 minutes, whisking constantly, then add rice milk and nutritional yeast. Combine well, bring to a boil, then lower heat and simmer until thickened, about 10 minutes. Working a handful at a time, stir in 3 cups of cheese, adding more when previous addition has melted. Stir in chiles and cayenne pepper.

3. Oil a 9×13-inch baking dish. Cut three tortillas in half. Layer four tortillas and two tortilla halves to cover bottom of casserole. Add half of Swiss chard mixture, half of black beans, and ⅓ of cheese sauce. Repeat an additional layer of four tortillas and two halves, then top again with remaining half of Swiss chard mixture, remaining half of black beans, and ⅓ of cheese sauce. Complete top layer of tortillas, then spread remaining cheese sauce over the top. Sprinkle with additional 1 cup cheese.

4. Cover casserole with aluminum foil, and bake until heated through and bubbly, about 45 minutes. Remove foil for last 10 minutes of baking to brown cheese topping. Serve immediately.

To freeze: Prepare through step 3. Cover with aluminum foil, then wrap tightly in several layers of plastic wrap, securing final layer with tape. Freeze for up to 3 months. To cook, defrost in refrigerator overnight, then bake as directed.

THE LOWDOWN

It's really easy and economical to make your own corn tortillas, and they will taste amazing, too! Simply mix 1¾ cups masa harina with 1 cup plus 2 tablespoons hot water. Knead until a smooth dough forms, then wrap in plastic wrap and set aside for 30 minutes. Heat a cast-iron pan over medium heat. Divide dough into 15 equal balls, keeping dough balls covered to retain moisture, then use a rolling pin or tortilla press to flatten each into a circle between two sheets of plastic wrap. Cook each tortilla in the dry cast-iron skillet for 30 seconds per side. Cover cooked tortillas with a towel to keep warm while you are working.

Ⓥ Quinoa-and-Mushroom-Stuffed Cabbage

Green cabbage leaves are stuffed with a savory mixture of mushrooms, onions, and nutty quinoa, then simmered in a tomato broth, for this eastern European comfort-food classic.

Yield:	Serving size:	Prep time:	Cook time:
12 cabbage rolls	3 cabbage rolls	10 minutes	1 hour and 15 minutes

1 cup uncooked quinoa

2 TB. safflower oil

1 large yellow onion, finely chopped

2 garlic cloves, smashed and finely chopped

1 (8-oz.) package fresh button mushrooms, finely chopped

½ tsp. ground allspice

½ tsp. chopped caraway seeds

¼ tsp. black pepper

1 tsp. fresh thyme leaves, finely chopped

1 tsp. kosher salt

12 large green cabbage leaves, plus 4 for lining pan

2 cups vegetable stock

2 TB. tomato paste

¼ cup dry white wine, such as sauvignon blanc

1 cup tofu sour cream, for serving (optional)

1. Heat a nonreactive sauté pan over medium heat, and add quinoa. Stir quinoa constantly until lightly toasted, about 5 minutes. Remove from heat, rinse quinoa well, and set aside to drain.

2. Heat safflower oil in a medium saucepan over medium heat. Add onion and cook until softened and translucent, about 5 minutes. Add garlic and cook 1 minute more. Add chopped mushrooms and cook, stirring frequently, until mushrooms have released their liquid and are lightly browned.

3. Add quinoa to pan and cook for 2 minutes, stirring often. Add allspice, caraway seeds, black pepper, thyme, salt, and 2 cups water. Stir well, and bring to a boil over high heat. Cover, reduce heat to low, and cook for 15 minutes. Remove from heat, cover, and set aside for 10 minutes.

4. Meanwhile, bring a large saucepan of water to a boil. Add cabbage leaves, and cook until tender, about 3 minutes. Drain thoroughly, and trim away tough stem end of each cauliflower leaf.

5. Fluff quinoa filling with a fork. Whisk vegetable stock, tomato paste, and white wine. Line a Dutch oven with a tight-fitting lid with four large uncooked cabbage leaves.

6. Fill each cooked cabbage leaf with about ⅓ cup filling. Fold the sides of each leaf over filling, then roll up beginning at the stem end. Tuck cabbage rolls into Dutch oven, pour vegetable stock mixture over, and bring to a boil over high heat. Cover, reduce heat to low, and cook for 30 minutes, stirring and basting often. Remove from heat and serve immediately with tofu sour cream (if using).

HEADS UP!

Don't skip the rinse! Quinoa has a bitter coating that must be rinsed off. It's up to you whether you rinse before or after toasting—I've found that quinoa rinsed after it is toasted tastes better. Just be sure to wipe the pan clean to remove any residue before you continue with the recipe.

Ⓥ Black Bean–Amaranth Burgers with Chipotle Mayo

Flavorful black bean burgers are served on crusty rolls with lettuce, tomato, and a lime-and-chipotle mayonnaise for a deliciously different burger.

Yield:	Serving size:	Prep time:	Cook time:
6 burgers	1 burger	10 minutes	15 minutes

2 TB. extra-virgin olive oil

½ cup yellow onion, finely chopped

½ cup green bell pepper, finely chopped

2 cloves garlic, smashed and finely chopped

½ tsp. ground cumin

¼ tsp. dried oregano

8 cups amaranth leaves, chiffonade cut

1 cup cooked brown rice

1 (15-oz.) can black beans, rinsed and drained

½ tsp. kosher salt

¼ tsp. freshly ground black pepper

2 TB. fresh cilantro, finely chopped

¼ cup dry bread crumbs

1 TB. safflower oil

1 canned chipotle chile, finely chopped

1 tsp. adobo sauce (from canned chipotles)

¼ cup vegan mayonnaise

1 tsp. lime zest

6 crusty round rolls

6 leaves romaine lettuce

6 slices beefsteak tomato

1. Heat olive oil over medium heat in a large sauté pan. Add onions and bell pepper, and cook until softened, about 5 minutes. Add garlic, cumin, and oregano, and cook 2 minutes more. Add amaranth leaves and cook until tender, about 5 minutes. Remove from heat and cool slightly.

2. In a food processor fitted with a metal blade, combine brown rice, black beans, amaranth mixture, salt, black pepper, cilantro, and bread crumbs. Process in 5-second pulses until well combined but still a little chunky.

3. Divide black bean mixture into six equal balls, then gently flatten each into a burger.

4. Heat safflower oil in a large nonstick or cast-iron skillet over medium heat. Cook burgers, turning once, for 5 minutes on each side.

5. Meanwhile, whisk chipotle pepper, adobo sauce, mayonnaise, and lime zest in a small bowl.

6. Carefully remove each burger to a bun, and top with lettuce, sliced tomato, and chipotle mayonnaise. Serve immediately.

DEFINITION

Chipotle chiles are jalapeño peppers that have been smoked over a wood fire. These dried peppers can be ground into a powder, or stored as dried chiles. Canned chipotles are dried chipotle peppers that have been rehydrated in a flavorful tomato sauce called adobo, and canned. This pantry staple adds a smoky heat to Mexican and Southwestern recipes. Once opened, chipotle chiles in adobo should be stored in the refrigerator in a tightly covered container, where they will keep for up to 2 months.

Greek Seitan, Spinach, and Brown Rice Casserole

Meaty seitan strips, nutty brown rice, spinach, and feta cheese star in this festive casserole, which has the flavors of spanakopita without all the butter and extra calories.

Yield:	Serving size:	Prep time:	Cook time:
1 9–inch-square casserole	⅙ of casserole	15 minutes	30 minutes

2 TB. extra-virgin olive oil	1 (8 oz.) package seitan strips, roughly chopped
1 large red onion, halved and thinly sliced	2 TB. fresh dill, finely chopped
3 cloves garlic, thinly sliced	1½ cups crumbled feta cheese
½ tsp. crushed red pepper flakes	1 TB. freshly squeezed lemon juice
1 lb. baby spinach	½ tsp. freshly ground black pepper
½ tsp. kosher salt	4 cups cooked brown rice

1. Preheat oven to 350°F. Heat olive oil in a large sauté pan. Add onion and cook until softened, about 5 minutes. Add garlic and crushed red pepper, and cook 1 minute more. Add spinach and salt, and cook until tender, about 5 minutes. Stir in seitan and continue to cook until heated through, about 5 minutes. Remove from heat and stir in dill, feta cheese, lemon juice, and black pepper.

2. Oil a 9–inch-square casserole dish. Fold cooked brown rice into spinach mixture, then spread evenly in casserole. Bake, covered, for 30 minutes. Serve immediately

MAKE IT VEGAN

Make an easy vegan substitute for feta cheese. Whisk together 1 teaspoon Dijon mustard, 1 tablespoon nutritional yeast, 1 tablespoon white miso, ½ teaspoon dried oregano, ¼ cup apple cider vinegar, and 2 tablespoons extra-virgin olive oil. Crumble ½ pound firm silken tofu into dressing, and marinate in refrigerator for 20 minutes. Use in spanakopita, casseroles, or salads. Store tightly covered vegan tofu in your refrigerator for up to 3 days.

Ⓥ Spicy Curried Greens with Chickpeas and Potatoes

This hot, savory, tomato-based curry is brimming with spicy mustard greens, nutty chickpeas and tender potatoes, with plenty of fragrant basmati rice to soak up the delicious sauce.

Yield:	Serving size:	Prep time:	Cook time:
8 cups	2 cups	20 minutes	15 minutes

2 TB. coconut oil

1 TB. curry powder

1 TB. turmeric

1 tsp. ground coriander

1 TB. freshly grated ginger

1 TB. black mustard seeds

¼ tsp. crushed red pepper flakes

2 yellow onions, halved and thinly sliced

1 serrano chile, seeded and finely chopped

4 garlic cloves, thinly sliced

1 large bunch mustard greens, tough stems trimmed, roughly chopped

1 cup canned diced tomatoes

2 cups vegetable stock

2 large Yukon gold potatoes, scrubbed, peeled and cut into ½-inch dice

1 (14-oz.) can chickpeas, drained and rinsed

½ tsp. kosher salt

1 tsp. freshly ground black pepper

2 cups basmati rice, for serving

1. Heat coconut oil over medium-high heat. Add curry powder, turmeric, ground coriander, ginger, mustard seeds, and crushed red pepper. Cook, stirring frequently, for 2 minutes. Add onions and serrano chile, and cook 5 minutes more, stirring frequently. Add garlic and cook 1 minute more. Stir in mustard greens and toss to combine well. Cook, stirring frequently, for 5 minutes.

2. Stir diced tomatoes, vegetable stock, and potatoes into mustard greens mixture. Bring to a boil, then reduce to a simmer and cook until potatoes and greens are tender, about 10 minutes. Stir in chickpeas, and season with salt and black pepper.

3. Divide basmati rice evenly among four serving bowls. Top each serving with curry, and serve immediately.

> **HEADS UP!**
>
> Curry is very fragrant when cooking because the spices release fat-soluble oils as they heat up. These fragrances are wonderful when you're cooking, but if you're making curries regularly, you may find that the pungent after-cooking odor is difficult to remove. If your home is haunted by the ghost of curries past, simmer equal parts of vinegar and water with a few whole cinnamon sticks and cardamom pods, and wipe down floors and surfaces with a cleaning solution of one part white vinegar to three parts water to remove the oils, and thus the unpleasant odors.

Spinach Risotto Cakes

Mixed with creamy fresh mozzarella, and fried to golden perfection, leftover risotto has never tasted so delicious!

Yield:	Serving size:	Prep time:	Cook time:
8 risotto cakes	2 risotto cakes	40 minutes, plus over-night chilling	10 minutes

1 recipe *Lemony Spinach Risotto*, chilled overnight (see Chapter 12)

1 cup fresh mozzarella, cut into ¼-inch cubes

1 cup freshly grated Parmesan cheese

1 large egg, beaten

2 TB. extra-virgin olive oil

2 cups tomato sauce (see Chapter 16)

1. Stir spinach risotto together with mozzarella, Parmesan, and beaten egg.

2. Divide risotto into 16 equal-sized balls, and flatten to form 3-inch cakes.

3. Heat olive oil in a wide sauté pan over medium heat. Add risotto cakes, and fry for 5 minutes per side, or until golden and heated through. Drain on paper towels.

4. Serve risotto cakes with tomato sauce.

To freeze: Make risotto cakes through step 3. Cool completely, then wrap in freezer paper, followed by several layers of plastic wrap. Freeze for up to 3 months. When ready to enjoy, place frozen risotto cakes on a parchment-lined baking sheet, and bake in a 375°F oven for 30 minutes, turning once.

Ⓥ Kale and Chickpea Falafel with Israeli Salad

Traditional falafel patties are combined with kale for a nutritious option, while Israeli salad adds a terrific acidic punch.

Yield:	Serving size:	Prep time:	Cook time:
4 sandwiches	1 sandwich	20 minutes	15 minutes

2 TB. extra-virgin olive oil

2 medium yellow onions, finely chopped

2 tsp. ground cumin

½ teaspoon ground cinnamon

½ tsp. kosher salt

½ tsp. freshly ground black pepper

1 bunch Tuscan kale, leaves only, chiffonade cut

2 (14.5-oz) cans chickpeas, drained and rinsed

4 TB. fresh lemon juice

1 cup fine dry bread crumbs

2 TB. grapeseed oil

1 medium cucumber, peeled, seeded, and cut into ¼-inch dice

½ small red onion, finely chopped

1 red bell pepper, cut into ¼-inch dice

2 plum tomatoes, halved, seeded, and cut into ¼-inch dice

¼ cup Italian parsley, finely chopped

6 whole-wheat pita loaves

1. Preheat oven to 375°F. Heat olive oil over medium-high heat in a medium sauté pan. Add onions and cumin. Sauté, stirring often, until softened and golden. Add cinnamon, and season with salt and pepper. Stir in kale and cook for 10 minutes, stirring occasionally. Remove from heat.

2. In a food processor fitted with the metal blade attachment, purée chickpeas with kale and onion mixture and 2 tablespoons lemon juice. Stir bread crumbs in by hand.

3. Use an ice-cream scoop or your hands to form eight equal patties, flattening with your hand to about 3 inches.

4. Heat grapeseed oil in a large nonstick skillet. Sauté burgers in hot oil, turning once, about 3 minutes per side. Place in oven on a parchment-lined sheet pan for 10 minutes.

5. Gently combine cucumber, red onion, bell pepper, tomato, parsley, and 2 table-spoons lemon juice. Split pita, and serve two falafel burgers and ¼ of Israeli salad for each sandwich.

> **THE LOWDOWN**
>
> If you can find fresh fava beans at your supermarket, try making a more traditional falafel. Fava beans are time-consuming to peel, but the flavor is incomparable. First, remove fava beans from the pod by snapping off the end of the bean, then pulling the "string" along the seam to release the beans. Steam the beans over boiling water for 1 to 2 minutes, then transfer to a bowl of ice water. Pop each fava bean out of its inner skin, and cook in boiling, salted water until tender.

Ⓥ Millet, Lentil, and Kale Loaf

This hearty vegan "meatloaf" is filled with tender vegetables, protein-packed lentils, millet, and herbs. Serve it with mashed potatoes and sautéed mushrooms, or on a sandwich with plenty of ketchup.

Yield:	Serving size:	Prep time:	Cook time:
1 8-inch loaf	¼ of loaf	20 minutes	45 minutes

2 TB. extra-virgin olive oil	1 cup brown lentils
1 medium yellow onion, finely chopped	2 cups vegetable stock
½ cup carrot, finely chopped	1 cup cooked millet
½ cup celery, finely chopped	½ cup walnuts, finely chopped
1 TB. fresh sage, finely chopped	½ tsp. kosher salt
1 tsp. fresh thyme, finely chopped	½ tsp. freshly ground black pepper
1 bunch curly kale, stems removed, roughly chopped	2 TB. fine cornmeal

1. Preheat oven to 375°F. Heat olive oil over medium-high heat in a medium saucepan. Add onion, carrot, and celery. Cook until softened, about 5 minutes. Stir in sage and thyme, and cook 2 minutes more. Stir in kale and cook for 5 minutes. Add lentils and vegetable stock, bring to a boil, cover, and reduce heat to low. Cook until lentils are tender and most of the stock has been absorbed, about 20 minutes.

2. Stir millet, walnuts, salt, and pepper into lentil mixture. Oil an 8-inch loaf pan, and sprinkle with cornmeal. Press lentil mixture gently into pan, cover with foil, and bake for 45 minutes. Allow loaf to rest for 10 minutes before slicing.

HEADS UP!

Depending on the kind of loaf pan you use, you may need to adjust your oven temperature. Glass and nonstick pans conduct heat more effectively than shiny aluminum pans, so you may wish to lower the oven temperature by 25°F if you find that foods or baked goods cook too quickly at your recipe's recommended temperature.

Deep-Dish Cabbage and Pierogi Pie

All of your favorite pierogi fillings, plus a flaky pie crust, make this a dish worth sharing.

Yield:	Serving size:	Prep time:	Cook time:
1 9-inch deep-dish pie	⅛ of pie	30 minutes	50 minutes

1 small head green cabbage, shredded

2 TB. plus 1 tsp. kosher salt

¼ cup unsalted butter

2 cloves garlic, thinly sliced

½ tsp. freshly ground black pepper

4 cups mashed potatoes with caramelized onions (see Chapter 16)

1/2 cup cream cheese

1 recipe pie pastry for a double-crust pie (see Chapter 16)

1 large egg, beaten

1. Preheat oven to 400°F. Place shredded cabbage in a large colander in your sink, and toss with 2 tablespoons kosher salt. Rub salt into cabbage with your hands, and drain for 20 minutes. Rinse and squeeze dry.

2. Heat butter in a large sauté pan over medium-high heat. When butter is sizzling, add cabbage and 1 teaspoon salt. Cook, stirring frequently, until cabbage is tender, about 15 minutes. Remove from heat and stir in black pepper.

3. In a large mixing bowl, use a rubber spatula to combine cabbage with mashed potatoes and cream cheese.

4. Butter a deep-dish pie pan. On a well-floured surface, roll one pastry dough round to a large circle. Fit carefully into pie dish, leaving a 1-inch overhang. Fill pie pastry with potato-cabbage mixture. Roll second dough round to a slightly smaller circle. Fit round over pie, pinch and crimp to seal edges, and use a sharp knife to cut 2-inch steam holes in five even spaces around pie.

5. Brush pie crust with egg wash and bake for 50 minutes, or until crust is golden brown. Serve hot or at room temperature.

MAKE IT VEGAN

Replace butter with extra-virgin olive oil, and use tofu cream cheese. Brush pie pastry with soy milk, and bake as directed.

Ⓡ Ⓥ Spinach and Almond Pesto with Zucchini "Noodles"

Tender young zucchini are sliced into ribbons and tossed with a raw spinach and almond pesto in this healthful take on a fattening classic.

Yield:	Serving size:	Prep time:	Cook time:
8 cups	2 cups	15 minutes	None

8 small, young zucchini

1 tsp. kosher salt

6 cups baby spinach leaves

1 TB. fresh lemon juice

1 TB. raw, unfiltered, cold-pressed olive oil

1 clove garlic, smashed and finely chopped

1 cup raw almonds, soaked in warm water for 10 minutes

2 TB. nutritional yeast

1 TB. Bragg Liquid Aminos

1. Using a mandoline or a vegetable peeler, slice zucchini into thin, lengthwise strips. Place in a colander in your sink with kosher salt, and toss gently to combine. Allow zucchini to release its liquid for 5 minutes, then rinse and drain.

2. Combine baby spinach, lemon juice, olive oil, garlic, soaked almonds, nutritional yeast, and liquid aminos in a food processor fitted with a metal blade. Process in pulses until smooth. Toss with drained zucchini and serve immediately.

Sides and Extras

Greens are the perfect complement to any meal. Part 6 brings you terrific side dishes, a wealth of pickling know-how, and the tools to make every meal homemade. If you need more information on how to make a truly memorable homemade meal, Chapter 16 will give you the tools to start from scratch with easy recipes and techniques that will add "wow" to your cooking.

Side Dishes

In This Chapter

- Sensational side dishes
- Crunchy coleslaws
- Sautés, braises, and gratins

Side dishes make the meal. You can serve all of these delicious dishes on the side, on their own as a light lunch, or grouped together to form a fun and different meal.

Vegetable gratins are excellent for a hearty winter supper, and are always a hit at pot-luck events. We'll travel the globe with sautés, braises, and cheesy greens from many countries. And, of course, we can't forget the coleslaw!

ⓥ Sweet and Sour Red Cabbage

The sweetness of apples and brown sugar is a delicious counterpoint to the tartness of cider vinegar in this warm and wintery pot of red cabbage.

Yield:	Serving size:	Prep time:	Cook time:
4 cups	½ cup	10 minutes	30 minutes

1 TB. extra-virgin olive oil

1 medium red onion, halved and thinly sliced

1 tart apple, peeled, halved, and thinly sliced (such as Granny Smith)

2 TB. light brown sugar

1 cup apple juice

¼ cup apple cider vinegar

1 (2-lb.) red cabbage, halved, cored, and cut into ½-inch chunks

1 TB. kosher salt, or to taste

½ tsp. freshly ground black pepper

1. Heat olive oil in a nonreactive Dutch oven with a tight-fitting lid. Add onion and apple slices, and cook, stirring frequently, for 5 minutes, or until onion is soft and translucent.

2. Add brown sugar, apple juice, apple cider vinegar, red cabbage, salt, and pepper. Bring to a boil, then reduce heat to a simmer. Cover and cook, stirring occasionally, until cabbage is tender. Serve hot or at room temperature.

THE LOWDOWN

A medium head of cabbage weighs about 2 pounds. If using raw, it will yield about 10 cups of cabbage. Once cooked, that 10 cups will reduce to about 4 cups. Plan on ½ cup of cooked cabbage, or 1 cup raw cabbage, per serving.

Red cabbage.

Ⓥ Tuscan Kale and Radicchio with Pickled Onions

This quick sauté of Tuscan kale and radicchio is enlivened with a last-minute addition of quick-pickled red onion slices.

Yield:	Serving size:	Prep time:	Cook time:
4 cups	1 cup	10 minutes	10 minutes

¼ cup red wine vinegar

2 TB. sugar

1½ tsp. kosher salt

1 large red onion, halved and thinly sliced

2 TB. extra-virgin olive oil

2 cloves garlic, thinly sliced

1 large bunch Tuscan (lacinato) kale, tough stems trimmed, thinly sliced

2 heads radicchio, halved, cored, and thinly sliced

½ tsp. freshly ground black pepper

1. Stir vinegar, sugar, and 1 teaspoon kosher salt in a small saucepan, and bring to a boil. Place red onion slices in a small, heatproof bowl, and pour vinegar mixture over. Mix well and set aside.

2. Heat olive oil in a medium sauté pan over medium-high heat. Add garlic and cook, stirring constantly, until golden and fragrant. Add kale, radicchio, remaining ½ teaspoon salt, and pepper. Cook, stirring often, until tender, about 7 minutes. Remove from heat.

3. Drain onions, discarding vinegar mixture. Stir pickled onions into warm kale and radicchio. Serve warm or at room temperature.

THE LOWDOWN

Radicchio has been cultivated in the Veneto and Trentino regions of northern Italy since the fifteenth century, and many varieties are named after the regions in which they are grown. You will find Chioggia, a round variety, and Treviso, which has an elongated head and resembles Belgian endive, in many grocery stores. If you'd like to try more exotic varieties, seek out heirloom Italian seeds, or visit your local farmers market to look for varieties such as Tardivo and Castelfranco, winter radicchio that resemble flowers, as well as other regional radicchio such as Trieste or Gorizia.

Potato and Kale Gratin

This cheesy potato casserole is studded with chunks of tender, garlicky kale.

Yield:	Serving size:	Prep time:	Cook time:
1 8-inch casserole	⅙ of casserole	20 minutes	30 minutes

5 TB. unsalted butter

2 cloves garlic, smashed and finely chopped

1 large bunch Tuscan kale, leaves only, roughly chopped

2 lbs. Yukon Gold or red potatoes, sliced very thin (⅛ inch)

2 cups half-and-half

⅛ tsp. freshly grated nutmeg

1 tsp. kosher salt

½ tsp. freshly ground black pepper

1 cup grated smoked Gouda cheese

1 cup grated Parmesan cheese

1. Preheat oven to 400°F. Rub an 8-inch baking dish with 1 tablespoon butter.

2. Heat remaining 4 tablespoons butter over medium heat in a large saucepan. Add garlic and cook, stirring frequently, for 2 minutes. Add kale and cook for 5 minutes more. Add potatoes, half-and-half, nutmeg, salt, and black pepper. Stirring constantly and carefully, bring mixture to a boil over medium-high heat, and cook for 10 minutes. Gently stir in smoked Gouda.

3. Pour potato mixture into prepared baking dish, top with grated Parmesan, and bake for 30 minutes. Allow casserole to rest for 10 minutes before serving.

HEADS UP!

Be sure to use a firm, somewhat waxy potato for this gratin. A baking potato, such as russet, is not a good choice, as it will fall apart during the cooking process. Slice potatoes carefully using a mandoline or a food processor. If slicing with a knife, take your time, and make the slices as thin and even as possible.

Spinach *Gratin*

Spinach is satisfying and savory when enriched with plenty of Gruyére, onions, cream, butter, and a hint of nutmeg in this cheesy French classic. This is definitely a special occasion calorie splurge!

Yield:	Serving size:	Prep time:	Cook time:
1 8-inch casserole	⅙ of casserole	20 minutes	30 minutes

4 TB. unsalted butter

1 medium yellow onion, finely chopped

5 lbs. tender young spinach, tough stems removed

1 tsp. kosher salt

2 cups heavy cream

⅛ tsp. freshly grated nutmeg

½ tsp. freshly ground black pepper

2 cups grated Gruyére cheese

½ cup panko bread crumbs

1. Preheat oven to 400°F. Rub an 8-inch baking dish with 1 tablespoon butter.

2. Heat 2 tablespoons butter in a large sauté pan over medium-high heat. Add onion and cook, stirring frequently, until onion is very soft and golden in color, about 8 minutes. Add spinach and salt, and increase heat to high. Stir until spinach is wilted and liquid has evaporated, about 5 minutes.

3. Add cream, nutmeg, and pepper to spinach mixture. Bring to a boil, then reduce heat to medium and cook for 5 minutes, or until slightly thickened. Stir in 1½ cups Gruyére, and immediately remove from heat.

4. Melt 1 tablespoon butter, and combine with panko and remaining ½ cup Gruyére. Pour spinach mixture into prepared baking dish, top with bread-crumb mixture, and bake for 30 minutes, or until golden and bubbly. Serve immediately.

Make it ahead: This recipe can be prepared through step 3 up to 2 days in advance. When ready to bake, prepare bread-crumb mixture and proceed as directed.

DEFINITION

A **gratin** is a dish that is topped with seasoned bread crumbs and/or cheese, and baked in the oven. The word "gratin" can also refer to the baking dish used to make gratinéed dishes, which is a shallow oval pan with handles at each end. If you don't have one of these dishes, a simple square or round 8-inch casserole dish works just fine.

Rainbow Chard with Olives, Pine Nuts, and Raisins

Sautéed Swiss chard gets a sweet and salty kick when studded with kalamata olives, toasted pine nuts, and chewy golden raisins. Enjoy as a side dish, or spread on bruschetta for a tasty appetizer.

Yield:	Serving size:	Prep time:	Cook time:
4 cups	1 cup	10 minutes	10 minutes

¼ cup pine nuts

2 TB. golden raisins

2 TB. extra-virgin olive oil

2 cloves garlic, thinly sliced

3 large bunches rainbow chard, tough ends of stems trimmed, chiffonade cut

¼ tsp. kosher salt

½ tsp. freshly ground black pepper

¼ cup pitted kalamata olives, thinly sliced

1. Heat a small sauté pan (don't use nonstick) over medium heat. Add pine nuts and toast, stirring almost constantly, until golden brown. Remove from heat and set aside.

2. Place raisins in a small, heatproof bowl, and cover with boiling water. Soak for 5 minutes, and drain.

3. Heat olive oil in a large sauté pan over medium-high heat. Add garlic and cook, stirring frequently, for 2 minutes. Add rainbow chard and salt, and continue to cook, stirring frequently, until chard is tender, about 7 minutes. Stir in black pepper, olives, pine nuts, and raisins. Serve hot or at room temperature.

Make it ahead: This recipe can be prepared through step 3 and stored in refrigerator for up to 2 days. Reheat gently when ready to serve, or just bring to room temperature.

> **HEADS UP!**
>
> Watch out for "pine mouth"! Some people experience a tingling, unpleasant, metallic sensation that can last for several days or even weeks after eating pine nuts. Recent research ties this "pine nut syndrome" to a particular species of pine nut grown in China. It is not yet known whether this species has a particular compound that causes this syndrome, or if the effect is caused by chemicals used in the shelling process. The FDA is currently researching this issue. Meanwhile, seek out pine nuts grown in the United States or Europe for their superior flavor and texture, minus the pine mouth effect.

Ⓥ Braised Brussels Sprouts with Toasted Pecans and Cranberries

Brighten your holiday season with this flavorful side dish. Fresh Brussels sprouts are braised in a sweet, flavorful stock and finished with tangy cranberries and toasted pecans.

Yield:	Serving size:	Prep time:	Cook time:
4 cups	1 cup	10 minutes	30 minutes

¼ cup pecans, roughly chopped

2 TB. extra-virgin olive oil

3 medium shallots, halved and thinly sliced

2 cloves garlic, thinly sliced

1½ lbs. Brussels sprouts, trimmed and halved

¼ cup dry white wine, such as sauvignon blanc

1 cup vegetable stock

1 TB. sugar

2 TB. dried cranberries

½ tsp. kosher salt

½ tsp. freshly ground black pepper

1. Heat a small sauté pan (don't use nonstick) over medium heat. Add pecans and toast, stirring almost constantly, until fragrant and golden, about 5 minutes. Remove from heat and set aside.

2. Heat olive oil in a large saucepan over medium-high heat. Add shallots and cook, stirring frequently, until softened, about 5 minutes. Add garlic and cook 2 minutes more, stirring often. Add Brussels sprouts and continue to cook until lightly browned, about 3 minutes.

3. Pour wine and vegetable stock over Brussels sprouts, and stir well to incorporate any brown bits *(fond)* at the bottom of the pan. Stir in sugar, cranberries, salt, and black pepper, and bring to a boil. Reduce heat to a simmer, and cook, covered, stirring occasionally, until Brussels sprouts are tender, about 20 minutes.

4. Remove Brussels sprouts to a serving dish, top with pecans, and serve immediately.

Variation: For **Dijon-Glazed Brussels Sprouts,** eliminate cranberries and pecans. When Brussels sprouts are tender, remove from cooking liquid with a slotted spoon. Increase heat to high, and whisk in 2 tablespoons Dijon mustard. When liquid has reduced to a thick sauce, return Brussels sprouts to pan and cook 2 minutes more. Serve immediately.

DEFINITION

The browned bits stuck to the bottom of the pan in this recipe are called the **fond,** and the method of scraping them up with boiling liquid is called deglazing. The word "fond" is French, meaning base or foundation, but it also means stock—a *fond vegetale* is vegetable stock.

Ⓥ Broccoli Aglio e Olio

This simple Italian preparation combines blanched broccoli with flavorful garlic and extra-virgin olive oil. Serve it as is, warm from the pan, or toss with spaghetti for a quick lunch or dinner.

Yield:	Serving size:	Prep time:	Cook time:
6 cups	1½ cups	10 minutes	15 minutes

1 large head fresh broccoli

2 TB. extra-virgin olive oil

2 cloves garlic, thinly sliced

½ tsp. kosher salt

¼ tsp. freshly ground black pepper

1. Trim tough end from broccoli stem. Separate florets and set aside. Peel stem and slice into ¼-inch rounds.

2. Bring a pot of salted water to a boil, and blanch broccoli and stems for 3 minutes. Cool quickly in ice bath, drain, and set aside.

3. Heat olive oil in a large sauté pan over medium heat. Cook garlic, stirring frequently, until golden, about 3 minutes. Add broccoli and salt, and cook until tender, stirring frequently, about 5 minutes more. Season with black pepper. Serve hot or at room temperature.

THE LOWDOWN

Broccoli is in season from October until April. Look for bright, fresh greens with tight buds and a moist stem. Do not use broccoli that has begun to flower—it will be bitter and past its prime. This simple preparation is also excellent with broccoli rabe, cauliflower, or hybrids such as "caulibroc" and purple cauliflower. Experiment with what you find at your local market, and you'll enjoy a seasonal variety of simply prepared greens throughout the winter season!

Ⓥ Spinach and Black-Eyed Peas with Caramelized Onions

This simple spinach dish is common in Lebanese kitchens. Serve it as a side dish, or mix a finely chopped clove of garlic and a few drops of lemon juice into some Greek yogurt and serve with warm pita bread for a light lunch or snack.

Yield:	Serving size:	Prep time:	Cook time:
4 cups	1 cup	10 minutes	25 minutes

2 TB. extra-virgin olive oil

2 medium yellow onions, halved and thinly sliced

2½ lbs. baby spinach, rinsed and drained in a large colander

½ tsp. kosher salt

½ tsp. freshly ground black pepper

1 (14-oz.) can black-eyed peas, rinsed and drained

1 TB. fresh lemon juice

1. Heat olive oil in a large sauté pan over medium-high heat. Add onions, stir to combine, and reduce heat to low. Cook, stirring occasionally, until onions are caramelized and dark golden brown, about 20 minutes.

2. Increase heat to medium high, and add spinach and salt. Cook until water clinging to spinach leaves has evaporated and spinach is tender, about 4 minutes.

3. Stir in black pepper, black-eyed peas, and lemon juice, and heat thoroughly, about 1 minute more. Remove from heat, and serve warm or at room temperature.

HEADS UP!

When caramelizing onions, keep the heat low, and don't stir too frequently. Some recipes suggest adding a bit of sugar to the pan and cooking at a slightly higher heat, and this will work if you're in a big hurry. It's worth it to take your time, though, as there is really no substitute for the sweet and savory flavor and melt-in-your-mouth texture of onions caramelized slowly in a little fat.

Ⓥ Amaranth Greens with Poblanos and Pepitas

Savory sautéed amaranth greens are spiced up with roasted poblano chiles and crunchy toasted pumpkin seeds. Serve as a side dish, or use as a filling for burritos, enchiladas, or quesadillas.

Yield:	Serving size:	Prep time:	Cook time:
4 cups	1 cup	10 minutes	10 minutes

½ cup hulled pumpkin seeds (pepitas)

2 large poblano chiles

2 TB. extra-virgin olive oil

2 cloves garlic, thinly sliced

3 large bunches (about 3 lbs.) tender young amaranth greens

½ tsp. kosher salt, or to taste

¼ tsp. freshly ground black pepper

1. Heat a small sauté pan (don't use nonstick) over medium heat. Add pumpkin seeds, and toast, stirring almost constantly, until fragrant and golden, about 5 minutes. Remove from heat and set aside.

2. Place poblano chiles under a broiler, or directly over a gas flame, and roast, turning frequently, until charred all over. Place in a small bowl, and cover with plastic wrap for 5 minutes. Carefully remove plastic wrap, and rub skin from peppers using a paper towel. Remove stem and seeds, and cut chile into thin strips. Set aside.

3. Heat olive oil in a large sauté pan over medium-high heat. Add garlic and cook, stirring frequently, until golden, about 2 minutes. Add amaranth, salt, and black pepper and cook until tender, stirring frequently, about 4 minutes more. Stir in poblano chile strips and toasted pepitas. Serve hot or at room temperature.

THE LOWDOWN

Pumpkin seeds, also known as pepitas, will plump up and pop in the pan as they are toasted. Stir frequently and carefully, and remove as soon as they are plump and golden. Toasted pepitas can be cooled to room temperature and stored for up to 2 weeks in an airtight glass jar. Store raw pepitas, and other infrequently used nuts and seeds, in the freezer in a tightly sealed container to keep them fresh.

ⓥ Roasted Radicchio and Belgian Endive

Seek out Treviso radicchio, which is similar in shape to Belgian endive, for this simple dish of roasted greens with a hint of garlic and sweet balsamic vinegar.

Yield:	Serving size:	Prep time:	Cook time:
8 cups	1 cup	15 minutes	15–20 minutes

3 TB. extra-virgin olive oil

2 cloves garlic, smashed and finely chopped

1 TB. balsamic vinegar

2 heads Treviso radicchio, trimmed and cut into 1-inch wedges

2 heads Belgian endive, trimmed and cut into 1-inch wedges

¼ tsp. kosher salt

¼ tsp. freshly ground black pepper

1. Preheat oven to 425°F. Stir olive oil, garlic, and balsamic vinegar together in a small bowl, and set aside for 15 minutes.

2. Toss radicchio and endive wedges with olive oil mixture, and season with salt and pepper. Spread on a rimmed baking sheet lined with parchment paper, and roast until tender, about 15 to 20 minutes. Serve hot or at room temperature.

THE LOWDOWN

This simple roasting method can be used for any vegetable you like. Browse the farmers market, and choose a mixture of seasonal veggies such as potatoes, broccoli, sweet potatoes, cauliflower, carrots, parsnips, celery root, cabbage, or whatever strikes your fancy. Roast hardier root vegetables for 15 minutes before adding your greens, and continue to cook until tender. Enjoy!

Ⓥ Roasted Broccoli with Garlic, Lemon, and Almonds

Broccoli becomes sweet and tender when roasted. Combined with toasty almonds and savory garlic, then finished with lemon juice, this quick and snappy side will soon become a favorite.

Yield:	Serving size:	Prep time:	Cook time:
8 cups	1 cup	10 minutes	None

3 TB. extra-virgin olive oil

2 cloves garlic, smashed and finely chopped

2 large bunches broccoli

½ tsp. kosher salt

¼ tsp. freshly ground black pepper

½ cup *blanched*, sliced almonds

1 TB. fresh lemon juice

1. Preheat oven to 425°F. Combine olive oil and garlic. Set aside for 10 minutes while you prepare the broccoli.

2. Trim tough end from broccoli stem. Separate florets, and set aside. Peel stem and slice into ¼-inch rounds. Toss broccoli with garlic mixture on a large rimmed sheet pan lined with parchment paper, and season with salt and pepper.

3. Roast broccoli for 15 minutes, stirring once. Add almonds, and roast for 5 minutes more, or until broccoli is tender and almond slices are lightly toasted. Remove from oven and toss gently with lemon juice. Serve hot or at room temperature.

DEFINITION

Blanched almonds are almonds that have been peeled and sliced, either in strips or thin slices. They can be found in the nut aisle of your grocery store. To blanch your own almonds, place raw almonds in a bowl, cover with boiling water, and let stand for 1 minute. Drain, then rinse and rub skins away. Be sure to drain almonds after 1 minute, as they will lose their texture if allowed to soak for too long. Chop blanched almonds as desired, and use immediately.

Ⓥ Ginger-Garlic Tastoi with Edamame

Tatsoi, or spoon lettuce, is quickly wilted in a warm ginger-garlic dressing, and tossed with edamame in this flavorful, protein-packed side dish.

Yield:	Serving size:	Prep time:	Cook time:
8 cups	2 cups	10 minutes	5 minutes

2 cups frozen, peeled edamame

1 TB. safflower oil

2 cloves garlic

1 TB. freshly grated ginger

1 tsp. Dijon mustard

1 TB. low-sodium soy sauce

12 cups tatsoi

1 tsp. light sesame oil

1. Defrost edamame according to package directions. Set aside.

2. Heat safflower oil in a medium sauté pan over medium-high heat. Add garlic and ginger, and cook for 1 minute, stirring constantly. Add Dijon mustard, soy sauce, and tatsoi, and cook, stirring frequently, until tatsoi is wilted. Stir in edamame and sesame oil, and serve immediately.

Tatsoi.

HEADS UP!

Be sure to look for organic edamame. Buying organic is the only way to avoid genetically modified (GMO) soy. While the full effects of GMO soy products will not be understood for generations to come, studies have linked allergies, liver problems, reproductive issues, and other serious health problems to the consumption of GMO soy.

Ⓥ Southern-Style Turnips and Greens

Earthy turnips are braised with onions, smoked paprika, and turnip greens in this vegan twist on a Southern staple.

Yield:	Serving size:	Prep time:	Cook time:
8 cups	2 cups	15 minutes	25 minutes

3 large turnips with greens attached

¼ cup extra-virgin olive oil

1 medium yellow onion, finely chopped

2 cloves garlic, smashed and finely chopped

1 tsp. smoked paprika

1 tsp. kosher salt

½ tsp. sugar

½ tsp. freshly ground black pepper

1. Separate greens from turnips. Scrub and peel turnips, and cut into ½-inch dice. Wash and roughly chop greens. Set aside.

2. Heat olive oil in a large saucepan. Add onion and cook until softened, about 5 minutes. Add garlic and smoked paprika, and cook 1 minute more. Add turnips, turnip greens, salt, and sugar, along with enough water to just cover. Bring to a boil, reduce to a simmer, and cook until turnips are tender, about 15 to 20 minutes. Season with black pepper and serve immediately.

HEADS UP!

Turnips, along with their cousin rutabaga, contain compounds called cyanoglucosides, which taste bitter and release very small, harmless amounts of cyanide. Some people have a genetically predisposed sensitivity to this compound—those who have two sensitive genes will find turnips twice as bitter as those who do not carry this gene.

Ⓥ Turnip and Mustard Greens Poriyal

Turnip and mustard greens are sautéed with curry spices and coconut in this spicy Indian side dish.

Yield:	Serving size:	Prep time:	Cook time:
4 cups	1 cup	5 minutes	15 minutes

2 TB. unfiltered coconut oil

½ tsp. black mustard seeds

1 large yellow onion, finely chopped

¼ tsp. crushed red pepper flakes

1 tsp. curry powder

¼ tsp. turmeric

2 cloves garlic, smashed and finely chopped

2 TB. unsweetened dried coconut

1 large bunch turnip greens, chopped into small pieces

2 large bunches mustard greens, chopped into small pieces

1. Heat coconut oil in a large sauté pan over medium-high heat. Add mustard seeds and stir until they pop. Add onion, crushed red pepper, curry powder, turmeric, and garlic, and cook for 5 minutes, stirring frequently.

2. Add coconut, turnip greens, and mustard greens to onion mixture, reduce heat to medium, and cook, stirring frequently, for 10 minutes. Serve immediately.

THE LOWDOWN

Poriyal is considered a "dry curry" in Indian cooking, as it is cooked in very little liquid, which allows the spices to coat the food with minimal sauce. Serve dry curries with Indian flatbreads such as naan, along with yogurt and *dal*, a spiced Lentil stew, for a delicious vegetarian meal.

Roasted Garlic and Kale Mashed Potatoes

Chunky mashed potatoes are studded with roasted garlic and sautéed kale for a different take on a comfort-food classic.

Yield:	Serving size:	Prep time:	Cook time:
4 cups	1 cup	10 minutes	25 minutes

4 large Yukon gold potatoes, peeled and cut into 1-inch dice

1 1/2 tsp. kosher salt, or to taste

1 large bunch curly kale, leaves only, torn into small pieces

1 cup whole milk

3 heads roasted garlic (see Chapter 16)

4 TB. unsalted butter

½ tsp. freshly ground black pepper

1. Place potatoes and 1 teaspoon salt in a large saucepan with water to cover by 1 inch. Bring to a boil, then reduce heat and simmer until potatoes are nearly tender, about 10 minutes. Add kale, and continue to cook until kale is tender and potatoes are easily pierced with a fork, about 5 minutes more.

2. Drain potatoes, and return to warm saucepan.

3. In a small saucepan over medium heat, combine milk, roasted garlic, and butter. Cook, stirring constantly, until butter has melted. Use a potato masher to incorporate the milk mixture into the potatoes. Mash to desired consistency, season with remaining salt and pepper, and serve immediately.

Variations: For **Wasabi Scallion Potatoes,** add 1 tablespoon wasabi powder to roasted garlic mixture, and stir in 1 cup scallions before serving. For **Curried Mashed Potatoes,** add 1 tablespoon curry powder to roasted garlic mixture. For **Broccoli Cheddar Potatoes,** replace kale with one bunch broccoli, separated into florets (reserve stems for another use), and add 1 cup cheddar cheese when mashing potatoes and garlic mixture.

If you prefer smoother mashed potatoes, cook potatoes and kale separately, and run cooked potatoes through a ricer, which presses the potatoes into small pieces that resemble rice for a perfectly smooth consistency. Stir kale in with roasted garlic mixture.

MAKE IT VEGAN

For a delicious vegan mashed potato, replace milk with rice milk, and use olive oil in place of butter. For extra flavor, add 1 tablespoon nutritional yeast flakes to roasted garlic mixture.

Ⓥ Ⓡ Sesame Ginger Collard Greens

Collard greens are "uncooked" in a savory mixture of garlic, ginger, and sesame oil for a spicy and delicious raw side dish.

Yield:	Serving size:	Prep time:	Cook time:
6 cups	1 cup	20 minutes	None

1 large bunch of collard greens, tough stems removed, thinly sliced

1 TB. freshly grated ginger

1 clove garlic, smashed and finely chopped

2 TB. Bragg Liquid Aminos

1 TB. dark sesame oil

1. Place collard greens in a large bowl. Use your hands to rub ginger, garlic, liquid aminos, and sesame oil into collards.

2. Place in refrigerator for at least 15 minutes. Serve immediately, or refrigerate for up to 6 hours.

THE LOWDOWN

Rubbing the dressing ingredients into the collard greens will help to tenderize and reduce them without cooking, making them tender and easily digestible. The longer you refrigerate them, the more flavorful they will be.

Ⓥ Ⓡ Asian Broccoli Slaw

Broccoli stems are shredded and tossed with carrots and ginger in this crunchy slaw.

Yield:	Serving size:	Prep time:	Cook time:
6 cups	1 cup	15 minutes plus 2 hours refrigeration	None

5 cups shredded broccoli stems (from about 3 large bunches broccoli)

1 cup shredded carrots

1 TB. freshly grated ginger

½ small red onion, halved and thinly sliced

2 TB. apple cider vinegar

2 TB. low sodium *tamari*

2 TB. light sesame oil

1. Combine broccoli stems, carrots, ginger, red onion, cider vinegar, tamari, and sesame oil in a large bowl. Toss well to combine.

2. Refrigerate for 2-4 hours, and serve.

DEFINITION

While **tamari** and soy sauce are both made from fermented soybeans, soy sauce is made with fermented wheat. Those on a low-allergen or gluten-free diet should use tamari, which is usually wheat-free (read the label to be sure!) and has a richer, more complex flavor than traditional soy sauce.

Spicy Tricolor Slaw

Crispy red and green cabbage mix with carrots in a chipotle buttermilk dressing for a deliciously spicy coleslaw with a kick.

Yield:	Serving size:	Prep time:	Cook time:
12 cups	1 cup	15 minutes plus 2 hours refrigeration	None

5 cups shredded green cabbage (from about ½ medium head)

5 cups shredded red cabbage (from about ½ medium head)

2 cups shredded carrot

1 tsp. kosher salt

2 TB. apple cider vinegar

1 TB. fresh lime juice

½ cup buttermilk

2 TB. extra-virgin olive oil

1 canned chipotle chile

1 TB. adobo sauce (from canned chiles)

½ tsp. freshly ground black pepper

1. Combine shredded green and red cabbage, carrots, and salt in a large colander. Toss gently, and drain for 10 minutes.

2. Meanwhile, process apple cider vinegar, lime juice, buttermilk, olive oil, chipotle chile, adobo sauce, and black pepper in blender until smooth.

3. Toss cabbage mixture and dressing in a large bowl. Cover and refrigerate for 2 hours. Serve well chilled.

Classic Coleslaw

This is an American classic—cabbage, red onion, and carrots in a vinegary dressing. Serve at picnics, parties, and barbecues for rave reviews!

Yield:	Serving size:	Prep time:	Cook time:
2 cups	1 cup	15 minutes plus 2 hours refrigeration	None

10 cups shredded green cabbage (from 1 medium head)

1 red onion, halved and thinly sliced

2 cups shredded carrot

½ cup sugar

1 tsp. kosher salt

½ tsp. celery seed

1 tsp. dry mustard

½ tsp. crushed caraway seeds

½ tsp. freshly ground black pepper

½ cup apple cider vinegar

½ cup grapeseed oil

1. Combine shredded green cabbage, red onion, and carrot in a large bowl.

2. In a small bowl, whisk sugar, salt, celery seed, dry mustard, caraway seeds, black pepper, and cider vinegar until well combined. Drizzle in grapeseed oil.

3. Pour dressing over coleslaw, and refrigerate until well chilled.

HEADS UP!

Eating raw cabbage offers tremendous health benefits, but sulphurous compounds in cruciferous vegetables cause intestinal distress for some. Try increasing your intake of raw cabbage gradually, and add a probiotic supplement if you find it troublesome. If you really can't digest it without discomfort, consider quickly blanching your cabbage in boiling water, then chilling in an ice bath. You'll miss the crunch, but keep most of the vitamin and antioxidant power!

Pickle It!

In This Chapter

- Pickling basics
- Quick pickles
- Fermentation 101

If it's a fruit or vegetable, chances are you can pickle it. Greens take particularly well to pickling, as evidenced by the proliferation of pickled cabbage recipes that span many cultures. But cabbage is not the only green you can pickle. Read on to experience pickles made from turnip and mustard greens, collards, radicchio, Brussels sprouts, and even broccoli stems.

All Around the World

Pickles have been on our tables for over 4,000 years. Both an art and science, pickling preserves food using acid and/or salt, while adding flavor, crunch, and savor to our meals.

The practice of preserving foods by pickling has been documented in Mesopotamia beginning around 2,500 B.C.E. Indian culture boasts the widest variety of pickles, with chutneys and *achar* (the Hindi and Punjab word for pickle) served at every meal. Indian cooks mix ginger, garlic, chiles, salt, and spices with fruits and vegetables to produce a dazzling array of fiery and sweet condiments.

Pickling is practiced by nearly every culture throughout the world. Many people think of pickles as just cucumbers in brine, but nearly any fruit or vegetable can be pickled! Pickling once ensured that fruits and vegetables were on the table throughout the long winter months. In eastern Europe, sauerkraut is only the beginning. Root vegetables, fruits, carrots, celery, mushrooms, and even pumpkins are pickled. Middle Eastern cultures offer pickled turnips, olives, and puckery and delicious preserved lemons. Asian culture offers us Japanese *tsukemono*, Chinese *bacai*, Indonesian *acar*, and Korean *kimchi*. Brits and Americans enjoy a melting pot of pickles, remnants of British Imperial culture and the American immigrant experience.

There are several methods of pickle making. Beginners will want to start with a quick pickle. To make quick pickles, fruits or vegetables are soaked in a flavored vinegar brine, and eaten within a few days. Chutneys and relishes are also easy to prepare; chopped fruits or vegetables are cooked in a spicy vinegar solution.

Fresh pack pickles are quick pickles that are covered in a hot brine, then preserved in a boiling water canner. It's important to observe proper food safety procedures when putting food up for long-term storage. Be sure to follow instructions carefully and sterilize your equipment.

Once you have a little experience under your belt, graduate to *fermented* pickles. To ferment pickles, fruits or vegetables are prepared in a brine of vinegar and salt, then fermented at room temperature for a period of several days. It's extremely important to understand the practices and pitfalls of fermentation, which occurs under very specific conditions, so follow instructions closely, and do not make changes to recipes.

DEFINITION

Fermentation is a curing process that produces lactic acid, which helps to preserve food. Food is placed in a brine, or curing solution, for one or more weeks. This process changes the flavor and texture of the food, kills bacteria and other spoilers, and preserves it for long-tem storage.

To Your Health

Lactic-acid-fermented pickles such as *kimchi* and sauerkraut offer significant health benefits. Live cultures and enzymes produced during the fermentation process support healthy digestion and immune function, help the body to absorb protein and iron, and stimulates cell metabolism.

Regular consumption of fermented foods reduces symptoms of asthma, skin problems, and autoimmune disorders. While studies have shown that fermented pickles inhibit the growth of certain cancers, a few others have linked unusual rates of esophageal and gastric cancers in China and Korea to these cultures' traditionally high consumption of fermented vegetables. While the World Health Organization has listed fermented pickles as a "possible carcinogen," it's important to remember that the population groups used in these studies rely extensively on pickled vegetables for nutrition. To date, no studies have shown a cancer risk from moderate intake of fermented vegetables that would outweigh the health benefits.

Fresh as a ... Pickle?

When pickling, as with any food preservation method, freshness counts. The best pickles are made from recently picked produce. An old saying suggests that the time period "from vine to brine" be no more than 24 hours. Plan your pickling to coincide with your garden's harvest, or a trip to your local farm or market. You can pickle foods from your supermarket as well, but it's best to use quick pickle methods and consume them as soon as possible, since produce on the supermarket shelf has traveled for weeks in order to arrive in your kitchen.

Choose firm, slightly immature specimens for pickling. Your greens should be crisp and fresh, with moist stems. When pickling cabbage, choose firm, mature specimens. Do not try to preserve produce that is wilted or on its way to spoilage. Wash all produce well. Food preservation does not improve the quality of foods—what you put in is what you get out.

The Right Stuff

Choosing the right ingredients is especially important when food is to be preserved. Follow these ingredient guidelines when preparing to pickle:

- Water: Hard water can alter the color and flavor of your pickles, and can inhibit the production of lactic acid. If you have hard water, use bottled water.

- Spices: Use fresh, whole spices. Spices are the only ingredient that may be adjusted in pickling recipes. You may substitute one spice for another, or decrease the total amount used. Avoid increasing the amount of spice in a recipe.

- Vinegar: The traditional choices for pickling are distilled white or apple cider vinegar. Both offer a guaranteed acidity level of 4 to 6 percent, which is essential to inhibit spoilers. White vinegar is a good choice if you don't want to add competing flavors to a dish. Apple cider vinegar adds a pleasing, fruity complexity to pickles, but may darken the resulting product.

- Salt: While any food-grade salt may be used for pickling, the best choices are pickling salt or kosher salt. Pickling salt is a pure, granulated salt that does not contain caking agents or iodine. Kosher salt is great for pickling, too, but bear in mind that as it is flaked, it measures at twice the volume of granulated salt. Unless the recipe specifically calls for kosher salt, you should double the amount of kosher salt used. Table salts that contain iodine or anti-caking agents can be used in a pinch, but they will darken foods and cloud brine, respectively. For reduced salt diets, look for recipes developed with potassium chloride. Do not alter the amount of salt called for in a quick pickle, and never change the salt concentration in a fermented pickle recipe. Salt is necessary in specific amounts for preservation, and proper fermentation will not occur without correct proportions of salt and other ingredients.

- Sugar: While pickles can be sweetened with white or brown sugar, bear in mind that brown sugar may darken your pickling liquid slightly. Honey may be substituted for sugar, but since it is sweeter, use one quarter less (1 cup sugar = ¾ cup honey). Do not substitute non-nutritive sweeteners unless you are using a recipe specifically developed for that purpose.

- Garlic: Use fresh, properly matured garlic for the best-looking pickles. Garlic that is immature or old will turn pink or purple when anthocyanins react with acid. This effect is undesirable from an aesthetic perspective, but it does not affect safety.

Equip Yourself

You'll want to gather the appropriate utensils when preparing to pickle. Heat pickling liquids in nonreactive cookware such as stainless steel, unchipped enamelware, or glass. Avoid copper pots, which may turn your pickles an odd shade of green, and galvanized cookware, which is treated with cadmium and may produce a toxic substance when reacting to vinegar or salt.

Fermented products can be prepared in glass, plastic, or stainless steel bowls or jars, or stoneware crocks. Whatever vessel you choose, you'll need to keep your food submerged using a clean, heavy plate and a weight. A plastic jar filled with brine makes a good weight, as does a plastic bag filled with the same pickling liquid you are using to ferment your pickles. Do not use stones or bricks to weight your pickles, as this may introduce unwanted impurities.

If you're planning to can your pickled foods, use standard canning jars and lids. Jars can be reused from year to year, but be sure to discard any with chips or cracks, as these can provide a hiding place for bacteria and other spoilers. Use new lids every time to ensure a safe seal. Jars are processed in a boiling water bath canner, which should be deep enough to allow the tops of your jars to be covered by 2 inches of simmering water. You will also need a rack to keep jars from touching the bottom of the canner. If you don't have a rack, try a layer of jar rings covered with a dish towel for an inexpensive solution.

Once you've gathered your equipment, read through the following recipes to familiarize yourself with the basics of pickling. Remember to keep your hands and utensils clean, follow instructions carefully, and get ready to enjoy the tangy, crunchy, appetite-enhancing world of homemade pickles!

ⓥ Pickled Collard Greens

Hardy greens such as collards are perfect for pickling. This recipe allows the flavor of the greens to shine through, in a simple brine of fruity apple cider vinegar, sugar, salt, spicy mustard seeds, and aromatic pink peppercorns.

Yield:	Serving size:	Prep time:	Cook time:
1 quart	½ cup	10 minutes	15 minutes, plus 1 hour cooling time

1 cup apple cider vinegar

1 cup water

1 TB. sugar

2 TB. kosher salt

¼ tsp. whole pink peppercorns

¼ tsp. black mustard seeds

1 lb. collard greens, tough stems trimmed, chiffonade cut

1 medium sweet onion, halved and very thinly sliced

1. Bring apple cider vinegar, water, sugar, kosher salt, pink peppercorns, and mustard seeds to a boil in a nonreactive stockpot.

2. Add collard greens and onion, and cook, stirring frequently, for 10 minutes, or until greens have softened enough to push below the surface of the brine.

3. Cool greens for 1 hour, then transfer to a clean glass jar or bowl. Cover and place in refrigerator to marinate for 2 to 3 days. Store pickled greens in refrigerator for up to 2 weeks.

Variation: Try this recipe with mustard greens, kale, or a combination of greens.

THE LOWDOWN

Pink peppercorns are not peppercorns at all, but the dried berries of the *Baies rose* plant. They will soften in the pickling liquid, and can be eaten whole.

Ⓥ Pickled Turnip Greens with Apples

Turnip greens are spiced with black peppercorns and allspice, and enhanced with the sweetness of apples in this fresh, fun quick pickle.

Yield:	Serving size:	Prep time:	Cook time:
1 quart	½ cup	10 minutes	15 minutes, plus 1 hour cooling time

3 whole allspice berries

½ tsp. black peppercorns

1¼ cups distilled white vinegar

1 cup water

2 TB. sugar

2 TB. kosher salt

1 lb. turnip greens, tough stems trimmed, roughly chopped

1 firm, sweet apple, such as Winesap, cored, peeled, and thinly sliced

1 small red onion, halved and thinly sliced

1. Wrap allspice berries and black peppercorns in cheesecloth, and tie with kitchen twine. Bring white vinegar, water, sugar, salt, and spice sachet to a boil in a large stockpot.

2. Add turnip greens, apple, and red onion to brine. Cook, stirring occasionally, for 10 minutes.

3. Cool mixture for 1 hour, then transfer to a clean glass jar or bowl. Refrigerate, covered, for 2 to 3 days, then remove spice sachet and enjoy. Greens will keep in refrigerator for up to 2 weeks.

HEADS UP!

Prepare bowls or jars for pickle storage. Cleanliness is essential. Run them through the dishwasher on the "pots and pans" setting, or simmer in a boiling water canner for 10 minutes. Pack hot foods in hot jars and cool foods in cool jars, to prevent breakage.

Ⓥ Garlicky Balsamic-Pickled Radicchio

Radicchio is quickly pickled in sweet balsamic vinegar and plenty of garlic for a crunchy and delicious condiment that pairs wonderfully with grilled foods.

Yield:	Serving size:	Prep time:	Cook time:
4 cups	½ cup	10 minutes	10 minutes

1 cup balsamic vinegar	1 tsp. brown sugar
½ cup apple cider vinegar	5 heads radicchio, cored and sliced (about 5–6 cups)
1 cup water	6 cloves garlic, thinly sliced
2 TB. kosher salt	

1. Bring balsamic vinegar, apple cider vinegar, water, salt, and brown sugar to a boil in a large stockpot.

2. Add radicchio and garlic, and cook for 10 minutes, stirring occasionally.

3. Cool mixture for 1 hour, then transfer to a glass bowl. Store in refrigerator for 24 hours, then enjoy. Pickled radicchio will keep for up to 3 days.

THE LOWDOWN

Balsamic vinegar and other specialty vinegars are usually not recommended for pickling because their acid level is often lower than the recommended 4 to 6 percent. Undesirable color changes are often a result, but since radicchio is the vegetable being pickled in this recipe, the mixture will already be pink. Since the radicchio and garlic will be eaten quickly, and not canned for long-term storage, balsamic vinegar is an acceptable choice, and will lend a flavorful sweetness to the bitterness of radicchio.

Ⓥ Spicy Brussels Sprout Pickles

Brussels sprouts are packed with spices in a vinegary brine in this easy-to-make recipe that is a great start for beginning home canners.

Yield:	Serving size:	Prep time:	Cook time:
2 pints	½ cup	25 minutes	10 minutes

1½ cups distilled white vinegar

1 cup water

2 TB. kosher salt

2 tsp. black peppercorns

½ tsp. crushed red pepper flakes

½ tsp. black mustard seeds

2 bay leaves

1 lb. Brussels sprouts, halved

1. Sterilize two pint-sized canning jars. Bring water to a simmer in boiling water canner, and place lids in a small pot of simmering water.

2. Bring vinegar, water, and salt to a boil in a small saucepan.

3. Combine peppercorns, pepper flakes, and mustard in a bowl. Divide spices evenly among sterilized jars. Place bay leaf in each pint. Pack halved Brussels sprouts tightly into jars, then pour boiling brine over sprouts, leaving ½ inch headspace at the top of the jar. Use a plastic utensil or wooden chopstick to gently press sprouts and remove air bubbles from jar.

4. Place lids on top of jars, and screw bands to fingertip tightness. Lower jars into simmering water, bring to a boil over high heat, and cover canner. Process jars for 10 minutes, then turn off heat and allow canner to stand for 5 minutes more. Carefully lift jars from boiling water bath, and place on cooling racks. After 48 hours, test seal by unscrewing bands and gently pulling at lids. Wipe jars clean, and store for up to 1 year.

HEADS UP!

Headspace is extremely important. Leaving too much space at the top of the jar will allow too much air to remain, exposing food to potential spoilers. Leave too little headspace, and your brine will boil over, destroying the seal, and your delicious pickles within. Follow headspace recommendations not only when canning, but when freezing foods as well, as expansion occurs during both of these preservation processes.

Brussels sprouts.

Ⓥ Ⓡ Quick-Pickled Gingery Cabbage and Carrots

Cabbage and carrots stay crunchy in a quick brine that is bursting with ginger flavor.

Yield:	Serving size:	Prep time:	Cook time:
8 cups	1 cup	15 minutes	None

½ head green cabbage, cored and cut into ½-inch slices

3 medium carrots, peeled and cut into diagonal ¼-inch slices

1 TB. kosher salt

1 (3–inch) piece ginger, peeled and finely chopped

1½ cups rice wine vinegar

½ cup apple cider vinegar

1 TB. sugar

1. Combine cabbage, carrots, and salt in a large colander. Rub salt in with your hands, and allow to drain and release liquid for 20 minutes. Press out excess liquid, then transfer to a heatproof bowl.

2. Place ginger in a small saucepan with rice wine vinegar, apple cider vinegar, and sugar. Bring to a boil, then pour hot vinegar over cabbage mixture.

3. Cover and refrigerate for 24 hours before serving. Will keep in refrigerator for up to 3 days.

THE LOWDOWN

You will find both rice vinegar and rice wine vinegar in a well-stocked Asian grocery. Both lend a sweet acidity to Asian-inspired dishes, and can be used interchangeably. Since the acidity of most rice and rice wine vinegar is around 4 percent, it's fine for quick refrigerator pickles, but should be avoided when canning for long-term storage.

Ⓥ Ⓡ Quick-Pickled Broccoli Stems

Enjoy the bold spices of Indian cuisine with this crunchy, spicy *achar* made with broccoli stems.

Yield:	Serving size:	Prep time:	Cook time:
4 cups	1 cup	10 minutes	30 minutes

¼ cup fresh lemon juice (about 2 lemons)

½ tsp. turmeric

1 pinch *asafoetida*

4 cups broccoli stems, peeled and thinly sliced (from about 2 large bunches)

2 TB. unfiltered coconut oil

1 tsp. black mustard seeds

1 tsp. whole cumin seeds

1 tsp. fenugreek seeds

1 TB. lightly packed fresh curry leaves, roughly chopped

2 tsp. chili powder, or to taste

1. Mix lemon juice, turmeric, and asafoetida. Toss in a nonreactive bowl with broccoli stems.

2. Heat a small sauté pan or cast-iron skillet over medium-high heat. Add coconut oil and heat for 1 minute. Add black mustard seeds, whole cumin seeds, and fenugreek. Cook until seeds begin to pop, about 1 minute. Stir in curry leaves and chili powder, and cook 30 seconds more. Pour oil mixture over broccoli stems, and mix well.

3. Cover bowl and place in refrigerator for 24 hours. Pickles will keep, refrigerated, for up to 7 days.

Variation: Replace broccoli stems with cauliflower, turnips, carrots, parsnips, cabbage, celery, green mango, or unripe papaya. Try fresh lime juice in place of lemon juice.

DEFINITION

Asafoetida is a spice used as a flavor enhancer and digestive aid. It has a strong odor, and is used in very small amounts in pickles and Indian cooking. Store asafoetida in a tightly sealed glass container to prevent its fragrance from contaminating other ingredients in your cupboard. Asafoetida is widely used in Indian cuisine to lend flavor and aroma to vegetarian dishes, and to reduce flatulence.

THE LOWDOWN

Fresh curry leaves, which come from the plant *Muraya koeniggi*, have nothing to do with curry powder, a mixture of turmeric, cinnamon, coriander, and other spices. You can find fresh curry leaves in the Asian or Indian aisle of your grocery store. Dried curry leaves are also available. Their flavor is much stronger, so start with 1 teaspoon of dried curry leaves for every 1 tablespoon fresh curry leaves called for in a recipe.

Ⓥ Ⓡ Napa Cabbage *Tsukemono*

Tsukemono is a speedy Japanese pickle that is eaten just about as soon as it is made. This version combines crisp Napa cabbage with salt, lemon zest, ginger, and a bit of heat from crushed chile peppers.

Yield:	Serving size:	Prep time:	Cook time:
8 cups	1 cup	10 minutes, plus 1 hour	None

1 small head Napa cabbage

1 tsp. sea salt

1 tsp. lemon zest

1 tsp. grated fresh ginger

¼ tsp. crushed red pepper flakes, or to taste

1 TB. fresh lemon juice

1. Core and shred cabbage, and place in a large colander. In a small bowl, combine salt, lemon zest, ginger, and crushed red pepper flakes. Use your hands to thoroughly rub salt mixture into cabbage (wear gloves, or wash your hands with care after handling hot pepper flakes).

2. Allow cabbage mixture to drain for 1 hour, pressing and tossing ingredients once or twice. Combine with lemon juice and serve immediately.

Ⓥ Ⓡ Traditional Kimchi

This fiery fermented condiment is a staple in Korean cuisine. It's easy to make, and safe to eat, as long as you follow the recipe precisely.

Yield:	Serving size:	Prep time:	Cook time:
2 quarts	½ cup	25 minutes plus 3–7 days fermentation time	None

1 large Napa cabbage (about 4 lbs.), cored and cut into 1- to 2-inch chunks

½ cup scallions, halved and roughly chopped (white and green parts)

6 cloves garlic, peeled and thickly sliced

2 medium carrots, julienne cut

1 2-inch piece fresh ginger, peeled and julienne cut

¼ cup pickling salt

1 tsp. sugar

3 TB. dried Korean chili powder

1 TB. soy sauce or tamari

1. Mix cabbage, scallions, garlic, carrots, and ginger in a large bowl. Add salt and sugar, and thoroughly combine with cabbage mixture.

2. Pack ingredients tightly into a fermenting crock or food grade plastic or glass container with straight sides. Place a double layer of cheesecloth over cabbage mixture, followed by a clean, heavy plate. Top plate with a food grade weight, such as a large mason jar filled with water. In order for kimchi to ferment properly, it must be submerged in the liquid that will quickly form, so be sure your weight is heavy.

3. Allow mixture to stand at room temperature (around 70 to 75°F is optimal) for 3 to 7 days. The progress of fermentation will be determined by the temperature in the room. Be patient. During the curing process, bubbles should form, generally after 3 to 4 days.

4. Taste the mixture daily once fermentation has begun, and when it has reached your desired level of sourness (no more than 7 days), drain excess liquid, mix in chili powder and soy sauce, and store in the coldest spot in your refrigerator for up to 30 days.

HEADS UP!

Do not adjust the amounts this recipe calls for, particularly the salt. Fermented pickles are created using specific ingredient percentages to encourage the formation of lactic acid, which is responsible for killing bacterial spoilers (such as botulism).

HEADS UP!

The first rule of home food preservation is, "When in doubt, throw it out!" Fermentation is an anaerobic form of food preservation; the lack of air in the process allows anaerobic bacteria such as botulism to grow if acidity levels are not high enough. If your kimchi turns black, seems slimy, develops a whitish gray film, or seems fizzy rather than bubbly, make the safe choice and start over. Properly fermented kimchi keeps best when stored under very cold conditions, as close to the freezing point of 32°F as possible, but definitely no warmer than 41°F. While kimchi will keep for 3 months at 32 to 34°F, most refrigerators are closer to the higher part of this range, so plan to consume your fermented kimchi within a month. When storing kimchi, remember that however slow the process, it will keep fermenting. Plan to leave a few inches of headspace at the top of your storage container to allow for expansion.

Ⓥ Ⓡ Sauerkraut

Sauerkraut has a distinct, sour cabbage flavor that is featured in many cuisines throughout eastern, central, and northern Europe. Try this fermented superfood in pierogi, soups, stews, or casseroles, or simply eaten as a side dish or sandwich condiment.

Yield:	Serving size:	Prep time:	Cook time:
2 quarts	½ cup	15 minutes plus 3–7 days fermentation time	None

5 lbs. green cabbage (about 2 medium), shredded

¼ cup pickling salt, plus 1 TB. for weight bag

1. Wash shredded cabbage in several changes of cold water, and drain well. Thoroughly mix shredded cabbage and pickling salt.

2. Pack cabbage tightly into a fermenting crock or food grade plastic or glass container with straight sides. A potato masher or clean hands are both great tools to ensure that cabbage is packed very tightly. Place a double layer of cheesecloth over cabbage mixture, followed by a clean, heavy plate. Top plate with a food grade weight, such as a heavy, well-sealed plastic bag filled with 1 quart water and 1 tablespoon pickling salt.

3. Allow mixture to stand at in a cool place (around 60 to 65°F is optimal) for 7 to 10 days. Once a day, tamp down cabbage mixture, ensuring that it is well covered with brine. Skim any scum that forms on top of the brine, and periodically wash cheesecloth and scald with boiling water. Keep cheesecloth moist by pouring 1 cup water mixed with 1 teaspoon pickling salt if it seems to be drying out.

4. When fermentation has occurred, and sauerkraut tastes pleasingly sour, pack into sterilized glass jars along with fermentation liquid. Sauerkraut can be stored in the refrigerator, or canned in a boiling water bath for 25 minutes (see the recipe for *Spicy Brussels Sprouts Pickles* for boiling water canning process). Either way, be sure to leave ½ inch headspace at the top of each jar to allow for expansion.

HEADS UP!

It's important to observe safe practices when fermenting and processing foods for long-term storage. Be sure that you are using a tested recipe that has been deemed safe by food scientists. The National Center for Home Food Preservation, your state's university cooperative extension, the USDA, and the Ball Mason Jar company are all good sources of information. See "Resources" in Appendix B at the end of this book, and consider picking up a book or taking a class with an expert if you are interested in learning more about safe home food preservation practices.

The Basics

In This Chapter

- Techniques and tips
- Foundations to build your repertoire
- Tools for truly homemade cooking

While it's easy to rely on purchased ingredients from the supermarket, it's just as easy to make your own kitchen staples. The recipes in this chapter are used as building blocks for recipes throughout this book. When possible, store-bought alternatives are suggested, but do try making your own. You'll notice a difference, and save some cash in the process.

Vegetable stock is made in about an hour, and costs pennies per serving, rather than three or four dollars per quart. Pizza dough, pie crust, and salad dressings are inexpensive—and a snap to prepare. And you simply can't beat the flavor and quality of homemade tomato sauce and salsa.

Your family or guests will appreciate food made from scratch. You can't go wrong with a little extra know-how in the kitchen, so we'll also explore some basics like roasting garlic and making citrus supremes.

Truly homemade food is the healthiest, most satisfying kind of food to serve and eat. Making it yourself ensures that you're using top-quality ingredients, free of pesticides, harmful additives, and genetically modified ingredients. Prepare to take your cooking to the next level.

HEADS UP!

Processed foods contain additives such as flavoring, color, and preservatives to extend shelf life. Many food additives have been shown to aggravate medical conditions such as autoimmune disorders, autism, and allergies, and even cause illnesses, including certain cancers. Even packaging can change the quality of your food. You should particularly avoid foods packaged in plastics, as BPA levels found in plastics and some cans produce undesirable health problems. Read your labels—if you can't pronounce it, you probably want to avoid it.

Ⓥ Quick and Easy Vegetable Stock

The flavor of homemade vegetable stock is simple and pure. Carrots, celery, leeks, and onions combine with a few herbs and spices to provide incomparable flavor that will complement your recipes without adding the strong, undesirable flavors and added sodium of processed stocks and broths.

Yield:	Serving size:	Prep time:	Cook time:
4 quarts	1–2 cups	10 minutes	1–2 hours

3 large leeks, halved lengthwise, washed and cut into 1-inch chunks

1 large yellow onion, unpeeled, halved, and trimmed of root end

4 medium carrots, scrubbed and cut into 1-inch chunks

5 large ribs of celery, cut into 1-inch chunks

1 bay leaf

½ cup parsley leaves and stems

3 sprigs fresh thyme

8 black peppercorns

1 tsp. kosher salt

1. Combine leeks, onion, carrots, celery, bay leaf, parsley, thyme, peppercorns, and salt in a large stockpot, and cover with 4 quarts of filtered water.

2. Bring to a boil over high heat, then cover and reduce heat to a simmer. Cook for 1 to 2 hours. Cool completely, strain, and pour into glass jars for storage. Stock will keep in refrigerator for up to 7 days.

To freeze: Pour strained stock into straight-sided Mason jars or BPA-free plastic containers with 1 inch headspace. Freeze for up to 6 months.

 Pie Pastry

Flaky, flavorful, and easy to roll out, this tender pie pastry will take your sweet and savory pies to the next level.

Yield:	Serving size:	Prep time:	Cook time:
1 double crust for a deep-dish pie	about ⅛ of pie	10 minutes, plus 30 minutes resting time in refrigerator	None

3 cups unbleached, all-purpose flour, well chilled

1½ tsp. kosher salt

1 tsp. sugar (optional, omit for savory recipes)

12 TB. nonhydrogenated organic shortening, partially frozen, cut into small cubes

½ cup ice water

1. Place flour, kosher salt, and sugar (if using) in bowl of food processor. Pulse five or six times to combine. Add half of shortening. Pulse five times, then run machine for 5 seconds. Add remaining shortening, and pulse until flour and shortening mixture resembles small pea-sized pieces. Alternately, you may cut in shortening using a pastry blender.

2. Transfer flour mixture to a large bowl. Working a few tablespoons at a time, drizzle ice water over flour, then gather together using a large kitchen fork. When mixture has nearly come together, use the heel of your hand to press dough against sides of bowl, until a cohesive mass has formed.

3. Separate dough into two equal pieces, wrap in plastic wrap, and use your hands to flatten into a disc measuring roughly 5 inches. Use the side of your hand to gently score dough in a tic-tac-toe pattern to ensure a tender crust.

4. Refrigerate dough rounds for 30 minutes. Proceed as directed in recipe.

To freeze: Wrap dough in plastic wrap, then place inside freezer-safe plastic bags. Store in freezer for up to 3 months. Refrigerate overnight to defrost, and proceed as directed in recipe.

THE LOWDOWN

Rolling pie crust is not as intimidating as it seems. Work on a cool, well-floured surface, such as a granite countertop or marble pastry board. Flour your rolling pin generously. Using your rolling pin, smack dough firmly, making quarter turns after each blow, to begin spreading the circle. Keeping your work surface and rolling pin well floured, begin to roll from the center, to nearly the edge of the dough. Think of the dough as a clock. Roll at 12:00, making a quarter turn each time. Reflour work surface, and roll once more all the way "around the clock," turning from 12, to 1, and all the way around until dough has reached desired size (a couple of inches larger than your pie pan). Lift the pin just before you reach the edge of the dough to prevent the edges from becoming thinner than the center. When you're ready to transfer your dough to your prepared pan, drape it carefully over your rolling pin, and gently transfer it, taking care to lift the edges when pressing dough into the pan. Practice makes perfect, so try again if you don't get it exactly right the first time.

Ⓥ Pizza Dough

Homemade pizza dough has incomparable flavor. The dough is kneaded and raised in one bowl in this recipe, so you don't have to worry about making a mess. In a pinch, stop by your local pizzeria and ask them to sell you some unbaked dough.

Yield:	Serving size:	Prep time:	Cook time:
1 pizza dough for a standard ½ sheet pan	⅛ of pizza	15 minutes, plus about 2 hours rising time	25 minutes

1 envelope (2½ tsp.) active dry yeast

1⅔ cups very warm water

3 TB. extra-virgin olive oil

1 tsp. sugar

4 cups all-purpose flour

1 TB. kosher salt

1. Sprinkle yeast over warm water, and allow to stand until foamy, about 8 minutes. Whisk in olive oil and sugar.

2. Combine flour and salt in a large mixing bowl. Using a rubber spatula, slowly stir the yeast mixture into the flour. Once the mixture forms a shaggy mass, use your hands to gently knead and press the flour in the mixing bowl for about 3 minutes. Turn it over a few times to be sure all flour from the bottom of the bowl is incorporated.

3. Cover dough with plastic wrap, and allow it to rise until doubled in size, 1 to 1½ hours.

4. When dough has doubled, oil a large (half sheet) baking pan. Use your spatula to scrape the dough onto the pan. Oil your hands, and gently spread the dough to the outer corners of the pan, working from the center outward. Cover dough with plastic wrap, and allow to rise until doubled, about 1 hour.

5. Preheat oven to 450°F. Top dough as directed in recipe, and bake until toppings are bubbly and bottom of crust is golden brown, about 25 minutes.

Variation: For **Rosemary Focaccia,** pour 1⅔ cups boiling water over 2 tablespoons fresh rosemary (or 1 tablespoon dried rosemary). Allow to stand until water reaches 110°F, then strain and proceed with recipe. After second rise, gently dimple dough with your fingers, and drizzle with 2 tablespoons extra-virgin olive oil and 1 teaspoon kosher salt. Bake as directed.

HEADS UP!

There's nothing worse than mixing up a recipe, and then finding that it didn't rise because your yeast was dead. Check expiration dates, and use the following method to proof your yeast. Measure the amount of warm water called for in the recipe, sprinkle yeast on top, and let it stand for 8 to 10 minutes. If it doesn't foam, your yeast is not active. Water should be around 110°F. If it's too cool, your dough will rise too slowly. If it's too hot, you'll kill the yeast. If you don't have a kitchen thermometer, simply place your finger in the water to test its temperature. It should be just hot enough to keep a finger submerged for 5 seconds before it becomes very uncomfortable.

Ⓥ Tomato Sauce

There's no need for sauce from a jar when you can quickly mix up this delicious sauce that is bursting with tomato flavor.

Yield:	Serving size:	Prep time:	Cook time:
6 cups	½ cup	5 minutes	30 minutes

2 TB. extra-virgin olive oil	1 (28-oz.) can peeled plum tomatoes, preferably San Marzano
½ cup yellow onion, very finely minced	¼ tsp. dried oregano
½ tsp. kosher salt	¼ cup dry white wine
2 cloves garlic, smashed and finely chopped	3 leaves fresh basil, torn
Pinch of crushed red pepper flakes, optional	¼ tsp. freshly ground black pepper

1. Heat olive oil in a large saucepan over medium-high heat. Add onion and salt, and cook, stirring frequently, until onion becomes soft and translucent, about 5 minutes. Add garlic and crushed red pepper (if using), and stir for 1 minute more.

2. Add tomatoes to onion mixture, and bring to a boil. Cook for 5 minutes, then use a potato masher or large fork to crush tomatoes. Add oregano and white wine, and continue to cook for 10 minutes, stirring frequently.

3. Reduce heat to a simmer, and cook 10 minutes more. Stir in basil and black pepper, and remove from heat.

To freeze: Prepare recipe as directed, eliminating oregano, basil, and black pepper. Cool completely, and pour into freezer-safe containers with ½ inch headspace to allow for expansion. Freeze for up to 6 months.

THE LOWDOWN

If you don't have fresh basil, leave it out of the recipe. Commercially dried basil has an undesirable flavor and aroma. If you have a garden, consider drying your own basil. The flavor will not be as delicious as fresh basil, but it will be better than anything you can buy in a store. Simply wash and dry basil leaves, and lay them on a sheet pan lined with a clean kitchen towel. Keep them in a warm, dry place, such as your unlit oven with the light turned on, for 24 to 48 hours, or until completely dry. Store in a sealed glass jar.

ⓥ Cheezy Toasted Bread Crumbs

This simple mixture of bread, almonds, and nutritional yeast for cheesy flavor creates the perfect vegan substitution for Parmesan cheese.

Yield:	Serving size:	Prep time:	Cook time:
2 cups	2 TB.	5 minutes	10 minutes

2 1-inch-thick slices country bread (or 4 slices French bread)

½ cup blanched almonds

2 TB. nutritional yeast

1. Preheat oven to 400°F. Place bread and almonds on a sheet pan lined with parchment paper. Place in oven until bread is toasted and almonds are golden, about 8 minutes.

2. Allow bread and almonds to cool for 10 minutes, then place in bowl of food processor fitted with metal blade. Add nutritional yeast, and pulse until mixture resembles coarse crumbs. Use immediately, or store in a glass jar for 5 days.

Variation: For **Cheezy Toasted Croutons,** cut bread into cubes. Pulse almonds and nutritional yeast in food processor with 2 TB. extra-virgin olive oil. Toss with bread cubes, and bake at 400 degrees until crisp, about 10 minutes.

THE LOWDOWN

Almonds are not nuts at all, but seeds (also known as tree nuts). This is good news for many people with nut allergies, as almonds are the only "nut" member of the plum family, and have the lowest incidence of allergic reactions among all nuts and tree nuts. Those with peanut allergies may not be allergic to almonds, but it's always best to see a physician for allergy testing, and proceed with caution.

Ⓥ Caramelized Onions

When onions are cooked slowly over low heat with a little bit of fat, they release their sugars, and become sweet and savory, with a beautiful dark golden brown color.

Yield:	Serving size:	Prep time:	Cook time:
2 cups	¼ cup	5 minutes	40 minutes

5 large yellow onions (about 4½ cups)	2 TB. extra-virgin olive oil
	½ tsp. kosher salt

1. Halve and peel onions, and cut into ⅛-inch slices.

2. Heat olive oil in a medium sauté pan over medium-high heat. Add onions and salt, stir, and reduce heat to low. Cook, stirring occasionally, until onions are softened and very dark golden brown, about 35 minutes. Caramelized onions can be used immediately, or refrigerated for up to 5 days.

Ⓥ Ⓡ Citrus Supremes

"Supremes" is just a fancy word for sectioned citrus that has been cut from its peel and membrane. Use this technique for salads, fruit compotes, marmalade, or desserts.

Yield:	Serving size:	Prep time:	Cook time:
1 orange or grapefruit	1 orange or grapefruit	10 minutes	None

1 orange or grapefruit

1. Using a sharp paring knife, cut about ½ inch from the top and bottom of the fruit. Carefully cut away the peel and *pith* of the fruit. You will now be able to see the membrane that separates the sections.

2. Use your paring knife to cut along the inside of each section, slicing as close to the membrane as possible. A neat supreme will pop out. Continue working your way around, until you are left with nothing but membrane.

Ⓥ Ⓡ Basic Vinaigrette

This simple vinaigrette is the original "French dressing." The balance of tart vinegar, flavorful mustard, and fruity olive oil is the perfect complement to any salad. Adjust the vinegar and oil quantities to suit your taste.

Yield:	Serving size:	Prep time:	Cook time:
1 cup	2 TB.	10 minutes	None

1 clove garlic, smashed

2 TB. shallot, finely minced (about 1 medium shallot)

½ cup white wine vinegar

½ tsp. kosher salt (or to taste)

1 TB. Dijon mustard

½ cup extra-virgin olive oil

½ tsp. freshly ground black pepper (or to taste)

1. Rub a small mixing bowl with the smashed garlic clove, and discard. Add shallots, white wine vinegar, salt, and mustard, and whisk to combine.

2. Working a few drops at a time, whisk olive oil into vinegar mixture. When all oil has been incorporated, whisk in pepper, then taste and adjust salt and pepper as necessary. Use dressing immediately, or refrigerate for 3 days.

Variation: Add fresh herbs to flavor this simple dressing. Try basil, thyme, tarragon, chives, or chervil, or find your own special blend! Add 2 tablespoons fresh herbs, or 1 teaspoon dried herbs, before oil is added.

THE LOWDOWN

Whisking the oil slowly into the dressing creates an emulsion. Oil and water do not want to mix, so adding a few drops at a time and whisking vigorously will suspend small drops of the oil in the vinegar mixture. When refrigerated, the dressing may separate. Just whisk or shake vigorously to recombine your dressing.

Ⓥ Roasted Garlic

Garlic becomes soft, sweet, and much less pungent once it has been roasted.

Yield:	Serving size:	Prep time:	Cook time:
3 heads of garlic	None	5 minutes	45 minutes

3 whole heads of garlic
3 TB. extra-virgin olive oil

½ tsp. kosher salt

1. Preheat oven to 375°F. Use a sharp knife to cut away the stem end of each head of garlic, exposing the cloves. (The stem end is the one that doesn't have a little fuzzy root—leave that side intact!)

2. Place garlic cloves, cut side up, on a double layer of heavy-duty aluminum foil. Drizzle with olive oil, sprinkle with salt, and bring sides of foil up and around garlic to enclose it completely. Place in a small baking dish, and roast for 40 minutes, or until garlic is soft and smells sweet and fragrant. Let stand, covered, for 10 minutes after removing from oven.

3. When garlic has cooled enough to handle, squeeze cloves from their skins. Use as directed in recipe, or store in refrigerator for up to 5 days.

THE LOWDOWN

Many people who are unable to digest raw garlic find that roasted garlic is much easier on the digestive system. Replace raw garlic with roasted garlic in any recipe.

Ⓥ Tomatillo Salsa

Tomatillo salsa is tart and tangy, with a kick from poblano peppers. Use it in recipes, or as a dip for tortilla chips.

Yield:	Serving size:	Prep time:	Cook time:
2 cups	None	10 minutes	20 minutes

2 poblano chiles

12 tomatillos

1 large yellow onion, roughly chopped

3 cloves garlic, smashed and roughly chopped

2 TB. extra-virgin olive oil

½ tsp. kosher salt

¼ tsp. freshly ground black pepper

¼ cup chopped fresh cilantro

1. Roast poblano chiles under the broiler or over an open flame until the skin is charred and blackened all over. Place in a bowl, cover with plastic wrap, and allow to steam for 5 minutes. Remove plastic wrap, and use a paper towel to rub skin from peppers. Remove core and seeds, and set aside. You may wish to wear gloves when handling hot peppers.

2. Remove papery husks from tomatillos, and wash well under running water.

3. Combine tomatillos, onion, and garlic on a large baking sheet. Drizzle with olive oil, and season with salt and pepper. Broil until tomatillos are softened and charred.

4. Place tomatillo mixture, poblano chiles, and cilantro in a food processor fitted with a metal blade. Pulse until salsa is smooth. Serve immediately, or refrigerate for up to 5 days.

To freeze: Prepare salsa as directed. Pour into freezer-safe containers with ½ inch headspace. Freeze for up to 6 months.

DEFINITION

Tomatillos are a member of the nightshade family, closely related to gooseberries. Once their papery husk is removed, a sticky coating remains. Wash well, and cook the tomato-like fruits to optimize their tart flavor. A high pectin content makes tomatillos a great choice for thick, rich-tasting salsas and sauces.

Glossary

al dente Italian for "against the teeth," this term refers to pasta or rice that's neither soft nor hard but just slightly firm when chewed.

all-purpose flour Flour that contains only the inner part of the wheat grain. It's suitable for everything from cakes to gravies.

allspice A spice named for its flavor echoes of several spices (cinnamon, cloves, nutmeg), used in many desserts and in rich marinades and stews.

amaranth A hardy annual herb grown for its leaves and seeds.

antioxidants A substance that is capable of counteracting the effects of oxidation in the body's tissues.

arborio rice A plump Italian rice used for, among other purposes, risotto.

artichoke heart The center part of the artichoke flower, often found canned in grocery stores.

arugula A spicy-peppery green with leaves that resemble a dandelion's and have a distinctive and very sharp flavor.

bake To cook in a dry oven. Dry-heat cooking often results in a crisping of the exterior of the food being cooked. Moist-heat cooking, through methods such as steaming, poaching, etc., brings a much different, moist quality to the food.

baking powder A dry ingredient used to increase volume and lighten or leaven baked goods.

balsamic vinegar Vinegar produced primarily in Italy from a specific type of grape and aged in wood barrels. It's heavier, darker, and sweeter than most vinegars.

basil A flavorful, almost sweet, resinous herb that's delicious with tomatoes and used in all kinds of Italian- or Mediterranean-style dishes.

baste To keep foods moist during cooking by spooning, brushing, or drizzling with a liquid.

beat   To quickly mix substances.

beet greens   The leafy tops of beet root.

Belgian endive   A pearly white, bitter leaf vegetable of the chicory family.

bioavailability   The degree to with a nutrient becomes available to your body tissue after consumption.

blacken   To cook something quickly in a very hot skillet over high heat, usually with a seasoning mixture.

blanch   1. To place a food in boiling water for about 1 minute or less to partially cook the exterior, and then submerge in or rinse with cool water to halt the cooking. 2. Process of cutting off light to plants to produce pale, tender leaves.

blend   To completely mix something, usually with a blender or food processor; slower than beating.

boil   To heat a liquid to the point where water is forced to turn into steam, causing the liquid to bubble. To boil something is to insert it into boiling water. A rapid boil is when a lot of bubbles form on the surface of the liquid.

bolting   Gardening term that describes the formation of a flower stalk at the end of a plant's growth cycle.

bok choy   A member of the cabbage family with thick stems, crisp texture, and fresh flavor. It's perfect for stir-frying.

bouillon   Dried essence of stock from chicken, beef, vegetables, or other ingredients. It's a popular starting ingredient for soups because it adds flavor (but often a lot of salt).

braise   To cook with the introduction of some liquid, usually over an extended period of time.

brine   A highly salted, often seasoned, liquid used to flavor and preserve foods. To brine a food is to soak, or preserve, it by submerging it in brine. The salt in the brine penetrates the fibers of the meat and makes it moist and tender.

broccoli   A cruciferous green vegetable with small, tight buds and an edible stalk.

broccoli rabe (or **rapini**)   A pungent, bitter green of the turnip family.

broil   To cook in a dry oven under the overhead high-heat element.

broth   *See* stock.

brown   To cook in a skillet, turning, until the food's surface is seared and brown in color, to lock in the juices.

brown rice   A whole-grain rice, including the germ, with a characteristic pale brown or tan color. It's more nutritious and flavorful than white rice.

bruschetta (or **crostini**)   Slices of toasted or grilled bread brushed with garlic and olive oil, often with other toppings.

Brussels sprouts   A cruciferous vegetable with tiny, cabbagelike heads on a large, inedible stalk.

bulgur   A wheat kernel that's been steamed, dried, and crushed and is sold in fine and coarse textures.

cabbage   Any of several cultivated varieties of *Brassica* with a short stem and a compact head of edible leaves.

cake flour   A high-starch, soft, fine flour used primarily for cakes.

canapé   A bite-size hors d'oeuvre usually served on a small piece of bread or toast.

caper   The flavorful buds of a Mediterranean plant, ranging in size from nonpareil (about the size of a small pea) to larger, grape-size caper berries produced in Spain.

capsaicin   The active metabolite that gives chile peppers their heat.

caramelize   To cook sugar over low heat until it develops a sweet caramel flavor, or to cook vegetables (especially onions) or meat in butter or oil over low heat until they soften, sweeten, and develop a caramel color.

caraway   A distinctive spicy seed used for bread, pork, cheese, and cabbage dishes. It's known to reduce stomach upset, which is why it's often paired with foods like sauerkraut.

cardamom   An intense, sweet-smelling spice used in baking and coffee and common in Indian cooking.

carob   A tropical tree that produces long pods from which the dried, baked, and powdered flesh—carob powder—is used in baking. The flavor is sweet and reminiscent of chocolate.

carotenoids   Powerful antioxidant, cancer-fighting substances, found in dark leafy greens and other plants.

cayenne   A fiery spice made from hot chile peppers, especially the cayenne chile, a slender, red, and very hot pepper.

chicory   A green with toothed, oblong leaves, cultivated for its leaves and root.

chickpea (or **garbanzo bean**)   A yellow-gold, roundish bean used as the base ingredient in hummus. Chickpeas are high in fiber and low in fat.

chiffonade   Method of finely shredding leaf vegetables or herbs, which are stacked, rolled, and sliced.

chile (or **chili**)   Any one of many different hot peppers, ranging in intensity from the relatively mild ancho pepper to the blisteringly hot habanero.

chili powder   A warm, rich seasoning blend that includes chile pepper, cumin, garlic, and oregano.

chive   A member of the onion family, chives grow in bunches of long leaves that resemble tall grass or the green tops of onions and offer a light onion flavor.

chop   To cut into pieces, usually qualified by an adverb such as "coarsely chopped" or by a size measurement such as "chopped into ½-inch pieces." "Finely chopped" is much closer to mince.

chutney   A thick condiment often served with Indian curries made with fruits and/or vegetables with vinegar, sugar, and spices.

cider vinegar   A vinegar produced from apple cider, popular in North America.

cilantro   A member of the parsley family used in Mexican dishes (especially salsa) and some Asian dishes. It should be used in moderation because the flavor can overwhelm. The seed of the cilantro plant is the spice coriander.

cinnamon   A rich, aromatic spice commonly used in baking or desserts. Cinnamon can also be used for delicious and interesting entrées.

clove   A sweet, strong, almost wintergreen-flavor spice used in baking.

cold frame   A small structure with a transparent roof used to protect plants from cold temperatures.

collards   A member of the cabbage family with large, thick, blue-green leaves.

compost   Plant matter and food waste that has been broken down to create fertilizer.

coriander   A rich, warm, spicy seed used in all types of recipes, from African to South American, from entrées to desserts.

cornstarch   A thickener used in baking and food processing. It's the refined starch of the endosperm of the corn kernel and often mixed with cold liquid to make into a paste before adding to a recipe to avoid clumps.

couscous   Granular semolina (durum wheat) that's cooked and used in many Mediterranean and North African dishes.

cream   To beat a fat such as butter, often with another ingredient such as sugar, to soften and aerate a batter.

crimini mushroom   A relative of the white button mushroom that's brown in color and has a richer flavor. The larger, fully grown version is the portobello. *See also* portobello mushroom.

cruciferous vegetable   A vegetable that belongs to the *Cruciferae*, or mustard, family of plants.

crudité   Fresh vegetables served as an appetizer, often all together on one tray.

cumin   A fiery, smoky-tasting spice popular in Middle Eastern and Indian dishes. Cumin is a seed; ground cumin seed is the most common form used in cooking.

cure   To preserve uncooked foods by either salting and smoking or pickling.

curly endive   A loose-headed, green leafy vegetable of the chicory family.

curry   Rich, spicy, Indian-style sauces and the dishes prepared with them. A curry uses curry powder as its base seasoning.

curry powder   A ground blend of rich and flavorful spices used as a basis for curry and many other Indian-influenced dishes. Common ingredients include hot pepper, nutmeg, cumin, cinnamon, pepper, and turmeric. Some curry can also be found in paste form.

dandelion   A plant commonly considered a weed, with edible, bitter green leaves and yellow flowers.

dash   A few drops, usually of a liquid, released by a quick shake.

deglaze   To scrape up bits of browned food and seasoning left in a pan or skillet after cooking. Usually this is done by adding a liquid such as wine or broth and creating a flavorful stock that can be used as a base for sauces.

dehydrating   A food preservation process that removes moisture from food to allow for long-term storage.

dice   To cut into small cubes about $\frac{1}{4}$-inch square.

Dijon mustard   A hearty, spicy mustard made in the style of the Dijon region of France.

dill   An herb perfect for eggs, salmon, cheese dishes, and, of course, vegetables (think pickles!).

dollop   A spoonful of something creamy and thick, like sour cream or whipped cream.

double boiler   A set of two pots designed to nest together, one inside the other, and provide consistent, moist heat for foods that need delicate treatment. The bottom pot holds water (not quite touching the bottom of the top pot); the top pot holds the food you want to heat.

dredge   To coat a piece of food on all sides with a dry substance such as flour or cornmeal.

drizzle   To lightly sprinkle drops of a liquid over food, often as the finishing touch to a dish.

dulse   A nutritious, red seaweed that adds the salty flavor of the ocean to foods.

edamame   Fresh, plump, pale green soybeans, similar in appearance to lima beans, often served steamed and either shelled or still in their protective pods.

electrolytes   Inorganic compounds that send impulses throughout your body, helping to regulate your heart and circulatory system, as well as your body's fluids and pH balance.

emulsion   A combination of liquid ingredients that do not normally mix well that are beaten together to create a thick liquid, such as a fat or oil with water. Creating emulsions must be done carefully and rapidly to ensure the particles of one ingredient are suspended in the other.

endive   A green that resembles a small, elongated, tightly packed head of romaine lettuce. The thick, crunchy leaves can be broken off and used with dips and spreads.

entrée   The main dish in a meal.

escarole   A broad-leafed, slightly bitter member of the endive family.

extra-virgin olive oil   *See* olive oil.

extract   A concentrated flavoring derived from foods or plants through evaporation or distillation that imparts a powerful flavor without altering the volume or texture of a dish.

falafel   A Middle Eastern food made of seasoned, ground chickpeas or fava beans formed into balls, cooked, and often used as a filling in pitas.

fennel   In seed form, a fragrant, licorice-tasting herb. The bulbs have a mild flavor and a celery-like crunch and are used as a vegetable in salads or cooked recipes.

fermentation   A process that produces lactic acid to preserve food.

fines herbes   A blend of parsley, chives, chervil, and tarragon traditionally used in French cooking.

flaxseed   The seed of the flax plant, which is grown for its meal as well as linseed oil.

flour   Grains ground into a meal. Wheat is perhaps the most common flour, but oats, rye, buckwheat, soybeans, chickpeas, and other grains can also be used. *See also* all-purpose flour; cake flour; whole-wheat flour.

fold   To combine a dense and light mixture with a circular action from the middle of the bowl.

freezer burn   Spoilage of frozen foods caused by exposure to air.

frisée   Young, tender curly endive with white, mild-tasting leaves.

frittata   A skillet-cooked mixture of eggs and other ingredients that's not stirred but is cooked slowly and then either flipped or finished under the broiler.

fry   *See* sauté.

garlic   A member of the onion family, a pungent and flavorful vegetable used in many savory dishes. A garlic bulb contains multiple cloves. Each clove, when chopped, provides about 1 teaspoon garlic.

ginger   A flavorful root available fresh or dried and ground that adds a pungent, sweet, and spicy quality to a dish.

Greek yogurt   A strained yogurt that's a good natural source of protein, calcium, and probiotics. Greek yogurt averages 40 percent more protein per ounce than traditional yogurt.

handful   An unscientific measurement, it's the amount of an ingredient you can hold in your hand.

headspace   Space left at the top of a container when canning or freezing food, to allow for expansion and maintain a proper seal.

hearts of palm   Firm, elongated, off-white cylinders from the inside of a palm tree stem tip.

herbes de Provence   A seasoning mix of basil, fennel, marjoram, rosemary, sage, and thyme, common in the south of France.

homocysteine   A toxic waste product that damages blood vessels and contributes to high cholesterol and heart disease.

hors d'oeuvre   French for "outside of work" (the "work" being the main meal), an hors d'oeuvre can be any dish served as a starter before a meal.

horseradish   A sharp, spicy root that forms the flavor base in condiments such as cocktail sauce and sharp mustards. Prepared horseradish contains vinegar and oil, among other ingredients. Use pure horseradish much more sparingly than the prepared version, or try cutting it with sour cream.

hummus   A thick, Middle Eastern spread made of puréed chickpeas, lemon juice, olive oil, garlic, and often tahini.

infusion   A liquid in which flavorful ingredients such as herbs have been soaked or steeped to extract their flavor into the liquid.

Italian seasoning   A blend of dried herbs, including basil, oregano, rosemary, and thyme.

jicama   A juicy, crunchy, sweet, large, round Central American vegetable. If you can't find jicama, try substituting sliced water chestnuts.

julienne   A French word meaning "to slice into very thin pieces."

kalamata olive   Traditionally from Greece, a medium-small, long black olive with a rich, smoky flavor.

kale   A cabbagelike member of the *Brassica* family, with curled or wrinkled leaves on slender, edible stalks.

knead   To work dough to make it pliable so it holds gas bubbles as it bakes. Kneading is fundamental in the process of making yeast breads.

kombu   A nutritious, dark-colored kelp used in Japanese cooking.

kosher salt   A coarse-grained salt made without any additives or iodine.

leaf lettuce   Lettuce with loosely curled leaves that do not form a compact head.

lentil   A tiny lens-shaped pulse (dried seed of a legume) used in European, Middle Eastern, and Indian cuisines.

locavore   One who endeavors to eat only seasonal foods grown or produced within 100 miles of his or her home.

magnesium   An important dietary mineral found in nuts, seeds, grains, and green vegetables.

mandoline   A kitchen tool with an adjustable blade that creates uniform, thin slices of food.

marinate   To soak food in a seasoned sauce, a marinade, that's high in acid content. The acids break down the fibers of the food, making it tender and adding flavor.

marjoram   A sweet herb, cousin of and similar to oregano, that's popular in Greek, Spanish, and Italian dishes.

masa harina   A flour that is made from field corn (maize) that has been treated with slaked lime, ground into a dough, and dried.

matcha   An edible powder made from ground green tea leaves.

meld   To allow flavors to blend and spread over time. Melding is often why recipes call for overnight refrigeration and is also why some dishes taste better as leftovers.

mesclun   Mixed salad greens, usually containing lettuce and other assorted greens such as arugula, cress, and endive.

millet   A tiny, round, yellow-colored nutty-flavored grain often used as a replacement for couscous.

mince   To cut into very small pieces, smaller than diced, about $\frac{1}{8}$ inch or smaller.

miso   A fermented, flavorful soybean paste, key in many Japanese dishes.

mizuna   A piquant, peppery green commonly used in Asian cooking.

mouthfeel   The overall sensation in the mouth resulting from a combination of the temperature, taste, smell, and texture of a food.

mustard greens   The spicy edible leaves of the *Brassica juncea*, commonly used in Southern cooking.

nutmeg   A sweet, fragrant, musky spice used primarily in baking.

olive   The fruit of the olive tree commonly grown on all sides of the Mediterranean. Black olives are also called ripe olives. Green olives are immature, although they're also widely eaten. *See also* kalamata olives.

olive oil   A fragrant liquid produced by crushing or pressing olives. Extra-virgin olive oil—the most flavorful and highest quality—is produced from the first pressing of a batch of olives; oil is also produced from later pressings.

oregano   A fragrant, slightly astringent herb used in Greek, Spanish, and Italian dishes.

orzo   A rice-shape pasta used in Greek cooking.

oxidation   The browning of fruit flesh that happens over time and with exposure to air. Minimize oxidation by rubbing the cut surfaces with lemon juice.

paella   A Spanish dish traditionally comprised of rice, saffron, rich broth, and herbs.

panko   Japanese-style bread crumbs with a light, crispy texture.

paprika   A rich, red, warm, earthy spice that lends a rich red color to many dishes.

parboil   To partially cook in boiling water or broth.

parsley   A fresh-tasting green leafy herb, often used as a garnish.

pesto   A thick spread or sauce made with fresh basil leaves, garlic, olive oil, pine nuts, and Parmesan cheese.

pith   The bitter white membrane located beneath the peel of citrus fruits.

phytoestrogens   Estrogen-like compounds that occur naturally in edible plants.

phytonutrients   Unique, protective compounds present in all plants that act as antioxidants in the body.

pickling   The process of preserving food using a combination of acid, salt, and/or fermentation.

pilaf   A rice dish in which the rice is browned in butter or oil and then cooked in a flavorful liquid such as a broth, often with the addition of meats or vegetables. The rice absorbs the broth, resulting in a savory dish.

pinch   An unscientific measurement for the amount of an ingredient—typically, a dry, granular substance such as an herb or seasoning—you can hold between your finger and thumb.

pine nut   A nut that's rich (high in fat), flavorful, and a bit pine-y. Pine nuts are a traditional ingredient in pesto and add a hearty crunch to many other recipes.

pita bread   A flat, hollow wheat bread often used for sandwiches or sliced pizza style. They're terrific soft with dips, or baked or broiled as a vehicle for other ingredients.

pizza stone   A flat stone that, when preheated with the oven, cooks crusts to a crispy, pizza-parlor texture.

poach   To cook a food in simmering liquid such as water, wine, or broth.

polenta   A mush made from cornmeal that can be eaten hot with butter or cooked until firm and cut into squares.

porcini mushroom   A rich and flavorful mushroom used in rice and Italian-style dishes.

portobello mushroom   A mature and larger form of the smaller crimini mushroom. Brown, chewy, and flavorful, portobellos are often served as whole caps, grilled, or as thin sautéed slices. *See also* crimini mushrooms.

preheat   To turn on an oven, broiler, or other cooking appliance in advance of cooking so the temperature will be at the desired level when the assembled dish is ready for cooking.

puntarelle   A long, thin, spiked Italian chicory.

purée   To reduce a food to a thick, creamy texture, typically using a blender or food processor.

quinoa   A nutty-flavored grain that's extremely high in protein and calcium.

radicchio   A perennial leaf vegetable with white-veined, red leaves.

reduce   To boil or simmer a broth or sauce to remove some of the water content, resulting in more concentrated flavor and color.

reserve   To hold a specified ingredient for another use later in the recipe.

rice vinegar   Vinegar produced from fermented rice or rice wine, popular in Asian-style dishes.

risotto   A popular Italian rice dish made by browning arborio rice in butter or oil and then slowly adding liquid to cook the rice, resulting in a creamy texture.

roast   To cook something uncovered in an oven, usually without additional liquid.

romaine lettuce   A sturdy, firm lettuce that grows in elongated heads with a central stem.

rosemary   A pungent, sweet herb used with chicken, pork, fish, and especially lamb. A little goes a long way.

roux   A mixture of butter or another fat and flour used to thicken sauces and soups.

saffron   An expensive spice made from the stamens of crocus flowers. Saffron lends a dramatic yellow color and distinctive flavor to a dish. Use only tiny amounts.

sage   An herb with a musty yet fruity, lemon-rind scent and "sunny" flavor.

sauté   To pan-cook over lower heat than what's used for frying.

savory   1. A popular herb with a fresh, woody taste. 2. Used to describe the flavor of food.

scald   To heat milk just until it's about to boil and then remove it from heat. Scalding milk helps prevent it from souring.

scant   An ingredient measurement directive not to add any extra, perhaps even leaving the measurement a tad short.

sear   To quickly brown the exterior of a food over high heat.

sesame oil   An oil made from pressing sesame seeds. It's tasteless if clear, and aromatic and flavorful if brown.

shallot   A member of the onion family that grows in a bulb somewhat like garlic but has a milder onion flavor. When a recipe calls for shallot, use the entire bulb.

shiitake mushroom   A large, dark brown mushroom with a hearty, meaty flavor. It can be used fresh or dried, grilled, as a component in other recipes, and as a flavoring source for broth.

short-grain rice   A starchy rice popular in Asian-style dishes because it readily clumps, making it perfect for eating with chopsticks.

simmer   To boil gently so the liquid barely bubbles.

skillet (also **frying pan**)   A generally heavy, flat-bottomed, metal pan with a handle designed to cook food over heat on a stovetop or campfire.

skim   To remove fat or other material from the top of liquid.

sorrel   A tart, lemony perennial herb cultivated for its leaves.

spinach   A plant, *Spinacia oleracea*, cultivated for its nutritious, dark-green leaves.

steam   To suspend a food over boiling water and allow the heat of the steam (water vapor) to cook the food. This quick-cooking method preserves a food's flavor and texture.

steep   To let sit in hot water, as in steeping tea in hot water for 10 minutes.

stew   To slowly cook pieces of food submerged in a liquid. Also, a dish prepared by this method.

stir-fry   To cook small pieces of food in a wok or skillet over high heat, moving and turning the food quickly to cook all sides.

stock   A flavorful broth made by cooking meats and/or vegetables with seasonings until the liquid absorbs these flavors. The liquid is strained and the solids are discarded. Stock can be eaten alone or used as a base for soups, stews, etc.

sumac   A spice with dark red color and a tart, lemony flavor that is frequently used in Middle Eastern cooking.

Swiss chard   A leafy plant, closely related to the beet root, which varies in color from white or green to ruby or rainbow hues.

tahini   A paste made from sesame seeds used to flavor many Middle Eastern recipes.

tapas   A Spanish term meaning "small plate" that describes individual-size appetizers and snacks served cold or warm.

tapenade   A thick, chunky spread made from savory ingredients such as olives, lemon juice, and anchovies.

tarragon   A sweet, rich-smelling herb perfect with seafood, vegetables (especially asparagus), chicken, and pork.

tatsoi (or **spoon lettuce**)   A dark, leafy Asian salad green with rosette-shaped leaves.

tempeh   An Indonesian food made by culturing and fermenting soybeans into a cake, sometimes mixed with grains or vegetables. It's high in protein and fiber.

thyme   A minty, zesty herb.

tofu   A cheeselike substance made from soybeans and soy milk.

turmeric   A spicy, pungent yellow root used in many dishes, especially Indian cuisine, for color and flavor. Turmeric is the source of the yellow color in many prepared mustards.

turnip greens   The leafy, edible top of the turnip root.

tzatziki   A Greek dip traditionally made with Greek yogurt, cucumbers, garlic, and mint.

udon   Thick, chewy wheat noodles used in Japanese cooking.

vegan   One who abstains from eating or animal flesh, and also abstains from eating or using products derived from animals, such as honey, leather, dairy products, eggs, and wool.

vegetable steamer   An insert with tiny holes in the bottom designed to fit on or in another pot to hold food to be steamed above boiling water. *See also* steam.

vegetarian   One who abstains from eating beef, pork, fish, shellfish, poultry, or animal flesh of any kind. *See also* vegan.

vinegar   An acidic liquid widely used as a dressing and seasoning, often made from fermented grapes, apples, or rice. *See also* balsamic vinegar; cider vinegar; rice vinegar; white vinegar; wine vinegar.

wasabi   Japanese horseradish, a fiery, pungent condiment used with many Japanese-style dishes. It's most often sold as a powder to which you add water to create a paste.

water chestnut   A tuber popular in many Asian dishes. It's white, crunchy, and juicy, and holds its texture whether cool or hot.

watercress   A leafy, semiaquatic perennial green with spicy flavor.

whisk   To rapidly mix, introducing air to the mixture.

white mushroom   A button mushroom. When fresh, white mushrooms have an earthy smell and an appealing soft crunch.

white vinegar   The most common type of vinegar, produced from grain.

whole grain   A grain derived from the seeds of grasses, including rice, oats, rye, wheat, wild rice, quinoa, barley, buckwheat, bulgur, corn, millet, amaranth, and sorghum.

whole-wheat flour   Wheat flour that contains the entire grain.

wild rice   Not a rice at all, this is actually a grass. It has a rich, nutty flavor and serves as a nutritious side dish.

wine vinegar   Vinegar produced from red or white wine.

yeast   Tiny fungi that, when mixed with water, sugar, flour, and heat, release carbon dioxide bubbles, which in turn cause the bread to rise.

zest   Small slivers of peel, usually from a citrus fruit such as a lemon, lime, or orange.

Resources

This appendix is provided as a resource for you in your search to find vegetarian and vegan foods and other products that will make your greens cooking an enjoyable experience.

Vegetarian and Vegan Cooking and Lifestyle

Feral, Priscilla. *The Best of Vegan Cooking*. Darien, Connecticut: Nectar Bat Press, 2009.

Madison, Deborah. *Local Flavors: Cooking and Eating from America's Farmers Markets*. New York: Broadway Books, 2002.

Moskowitz, Isa and Romero, and Terry Hope. *Veganomicon*. Cambridge, Massachusetts: Da Capo Press, 2007.

Schneider, Elizabeth. *Vegetables from Amaranth to Zucchini*. New York: Harper Collins, 2001.

Thomas, Anna. *The New Vegetarian Epicure*. New York, NY: Knopf, 1996.

Walters, Terry. *Clean Food: A Seasonal Guide to Eating Close to the Source*. New York: Sterling Epicure, 2007.

Waters, Alice. *Chez Panisse Vegetables*. New York: Harper Collins, 1996.

veganmeans.com, Friends of Animals

cok.net, Compassion Over Killing

vegansociety.com, The Vegan Society

theppk.com, Post Punk Kitchen

vrg.org, The Vegetarian Resource Group

navs-online.org, The North American Vegetarian Society

Nutrition

Hever, Julieanna. *The Complete Idiot's Guide to Plant-Based Nutrition.* New York: The Penguin Group, 2011.

Mahan, L. Kathleen and Sylvia Escott-Stump. *Krause's Food & Nutrition Therapy, Twelfth Edition.* St. Louis, MO: Saunders Elsevier, 2008.

Pitchford, Paul. *Healing With Whole Foods: Asian Traditions and Modern Nutrition, Third Edition.* Berkeley, California: North Atlantic Books, 2002.

http://www.mayoclinic.com/health/nutrition-and-healthy-eating/MY00431, Mayo Clinic

livestrong.com, LIVESTRONG Foundation

garynull.com, Gary Null, PhD

drweil.com, Andrew Weil, MD

Gardening

Alexander, Stephanie. *Stephanie Alexander's Kitchen Garden Companion.* New York: Penguin Group, 2009.

Crockett, James Underwood. *Crockett's Victory Garden.* Canada: Little, Brown and Company, 1977.

Jeavons, John. *How to Grow More Vegetables (And Fruits, Nuts, Berries, Grains, and Other Crops), 8th Edition.* Berkeley, California: Ten Speed Press, 2012.

Trail, Gayla. *Grow Great Grub: Organic Food From Small Spaces.* New York: Clarkson Potter, 2010.

homegrown.org, HOMEGROWN (an online community created by FarmAid)

gardening.cornell.edu, Cornell University

squarefootgardening.org, Square Foot Gardening Foundation

garden.org, National Gardening Association

nybg.org, The New York Botanical Garden

kgi.org, Kitchen Gardeners International

verticalgardeninstitute.org, The Vertical Garden Institute

howtocompost.org, Online Composting Resource

compostingcouncil.org, U.S. Composting Council

mastercomposter.com, Home Composting Information

Food Preservation

Andress, Elizabeth and Judy Harrison. *So Easy to Preserve, New & Revised Edition*. Augusta, Georgia: University of Georgia Cooperative Extension Service, 2006.

Cancler, Carole. *The Home Preserving Bible*. Indianapolis: Alpha, 2012.

Kingri, Judi and Laura Devine. *Ball Complete Book of Home Preserving*. Canada: Robert Rose, 2006.

U.S. Department of Agriculture. *Complete Guide to Home Canning and Preserving (Second Revised Edition)*. Mineola, New York: Dover Publications, 1999.

nchfp.uga.edu, National Center for Home Food Preservation

usda.gov, U.S. Department of Agriculture

Kitchen Equipment

cuisinart.com, Food processors

energystar.gov, Energy Star–rated appliances

kitchenaid.com, Mixers and food processors

lodgemfg.com, Cast-iron cookware

scanpan.com, Scanpan titanium nonstick cookware

vitamix.com, Vitamix Corporation

waringproducts.com, Blenders and kitchen equipment

Index